Sesame Street Around the World

RECENT TITLES IN
OXFORD STUDIES IN CULTURE AND POLITICS
Clifford Bob and James M. Jasper, General Editors

Sesame Street Around the World

Culture, Politics, and Transnational Organizational Partnerships

Tamara Kay

OXFORD
UNIVERSITY PRESS

OXFORD
UNIVERSITY PRESS

Oxford University Press is a department of the University of Oxford.
It furthers the University's objective of excellence in research, scholarship,
and education by publishing worldwide. Oxford is a registered trade mark of
Oxford University Press in the UK and in certain other countries.

Published in the United States of America by Oxford University Press
198 Madison Avenue, New York, NY 10016, United States of America.

CIP data is on file at the Library of Congress

ISBN 9780197840924

ISBN 9780190844295 (hbk.)

DOI: 10.1093/9780190844325.001.0001

Paperback Printed by Marquis Book Printing, Canada

The manufacturer's authorized representative in the EU for product safety is
Oxford University Press España S.A. of Parque Empresarial San Fernando de Henares,
Avenida de Castilla, 2 – 28830 Madrid (www.oup.es/en or product.safety@oup.com).
OUP España S.A. also acts as importer into Spain of products made by the manufacturer.

MIX
Paper | Supporting
responsible forestry
FSC
www.fsc.org   FSC® C103567

For Mireya Rebecca Toro Kay

Contents

Preface

Every research project is a leap of faith. But some require a bigger leap, or a lot more faith. In 2007, I had the opportunity to embark on a new project focused on how Sesame Workshop, a nonprofit organization based in the US, builds and maintains relationships with its partners around the world to create local *Sesame Street* programs together. Taking this leap meant that I would turn temporarily away from my primary research area, to which I have a strong intellectual and ethical commitment: labor and workers' rights. Pivoting to a project on organizations, development, and culture would also require getting up to speed in all of these extensive and multidisciplinary fields. After consulting trusted colleagues about pursuing Sesame Workshop as a case, their encouragement and enthusiasm provided the extra faith that I needed to make that leap.

While at first it may seem that this new project was a total departure from my earlier work, in fact, there are strong connections between them. Exploring possibilities for the construction of more equitable transnational relationships is the thread that runs through much of my work. Both my first and second books explored how different social movement organizations forged new cooperative and collaborative relationships—North American labor unions in the former (Kay 2011), and environmental organizations and labor unions in the latter (Kay and Evans 2018)—in order to confront the threat posed by the North American Free Trade Agreement. Although in this book I examine a different kind of organization—an educational media nonprofit engaged in development work—I still ask very similar questions about how more equitable partnerships among organizations in low- and high-income countries can be forged and sustained. I hope that the analysis in this book can more generally inform our understanding of transnational organizational partnerships—particularly among partners with significant economic and cultural differences and asymmetries in power.

The seed of the idea that would grow into this book was planted in 2006 when I opened a red Netflix envelope and popped the documentary film *The World According to Sesame Street* into my DVD player. I was mesmerized by this film about how three local Sesame *Street* programs were coproduced in Kosovo, Bangladesh, and South Africa. As I watched New York staff and partners on screen develop curricula, create new characters, and negotiate with government officials, I was fascinated by the questions: How did they do this? How did they make this work with their partners, and why did audiences love it? When the film ended, I knew that I had to study this organization.

But I also knew that convincing Sesame Workshop to grant me access to the organization and its staff and partners would be challenging. It took me months to develop what I thought was the perfect pitch and find the right person to pitch it to, which, ultimately, was Cooper Wright. She had been a producer, then was in charge of international production, and at that time was an executive producer and creative consultant. She agreed to meet me on June 21, 2007, in New York, at Josephina Restaurant, just outside of Sesame Workshop's office on Broadway across from Lincoln Center. She also invited Dr. Charlotte Cole, then Senior Vice President of Global Education. As we talked and got to know each other, I felt hopeful. And by the time I made the pitch, they seemed to instantly understand what I wanted to do. And they liked it.

They still needed to secure the support of Gary Knell, then President and CEO of Sesame Workshop. I suggested we invite him to give a talk at Harvard—where I was a faculty member—co-sponsored by the School of Education and the Weatherhead Center for International Affairs. After months of preparation, Knell gave his talk in November 2007 to a packed auditorium at the Harvard School of Education. At dinner that night, he said to me, "I think you understand what we're doing." And then he told me I could travel with New York staff, attend meetings and workshops, and interview any New York staffer and partner on my wish list. I finally had access to Sesame Workshop.

While I worked on this project, the world changed dramatically. In the US, the hope generated by Barack Obama's election in 2008 eventually gave way to cynicism, divisiveness, and a more polarized electorate. The rise and success of right-wing populism and parties not only emerged in the US, with the 2016 election, but also in countries where I had done fieldwork: Brazil, Israel, and India. These parties exploited populist attitudes among their populations, including "economic discontent, hostility to immigrants, distrust in government" (Sides 2024). Then, in 2020, the COVID-19 pandemic wreaked havoc across the planet, killing millions and disrupting the economy, education, and social life.

In the US, the 45th president and his administration pushed policies that created deeper divisions within the country and led to greater inequality by restricting health care (including reproductive health and rights), undermining environmental protections, scapegoating immigrants, and benefitting the wealthy at the expense of the poor, working, and middle classes. One of the most disturbing qualities of the 2016 Republican presidential candidate was the effortlessness of his fluency in hate—directed at people of color, women, the LGBTQ community, immigrants, people with disabilities, and many others when it served his political needs—the denigration of whom he took up with even greater zeal during the 2024 election. Perhaps most distressing has been the willingness of some to participate in the malevolence, and others to capitulate to it.

As the hate spirals out of control and wreaks havoc in the US and around the world, organizations like Sesame Workshop that are dedicated to resisting it become even more relevant and critical. That work is difficult, and no organization will get it right every time. But contributing to a culture of kindness and mutual respect acts as a strong counterbalance to the divisiveness, reminding us that another world is always possible.

New York, New York

Acknowledgments

There are many people who made this project possible, and to whom I am profoundly grateful. First and foremost are the Sesame Workshop staff and partners who generously gave me inordinate amounts of their time and shared invaluable insights and knowledge. All of the partners I visited were wonderful, but something inside me shifted when I met the Palestinian team. In no other place except Palestine was I repeatedly welcomed into partners' homes to spend time with them and their extended families. *Shara'a Simsim* producer and renowned journalist Daoud Kuttab welcomed me into his, where I met his wife and children. His eldest daughter Tamara and I had an instant rapport—and not simply because we share a name. She invited me to meet her maternal grandparents in Jericho. There, her grandmother made maqluba for us and showed me how to perfectly flip it, and her grandfather took me to see Zacchaeus' sycamore tree.

Soon after my arrival in Ramallah, I met with Layla Sayegh, *Shara'a Simsim's* project manager. On that very special day, she was awaiting the arrival of her brother, whom she had not seen in years. He had left Palestine and was living in Guatemala with his family. While Layla and I were talking, family members called every few minutes to update her on his progress from Ben Gurion airport. She was beside herself with joy but anxious that he would be stopped at a check point and turned back, which would end the reunion before it began. She invited me to a large family celebration for him that night, but, assuming she was just being polite, I thanked her and declined. She insisted. I contemplated what the culturally appropriate response was—and had absolutely no idea. Ultimately, her sincerity persuaded me. When I arrived at her home, Layla introduced me to her brother, and I had the opportunity to talk to him (in Spanish, which amused everyone) about his life in Guatemala and his longing for his family, and his homeland. It was an evening filled with family, food, music, laughter, and warmth, and I felt so fortunate to experience it. These are but a few of the many special moments I spent with the Palestinian team, and I thank them and express my profound gratitude for their generosity, kindness, and hospitality.

I also offer my great thanks to friends and colleagues who offered invaluable advice on the manuscript and the ideas that preceded it, as I walked this street beginning in 2007: Joshua Bloom, Bart Bonikowski, James Collins,

Frank Dobbin, Peter Evans, Malcolm Fairbrother, Roberto Fernandez, Robert Fiala, Neil Fligstein, Duana Fullwiley, Tim Hallett, Heather Haveman, Mala Htun, Kendra Koivu, Julia Kowalski, Michèle Lamont, Peggy Levitt, Omar Lizardo, Isaac Martin, Elizabeth McClintock, Erin McDonnell, Terry McDonnell, Rory McVeigh, Ann Mische, Sara Niedzwiecki, Abi Ocobock, Atalia Omer, Susan Ostermann, Mark Peceny, Jeff Sallaz, Sarah Soule, Jason Spicer, William Stanley, Sid Tarrow, Kim Voss, and Richard Wood. Special thanks to my great friend Marshall Ganz, who offered steady encouragement through regular, enthusiastic emails—notably the one that opened with: "What's the status of the *Sesame Street* project which remains one of the coolest things I've ever heard of?" I am also grateful to Michael Burawoy, who supported this project from the beginning. In 2011, Michael asked me to write what became my first publication from it, for the International Sociological Association's magazine *Global Dialogue* (Kay 2012). He responded to the finished piece with his affirming signature phrase: "Absolutely bloody brilliant . . . Beautifully written. Exactly the ticket!" As he knew it would, this early praise gave me the confidence I needed to forge ahead with this book. I wish he could have seen what it became.

Many then-undergraduate and graduate students contributed their time and ceaseless energy to the project, including: Asad L. Asad, Bryanna Beamer, Giampaolo Bianconi, Anna Calasanti, Anmol Chaddha, Siri Colom, Oana Dan, Sarika Gupta, Nicole Arlette Hirsch, Simone Ispa-Landa, Isabel Jijon, Jing Li, Audrey Lindemann, Saloni Malik, Ami Nash, Carli Steelman, Jessica Tollette, En-Ya Tsai, and Catherine Turco.

Jodi Lefkowitz deserves special thanks for organizing my many visits to Sesame Workshop's New York office to interview staff, Jane Jones for editing the initial book proposal, Laura Thomas for transcribing interviews, Beatrice Chow for arranging follow-up interviews and access to Sesame Workshop photographs and visuals, Estee Bardanashvili for meticulously fact-checking the final manuscript, and Nina Katz for creating the index. The editors and staff at Oxford University Press have been extraordinary, and I am so grateful for their stewardship of this book. This is the second book that I had the good fortune to publish with James Cook. I thank him, Phoebe Aldridge-Turner, and reviewers for the time they devoted to the manuscript. I also wish to express my gratitude to the anonymous Oxford reviewer whose feedback was, in a word, phenomenal. It is a gift to have a reviewer who understands where you are trying to go and helps get you there with their insightful, thoughtful advice. This research is made possible, in part, by support from Harvard Medical School, the Harvard Academy for International and Area Studies, and the David Rockefeller Center for Latin American Studies, Harvard University. I also thank my closest friends and family who are a constant source of support, love, and strength. I love you and am so grateful for you.

I started this project four years before my daughter was born. So many of the brilliant and creative people I interviewed in the US and in every country I visited spoke about their work on *Sesame Street* in relationship to their own children and their hopes and dreams for them. It wasn't until I had a child that I could fully understand the depth of their commitment to creating something that they believed could make the world a better place for everyone's children. My daughter has strengthened my own commitment to contribute to that better world, and she gives me hope every day that it can be achieved. And so I dedicate this book to her.

1

Introduction

Coproduction and *Sesame Street*: Culture in Transnational Interaction

The clock is ticking, and the auditorium is filled with a nervous excitement. The heavy purple velvet draperies have been pulled back, letting the dappled light settle onto the floor. At the front of the room is a makeshift stage. The backdrop is a colorful farm scene with smiling cartoon cows and horses. A display board with various items pictured—flowers, fruit, animals, and the Arabic letters they each begin with—is centered on the stage. The children fidget in their chairs, look expectantly at doting teachers, until suddenly, the auditorium doors open. As Haneen (a bright orange and pink girl monster Muppet) and Kareem (a green and blue rooster Muppet with a multi-colored tail) enter the room, the children clamor to stand on their seats, their voices joining and nearly eclipsing the theme song to *Shara'a Simsim* that erupts through the loudspeakers.

It is 2009, and we are in an elementary school in Ramallah, Palestine. The scene here is one I have experienced before and will experience every time I travel to a country with a local *Sesame Street* program.[1] Children across the globe respond to the characters with wonder and awe, blissfully unaware that the fluffy and vibrantly colored Muppet characters are simply vehicles used to achieve larger educational goals. In urban slums in India, they huddle around a vegetable cart fitted with a television and DVD player transfixed to characters who sing about the letter "ma" in Hindi. In Tanzania, they listen to a radio program that teaches them how to treat a mosquito bed net to help prevent malaria. And in South Africa, where one in ten children has lost a parent to

---

[1] Sesame Workshop has historically referred to local *Sesame Street* programs as "coproductions." Because this book focuses on analyzing the *process* of coproduction, I use the terms "local *Sesame Street* programs" or "local programs" to minimize confusion. The term local can also be problematic in reference to *Sesame Street* programs and partners because it centers Sesame Workshop and New York staff, who, of course, are also "local." Distinguishing between the people who work in New York and those who work in other countries and areas, however, is essential here, and "international" and "transnational" in relationship to programs and partners does not capture their uniqueness and rootedness in a specific place. I therefore opt to use the term local with the acknowledgment that it is not a perfect term either.

Sesame Street Around the World. Tamara Kay, Oxford University Press. © Oxford University Press (2025). DOI: 10.1093/9780190844325.003.0001

HIV/AIDS, an HIV-positive Muppet named Kami, who has lost her mother to the disease, destigmatizes it and helps them deal with loss. All of these children have at least two things in common: they will be way behind more advantaged children if and when they attend school, and their local version of *Sesame Street* was created to help mitigate the disadvantages they face.

The Birth of Sesame Street in the United States

The producers of *Sesame Street* had the same target audience and goals for the program in the US. The program was birthed by a trifecta of factors that came together in the late 1960s. The civil rights movement was exposing enormous inequalities across the country, particularly in schools. Poor and minority children had little access to quality preschool or pre-kindergarten, and their mothers had always worked outside their homes to provide or supplement family incomes. Many of them arrived unprepared for school. As more middle-class women entered the workforce by necessity or choice, there was a growing number of latchkey kids—children who arrived from school to a home with no adult supervision, and whose sole babysitter was often the television. And in the late 1960s, there were few viewing options for young children.

The three primary commercial television channels catered to an adult market. Children were exposed to violence in programs and on the nightly news. Even Hanna-Barbera and Looney Tunes cartoons featured violence. Most importantly, as the creators of *Sesame Street* realized, they lacked educational value. Children's programming was practically nonexistent, and what did exist was made purely for entertainment. *Sesame Street* was created to fill that void. Its goal was to prepare children for school. Its creators—Joan Ganz Cooney and Lloyd Morrisett—also believed that the program should highlight diversity and prosocial values. So they set it on a diverse urban street. The primary cast included Latino and African American couples, and over the years featured an actress who is deaf, and people who use wheelchairs. This effort to normalize diversity was not without controversy. In 1970, soon after it premiered, the state of Mississippi initially banned *Sesame Street* because it had an interracial cast.

The idea that children's television should educate rather than simply entertain was innovative and groundbreaking. In order to prepare preschool age children for school, *Sesame Street's* creators developed a "whole child" curriculum that is divided into three broad categories: cognitive learning (literacy, numeracy), socio-emotional learning (mutual respect and under-standing), and physical well-being (health and wellness, such as nutrition, personal hygiene, safety). Each *Sesame Street* episode was divided into seg-ments that included: 1) animation; 2) studio scenes with actors and/or puppets); and 3) live-action documentary segments depicting real events, such as a child's first day of school. Each segment incorporates at least one and usually multiple curricular goals. For example, a segment might include Cookie Monster teaching shapes using cookies (cognitive learning goal), while highlighting that cookies are not an everyday food (health and wellness goal).

From the beginning, Sesame Workshop (originally called the Children's Television Workshop), the nonprofit organization formed to create *Sesame Street*, utilized a content-production-research model to achieve its educa-tional goals. The model combines: 1) educational content developed by experts in education, child development and psychology, medicine, public health, among many others; 2) production, created by writers, directors, pro-ducers, artists and animators, musicians, and puppeteers, and; 3) research conducted by scholars that tests the effectiveness of the content, and mea-sures and analyzes the program's educational outcomes. Sesame Workshop's innovation in children's television has been chronicled in the popular press (Gladwell 2000). Indeed, *Sesame Street* is the most researched television pro-gram in the world. Countless academic studies conducted during the last 57 years consistently demonstrate the program's positive effects on children's educational outcomes and social skills; *Sesame Street* improved children's performance in school (Kearney and Levine 2019). Preschool viewers score higher on literacy and numeracy measures than nonviewers (Wright et al. 2001), earn higher grades in high school, read more books for pleasure, and place higher value on academic achievement (Anderson et al. 2001). Viewers also develop more sophisticated social skills and greater respect for diver-sity and differences compared to nonviewers (Bogatz and Ball 1971; Gorn et al. 1976; Zielinska and Chambers 1995; Mares and Pan 2013; Cole and Lee 2016). Sesame Workshop's educational model, which combines a curriculum with ongoing testing of its effectiveness, has proven results: it helps educate children.

And yet, the research shows that *Sesame Street* did not only help prepare poor and disadvantaged children for school. Indeed, the rising tide Sesame Workshop created lifted all boats. Middle class and wealthy children, those with access to preschool programs, and those with educated parents all ben-efited from viewing the program. *Sesame Street's* universal impact, and its universal appeal, quickly made it an iconic US cultural innovation. Since the 1970s, it has been famously parodied across the entertainment landscape from *Saturday Night Live* and *The Daily Show* to Broadway (*Avenue Q*), and has been invoked during presidential elections and debates. Most Americans[2] can hum its theme song, recognize its characters, and locate its resonance at key moments in their lives, and even their children's lives. In the US, *Sesame Street* is a cultural reference point.

How, then, can we explain the effect Haneen and Kareem had on that roomful of children in Palestine? How can we understand why local *Sesame Street* programs became iconic in Egypt, Germany, and the Netherlands? How can we appreciate why airline passengers in Mexico spontaneously began singing the *Plaza Sésamo* theme song when they realized Pancho and the puppeteer who played him were on their flight? How do we reconcile why thousands of South African children flocked to a soccer stadium for a rally with the HIV-positive Muppet Kami, who appeared with Nelson Mandela and Desmond Tutu on *Takalani Sesame*? How has *Sesame Street* escaped its cultural bonds to become a global phenomenon that embodies universal goals and messages while at the same time being very particularly localized—meaning made resonant, salient, and meaningful for local users and audiences—in every country in which it spreads?

To put it more simply, given the extraordinary politicization of culture in an era of globalization, how can we explain why and how *Sesame Street*, an iconic US cultural innovation, has gained acceptance and legitimacy in more than fifty countries during the last five decades by promoting both universality and particularity at the same time? The goal of this book is to answer that question.

Sesame Street is an iconic US cultural product that emerges out of a Western educational philosophy and curriculum rooted in very particular visions of childhood and society. And there are many different definitions of and sociocultural approaches to childhood around the world (Rogoff 2003; Lareau 2003; Cole 2005; Cole and Durham 2007; LeVine and New 2008; Lightfoot et al. 2018; Berman 2019). Those definitions and approaches also change over time (Zelizer 1994; Cole and Durham 2008; Mukerji 2016). In addition, educational experiments meant to bridge cultural divides do not frequently succeed (see Sims 2017; Ames 2019). Given the varieties in these approaches, and that *Sesame Street* is centered on children's education—which is particularly important, meaningful, and potentially contentious for local populations—the spread of *Sesame Street* is unexpected and surprising. It is therefore important to understand how local *Sesame Street* programs are

---

[2] Because all citizens of North, Central, and South America fall under the broad category of "American," I use the adjective "US" throughout the book. Because in English there exists no noun except "American" to describe US citizens, I use it when necessary.

created and the tensions that emerge at the local level as people in diverse countries all over the world strive to make *Sesame Street* their own.

Big Bird Goes to Bangladesh

Outside the building, there was no sign announcing that you had successfully figured out how to get to *Sesame Street*—or at least its office in New York. But if you looked up while standing on Broadway or Columbus Avenue, you could see the furry Muppets grinning at you from the building's windows. Inside, the offices of Sesame Workshop were a colorful wonderland when I arrived to conduct my first interviews for this book. Nadine Zylstra, a South African woman who was one of the directors of *Takalani Sesame*, was the first to greet me that day. She led me from the reception area—decorated with Emmy Awards, photographs, and a kiddie ride featuring Elmo on a train—into Sesame Workshop's labyrinthine hallways and back offices.

One hallway was painted in blackboard paint, upon which Sesame Workshop's artists and animators had drawn *Sesame Street's* main characters. Another hallway featured street signs and characters from all over the world. As we followed the carpet's blocks of primary colors through a maze of cubicles and modular offices decorated with family photos and toy Grovers and Elmos, I told Nadine I would never be able to find my way back. "It takes people weeks to learn how to navigate through here. No worries, we'll make sure you get where you need to go today," she reassured me.

When we finally reached her bright office, whose shelves were lined with mementos from all over the world, Nadine eagerly explained to me how *Sisimpur*, the Bangladeshi version of *Sesame Street*, was born. What fascinated me the most was not her description of how her local counterparts in Bangladesh embraced the project, but rather, how skeptical they were at the beginning of it, "The Bangladeshis did feel very anxious about us as an American company coming in and just railroading over who they were." Intrigued, I asked her, "How did that manifest, did they say things?" She responded:

That discussion session we had after the curricular seminar was very tense—to the point that the Chief Creative Advisor was even asking, why do all the Muppets have the same eyes? It was very suspicious. There was definitely a defensive thing, particularly around the puppetry element, about this idea that we were bringing in our puppets and sidelining theirs and there was definitely subtext happening. It was the Chief Creative Advisor and our head writer, you could feel it, coming from them. And they would say it, "We have our own stories." They were very vocal. And to their credit, they were vocal about it but they didn't want to feel the pressure to make it American and I would say they even laid that out there.[3]

I asked Nadine how she allayed their fears. "I was already then saying we don't want it to be American, this is about your stories," she explained.

One cannot understand the *Sisimpur* team's trepidation without understanding key elements of the country's history, culture, and political system. Bangladesh's battle for independence from Pakistan and the movement that preceded it centered, in large part, on its cultural and political distinctiveness, particularly its language. Activists died fighting for the right to use their own language. Although *Sesame Street*'s focus on literacy dovetailed with the Bangladeshi team's goals of inculcating children with a love and appreciation for their alphabet and language, the question remained: would the vehicle used to achieve this goal—an iconic US educational program with distinctive songs and puppets—be their own? Chief creative advisor Mustafa Monwar, a renowned puppeteer and artist, expressed confidence that it would: "We feel that when we are expressing ourselves—whether it is *Sisimpur*, whether it is theater, whether it is song, whether it is dance—we are actually connecting to our identity as Bengalis and to the Bangla language."[4]

Nadine Zylstra's vignette about *Sisimpur* perfectly captures the complicated set of dynamics that motivates the primary questions in this book about how an iconic US cultural innovation is translated and transformed as it moves around the world. The vignette also highlights how cultural differences and conflicts emerge and are managed in the process of constructing a *Sesame Street* program in a new context.

Coproduction: Sesame's Secret Sauce

It starts with a simple question: What is the vision of the street? On a light-filled morning in Dhaka, Nadine Zylstra posed this question to the Bangladeshi team. The group was a who's who of nationally recognized talent, including artists, educators, and activists. In addition to Mustafa Monwar, who had also been the director general of state-owned Bangladesh Television, it included Sara Zaker, an award-winning actress and feminist with a national reputation, and Dr. Mahtab Khanam, a prominent psychologist, among many others. They were gathered with New York staff to develop the goals and themes of their new program, *Sisimpur*. In the following exchange,

[3] Personal Interview, New York: 1/14/08.
[4] Quoted in the film The World According to Sesame Street, 2006.

captured on film in real time,[5] Nadine leads a discussion with the Bangladeshi team about what they want *Sisimpur* to say and to represent:

ZYLSTRA: What is the vision of the street? Before we can decide who needs to be on the street, what is not just the street, but what is *Sisimpur*?

MONWAR: It is the most friendliest street in our Dhaka City.

MALE #2: *Sisimpur* is joyful.

MALE #3: The street is a safe place, joyful.

MALE #4: Lots of fun.

ZAKER: Put in the idea that equality. Because our society is so much demarcated by . . . .

ZYLSTRA: So its a place where everybody's equal.

ZAKER: Equal, you know ... Gender equity is another issue. Just like class equity is an issue.

FEMALE #2 Most children don't really have a childhood. By the time they you are five you end up working and supporting your family.

MALE #3: Right to safety, security. Right to go to school. These are basic things.

ZYLSTRA: Well and can I just jump off that, because that brings us to, when children switch on the tv, what do we want to leave them with?

ZAKER: I would like to say that look, this world is as much yours as any other privileged child.

ZYLSTRA: That's beautiful.

FEMALE: That's it.

This exchange reveals a tremendous amount about how New York staff conceptualize and explain the *Sesame Street* model, how the Bangladeshi team conceptualizes and explains their priorities and vision, and how the two teams interact as they try to align their goals and interests. Through this exchange, we see the dance that occurs as New York staff try to guide their partners as they make decisions about their themes and curricula so they are in line with the Sesame Workshop model, but acceptable and resonant in the local context. And these interactions are laden with asymmetrical power dynamics between Sesame Workshop and partners around the world, making the dance even more complicated.

The key to Sesame's spread, what makes it work, is how Sesame Workshop choreographs this dance with its partners. Therefore, in order to answer the question of how *Sesame Street* has gained acceptance and legitimacy internationally, we must first answer a second question about how organizations like

---

[5] Quoted in the film The World According to Sesame Street, 2006.

Sesame Workshop that produce a hybrid cultural product as a transnational team work together on the ground.

What is Coproduction?

Sesame Workshop's secret sauce is that it engages in *coproduction*. Although the term has been defined in different ways and used in various contexts,[6] in this book I define coproduction as the process by which two or more organizations working together as a transnational team coproduce—meaning *jointly* create—a hybrid cultural product. Coproduction involves partners working together in real time.[7] The *process* of coproduction involves cooperation, and the *result* of coproduction is a hybrid form of mixed knowledge. Many concepts have emerged to describe how cultural products that originate in one place are modified in another, including local adaptation, hybridization, localization, glocalization, indigenization, vernacularization, and creolization, among others (Hannerz 1987; Robertson 1994; Appadurai 1996; Boellstorff 2003; Acharya 2004; Kraidy 2005; Molnár 2005; Burke 2009). While these terms tell us that a cultural product is being transformed, they do not tell us *who* is engaged in that transformation. For example, the original creator, or originator, of the cultural product can locally adapt or hybridize it at the point of production alone, or the adopter of the cultural product can do so at the point of consumption.[8] The concept of coproduction, however, goes one step further by telling us *who* is engaged in that transformation—originators and adopters working together to jointly create a new hybrid cultural product. Analyzing the complexities of how coproduction works, then, illuminates how decisions are made on the ground about how cultural products are modified in local contexts by transnational teams.

Many organizations coproduce, but Sesame Workshop does so in very specific ways. For this case, coproduction centers on how people from different cultures who do not share collective identities and meanings are able to construct them as they engage each other. Coproduction then, depends on the way both the product (in this case, local *Sesame Street* programs) and the relationships between its creators (Sesame Workshop and its partners) are produced.

---

[6] Elinor Ostrom, for example, defines coproduction as "a process through which inputs from individuals who are not 'in' the same organization are transformed into goods and services" (Ostrom 1996:1073).

[7] Some data and ideas in this book were originally published as "Culture in Transnational Interaction: How Organizational Partners Coproduce Sesame Street" in *Theory and Society* (2023).

[8] The terms originator and adopter are used in the literature on diffusion and local adaptation (see Rogers 2003).

In this book, I will trace the successive processes of coproduction, beginning with the imagination of the cultural product, to its disassembly,[9] reconstitution, and dissemination. All of these processes affect both the cultural product itself and the relationships among its creators. The process of creating *Sesame Street* involves the exchange of complex cultural knowledge. And yet it moves beyond mere exchange. The process privileges the creation of *new* knowledge that emerges from transnational interaction, and that is used to coproduce a product that is transformed into more than the sum of its parts. The *Sesame Street* case, then, allows us to grapple with "culture in interaction" at the transnational level, shedding light on *culture in transnational interaction*. By foregrounding interactions among people working in organizations, we can analyze "the cultural bases of diffusion" and develop a cultural approach that replaces "a theory of connections with a theory of connecting" (Strang and Soule 1998:276; Kaufman and Patterson 2005). At its core, this model of how organizational partners jointly create hybrid cultural products is an initial attempt to lay the foundation for understanding transnational interaction in relationship to cultural coproduction, and an invitation for other scholars to build upon it.

Global and Transnational Cultural Production

I conceptualize coproduction as a distinctive form of global and transnational cultural production, and *Sesame Street* as a specific case of coproduction characterized by joint creation and production among two or more organizations. The vast literature on cultural production at the transnational or global level is interdisciplinary, cutting across sociology, political science, anthropology, communication and media studies, and cultural studies, among others. The research tends to focus on how cultural products are created and diffused, and how they are adapted and translated in new locations.

World society approaches in sociology focus on the development of world culture, suggesting that it develops from a convergence of similar policies, practices, and products around the globe. Nations, multilateral and global governance institutions, international organizations, and transnational networks facilitate this cultural convergence, which emerges largely from consensus (Boli and Thomas 1997; Meyer et al 1997; Jameson and Miyoshi 1998; Lechner and Boli 2005; Meyer 2010; Bromley, Schofer, and Longhofer 2020).

---

[9] I define disassembly as breaking down the essential characteristics of the cultural product (e.g. form, content, structure), the rules governing it, and its relationship to the environment it is entering.

Scholars critical of world society frameworks argue that cultural convergence is never frictionless. Global culture, they assert, reflects the imposition and dominance of Western values, institutions, and cultural icons—from Walmart and McDonald's to megachurches and Madonna—that eclipse local power, culture, and agency (Hamelink 1983; Robertson 1994; Ritzer 1995; Cowen 2004). Others point out that hybrid cultures and identities emerge as locals resist (fully or partly) a hegemonic global culture, combining transnational influences with local specificity (Nederveen Pieterse 1994; Appadurai 1996; Hannerz 1996; Yúdice 2004; Kymlicka 2007). The theoretical and philosophical grounding of much of this work emerged from humanities and cultural studies scholars, particularly those interested in culture and globalization (Bhabha 1994; Storey 2003).

World society scholars have made important contributions that inform the analysis in this book by foregrounding organizations as conduits for the spread of global culture. But because their research focuses on macro-level analyses, it cannot adequately explain how world culture—and the products and policies that constitute it—get incorporated, transformed, and spread at the local level. Another group of scholars of global and transnational cultural production, however, helps us understand how cultural products are translated for local contexts and audiences. A significant strand in this literature focuses on the translation of media, a particular kind of cultural product, in the context of "cultural globalization" (Crane et al. 2002). Scholars in this arena examine how media (including books, comics, and magazines) are translated and the political and cultural factors that affect their translation (Ang 1985; Griswold 1987; Davis 2002; Kuipers 2015; Brienza and Revers 2016).

A rich body of research in communications and media studies examines processes of translation and interpretation of television programs once they arrive in a new locale. We therefore understand a lot about what makes particular genres and programs successful, both in the US and internationally (Grindstaff 2002; Abu-Lughod 2005). We also know how television programs such as *Dallas* or *The Nanny* are translated and the political and cultural factors that affect those translations (see Ang 1985; Liebes and Katz 1990; Kuipers 2015). We know very little, however, about how hybrid versions of television programs with local plots, themes, and characters are constructed by partner organizations. This paucity of knowledge results in part from the fact that many more programs are dubbed or translated than are coproduced as hybrids.

In addition to the translation approach, a robust literature on local adaptation examines how cultural products are fundamentally transformed by adopters. In contrast to translation approaches, local adaptation scholarship focuses on the creation of hybrid cultural products, specifically on how they are reinterpreted, adapted, and transformed at the local level (Risse, Ropp, and Sikkink 1999; Rosenau 2003). Scholars usually employ qualitative methods to analyze the malleability of culture, the multi-directionality of transnational practices, and the reconfiguration of global norms to suit local needs (Thayer 2000; Saguy 2002; Zwingel 2011). They foreground full or partial resistance to global culture, examining how adopters fuse the transnational and the local (Naples and Desai 2002). Merry (2006), for example, examines the UN negotiations that determine cultural norms at the global level, and how their "vernacularization" is critical to their ability to gain traction and resonance locally.

Translation and local adaptation research has been essential to understanding cultural production at global and transnational levels, particularly how cultural brokers who translate cultural products make new ideas intelligible for local audiences (Levitt and Merry 2009; Liu, Hu, and Liao 2009; Kuipers 2015; Lavie and Varriale 2019; Menon 2019; Sedano 2019; Levitt 2020; Fang 2024). This focus on cultural brokers informs my analysis of coproduction because it insists that we analyze what skilled actors with agency actually do on the ground to translate and transform cultural products.

Although scholars engaged in research on global and transnational cultural production using all of these approaches provide compelling insights into how cultural products change and spread, they all primarily examine what originators or adopters do in isolation from each other. They are not asking questions about how *partners work together* on the ground. This is not surprising; the bird's eye view of world society researchers focuses their attention on macro-level questions. And translation and local adaptation scholars' concern with resistance to global culture has rightly centered their focus primarily on meso-level processes. From each of their very different vantage points, however, they cannot see how partners are working on the ground and why it is important to understand what they are doing.

Methodological choices also prevent scholars from observing partners on the ground in real time. The vast majority of research on global cultural products, particularly media, are reception studies centered on processes of translation, interpretation, and acceptance at the point of consumption in a new location (Liebes and Katz 1990; Abu-Lughod 2005). Retrospective or ex post facto analyses that compare original innovations to local adaptations after (rather than during) their creation lack critical data about how vital decisions were made. Studies of McDonald's and Disneyland, for example, focus on how versions in other countries resemble or differ from their US counterparts and how this affects consumers' acceptance (Van Maanen 1992; Ritzer 1995; Watson 1997). Although ex post facto analyses offer hypotheses of why an adaptation mimics or strays from its original—for example, why McDonald's serves different food in India—few studies can trace the nature of the interactive process that resulted in the innovation's final form—for example, how McDonald's and its Indian franchisees made decisions together about food options there. In other words, the discussions and negotiations among organizational partners in real time that shaped these decisions at the point of production were not observed.

I build upon these three important research traditions by introducing a new question: What do partners do together on the ground? My methodological approach, combining interviews with observations of partner interactions in real time, is conducive to seeing what is happening on the ground. And what does it reveal? The importance of organizations involved in coproduction.

Organizations and Coproduction

The focus on coproduction in organizational contexts makes this book distinctive from other research on global cultural production. It is also useful because it reveals how the ability of organizations in different countries to *jointly* create a hybrid cultural product depends on their ability to align their interests and exchange different kinds of complex cultural knowledge in real time. In the extensive body of cross-disciplinary research on organizations, there are retrospective studies focused on the ways in which individual firms and for-profit organizations create subsidiaries, and local franchises transform products for global markets (Guillén 2000; Sklair 2001; Tihanyi et al. 2005; Lanchimba et al. 2025).

There is also a substantial amount of research on what makes teams effective (Hackman 2002; Felps et al. 2006; Hackman 2011), including a smaller body of work examining the structure, performance, and effectiveness of transnational teams (Snow et al. 1996; Earley and Mosakowski 2000; Verhoeven et al. 2017; Bjorvatn and Wald 2024). Research focused on transnational teams generally employs quantitative methods to examine firms and the collaborative creation of profit-generating products, from clothing to pharmaceuticals. This scholarship is important in analyzing the *Sesame Street* case because it illuminates how cultural differences can affect transnational team performance and shows that building trust and managing conflict are essential to creating an effective transnational team. These scholars, therefore, provide a strong foundation for analyzing how transnational teams engage in cultural production. They fall short, however, in expanding our understanding of how transnational teams construct *hybrid cultural products* in real time on the ground, and the underlying processes that mediate the interactions involved in managing cultural differences, building trust, and managing conflict.

Research on nonprofit and nongovernmental organizations (NGOs) engaged in spreading cultural products usually focuses on whether they succeed or fail—often in the context of development projects (Ferguson 1994; Campbell 2003; Swidler and Watkins 2017; Barrington 2025). Billions of dollars of global aid money are poured into public health awareness campaigns, intended, for example, to prevent HIV transmission by convincing people to use condoms. These campaigns have dubious effects at best (McDonnell 2016), and are often "thin" attempts at diffusion—devoid of substantive efforts to locally adapt cultural products (for example, by placing local actors in appropriate clothing in the background photo behind the "use a condom" message).

Few studies, however, examine the nature of the organizations that implement these projects, their relationship to local partner organizations charged with assisting or directing development programs, and how organizational relationships influence development outcomes. We therefore know little about how transnational organizations work with local partners to design and implement projects. Moreover, because most research does not analyze the building of collaborative organizational ties, it misses the cultural environment in which transnational partnerships are constructed.

These gaps are surprising given that critics frequently blame the failure of development programs on US organizations' lack of understanding of local cultural practices and imposition of Western values on local communities and organizations (Ferguson 1994; Morfit 2011). While the idea that cultural ignorance contributes to or is responsible for developmental failure is widespread, few scholars have analyzed what exactly leads to the disarticulation between developmental strategies and local cultural environments in real time on the ground.

A Framework for Understanding Culture in Transnational Interaction

The *culture in transnational interaction* framework I introduce here traces the successive processes of coproduction, beginning with the imagination of the cultural product, to its disassembly, reconstitution, and dissemination. As we will see, the processes at each of these stages involve both the cultural product itself and the relationships among those creating it.

Sesame Workshop and its partners coproduce a hybrid cultural product that involves the exchange of complex cultural knowledge. My theoretical framework is therefore meant to address the processes by which organizations working together as a transnational team *jointly* create a hybrid cultural product. Partners who coproduce hybrid cultural products together in real time engage fundamentally different processes than originators or adopters who tweak or transform them in isolation from each other.

There are innumerable forms of hybridity. Hybrids can be objects that occupy physical space and reflect material culture (e.g. magazines, clothing, food, architecture), and those that reflect non-material culture (e.g. ideas, norms, values). Theorizing and analyzing hybridity is prevalent in science studies (Latour 1993), feminist theory (Haraway 1985), and in their intersection. Scholars show that the nature of objects impacts the social processes in which they are involved (Haraway 1976; Latour 2000). In my culture in transnational interaction framework, Nederveen Pieterse's dual understanding of hybridity is the most useful: "Structural hybridisation, or the emergence of new practices of social cooperation and competition, and cultural hybridisation, or new translocal cultural expressions, are interdependent: new forms of transnational cooperation require and evoke new cultural imaginaries" (Nederveen Pieterse 1994:180). In the case of *Sesame Street*, cooperation in the form of coproduction is inextricably linked to new cultural expressions in the form of unique local programs.

My goal here is to understand how hybrid products involving complex cultural knowledge are coproduced by a transnational team. *Sesame Street* is the paradigmatic example of hybridity—a cultural product tailored to fit the needs and requirements of different audiences. *Sesame Street* programs are not established once; they are created and iterated over and over again through regular and intensive interactions among transnational organizational partners. *Sesame Street*, therefore, looks and sounds very different in India, Mexico, South Africa, and the United States; each country has its own content, format, and educational priorities.

A variety of sociology of culture approaches are useful in understanding the *Sesame Street* case. The theory of fields developed by Bourdieu—including global fields elaborated in his later work and expanded upon by subsequent scholars—reveals how power operates within fields that span national boundaries (Dezalay and Garth 2002; Bourdieu 2005; Go 2008; Buchholz 2016). Becker's approach in *Art Worlds* (1982) helps us understand how creators negotiate aesthetic conflicts in order to accomplish the work of creating collectively. And Peterson's production of culture perspective (1976) offers insights about how local *Sesame Street* programs are made. Although these approaches could, respectively, help analyze the power dynamics between New York staff and partners, how they negotiate creative conflicts, and how their decisions are shaped by children's media markets, new digital technologies, and shifts to streaming services across the entertainment industry, they would not adequately illuminate and explain the transnational processes that affect coproduction.

The book's central framework—culture in transnational interaction—is situated within two sets of theoretical approaches that could be extended to capture these transnational processes: *culture in interaction* (a meso-level analysis of culture following the symbolic interactionism tradition) and *inhabited institutionalism* (an integration of symbolic interactionism and new institutionalism). My primary intervention is to put them in conversation with each other in the transnational context, and to develop a new framework that can be used to analyze the processes by which transnational organizational teams coproduce hybrid cultural products together.

Culture in interaction, Eliasoph and Lichterman's groundbreaking approach, built upon symbolic interactionism by offering an analysis of culture at the meso-level (2003). Using two cases—a group of suburban environmental activists, and patrons in a bar—they examine how groups communicate collective representations—defined as "vocabularies, symbols, or codes—that structure people's abilities to think and act" (2003:735). It is through interactions within groups that collective representations and meaning are made and transmitted, producing culture in interaction (2003:737). The concept of culture in interaction is quite useful in analyzing global/transnational cultural production because it captures how interactions within groups forge collective representations and meaning, resulting in particular "group styles." But the approach falls short in explaining how people who do not share a common culture might construct collective representations, meaning, and group styles through their transnational interactions. Moreover, it cannot elucidate how they utilize collective representations to create a hybrid cultural product together.

Scholars who use an inhabited institutionalism approach also prioritize social interactions among people, but they focus on interactions within organizations, their relationship to outside institutions, and how those interactions shape meaning-making within them (Hallett and Ventresca 2006; Binder 2007; Morrill 2008; Hallett and Hawbaker 2021). They examine meaning that can be routine or emergent, and how it is contested and resolved (or not) through interaction. Haedicke (2012), for example, shows how members and leaders of natural food co-ops interpreted and responded to market pressures that threatened their practices as a mission-driven organization. He also reveals the interconnectedness of external institutional environments, organizations at the local and national levels, and interactions among people in both.

Inhabited institutionalism is also quite helpful in examining global/transnational cultural production because it reveals how, through interacting within organizations, people manage, interpret, and resolve tension and conflict. Indeed, Hallett and Hawbaker emphasize that: "Interests are often 'figured out' and contested during interactions" (2021:18). Research thus far that employs an inhabited institutionalist approach, however, focuses largely on organizations and the people that inhabit them at the local or national level.[10] Like Eliasoph and Lichterman's suburban activists and bar patrons, the people in these organizations already have considerable common ground for interaction, including shared language(s), histories, political systems, and cultural reference points, including stories, music, and humor etc. But what about people in organizations that cross national boundaries who have few, if any, shared collective representations, meanings, and culture? What is the nature of their interactions as they engage in collaborative work, such as coproduction? Concerns with the rapid progression of globalization raise questions about the nature of interactions among people who engage each other as part of transnational organizational teams.

The *Sesame Street* case provides an opportunity to extend culture in interaction and inhabited institutionalism to the transnational level in order to understand how New York staff and partners around the world create a hybrid cultural product together. The ideas that collective meaning is constructed through group interaction and that organizational interactions allow people to manage, interpret, and resolve tension and conflict in order to work together provide a foundation for my analysis of the *Sesame Street* case. The transnational context in which New York staff and partners work challenges the parameters of culture in interaction and inhabited institutionalism by suggesting that in the case of transnational organizations, new group styles, collective representations, and meaning must be constructed and negotiated. How that process works on the ground, including how interests are "figured out" and contested during interactions, is not well understood. Nor do we know how the larger outside institutional environments—from childhood education to global media production—in which transnational teams are embedded, affect that process.

My approach marries insights from inhabited institutionalism to cultural sociology by expanding them to the transnational level and examining "culture in interaction" among people who do not share collective representations and must somehow construct them as they engage each other in

---

[10] See Kameo 2024 for an excellent exception.

organizations. It also allows us to examine "culture in interaction" at the transnational level and to theorize *culture in transnational interaction* at the organizational level.

Here I offer a framework for understanding culture in transnational interaction that shows how organizational partners who do not share collective representations create them together through coproduction by: 1) constructing value to align their interests, 2) exchanging complex cultural knowledge to customize, and 3) exchanging complex cultural knowledge to build alliances. This occurs during three successive processes of coproduction—disassembly, reconstitution, and dissemination. Table 1.1 details these processes at each

Table 1.1 Culture in transnational interaction at the organizational level

	Constructing Value to Align Interests	Exchanging Cultural Knowledge to Customize	Exchanging Cultural Knowledge to Build Alliances
Process	Disassembly	Reconstitution	Dissemination
Status of hybrid?	Imagined	Produced	Disseminated
Questions faced?	Will we coproduce?	What will it look like?	How will we get it to people?
Challenges confronted?	moral landmines; high-level values; Sesame Workshop prohibitions	technical challenges; navigating local culture	accessing local networks
Participants involved?	New York staff (decision makers); local experts and gatekeepers	New York staff and partners (technical and creative)	New York staff; local brokers
What happens to hybrid?	Disassembled: break down essential characteristics and rules to align interests *and* construct value	Reconstituted: customize and construct collective meanings	Disseminated: introduce into new locale by building alliances and networks
Resources exchanged by Sesame Workshop?	flexible model financial resources	financial resources technical knowledge	financial resources ability to leverage networks
Resources exchanged by partners?	local cultural knowledge (cultural capital)	local cultural knowledge (cultural capital)	local networks and brokers (social capital)
How New York staff and partners practice flexibility, trust, and mutual learning?	willingness to disassemble and set boundaries on core goals and values	willingness to thickly adapt, "bend" rules, and share local knowledge	willingness to share networks

stage, and shows how they involve both the cultural product itself and the relationships among its creators:

The framework of culture in transnational interaction moves beyond established consensus in the literature that cultural products are often valorized and customized before they diffuse, by addressing the underlying processes at work: What do *partners* (as opposed to individual originators and/or adopters) see as valuable, how and why do they customize, and how do they reach sufficient consensus to be able to construct a hybrid cultural product together? Examining these processes reveals how partners' crucial knowledge allows them to recalibrate the scales, mitigating—but not completely eliminating—the power differential with Sesame Workshop.

Creating a *Sesame Street* program is incredibly difficult relationally and organizationally. New York staff cannot simply send partners written instructions about the program, its goals, and its values, and expect them to be able to coproduce a hybrid version. The cultural knowledge needed to do so is complex, meaning it is based on abstract, tacit, and/or symbolic meanings and understandings (Polanyi 1958). Transmitting this knowledge requires extensive and regular personal interaction and the construction of shared understandings through engagement in real time.

This cultural knowledge exchange occurs in two directions among New York staff and partners. Both possess valuable knowledge—one at the point of production and one at the point of consumption. New York staff must communicate Sesame Workshop's culture and the goals and values of *Sesame Street*. The program as a cultural product inheres explicitly normative content and may challenge cultural and moral frameworks. Partners must communicate their goals and values, and those of the local culture—including needs, norms, taste, values, humor, etc. *Sesame Street* programs are not established once; they are created over and over again through these interactions. The nature of this complex cultural knowledge, therefore, demands cooperation; organizational partners must continuously build tacit knowledge together and establish shared understandings through social networks.

Disassembly: Constructing Value to Align Interests

The first step in creating a new *Sesame Street* program is deciding whether to coproduce or not. During initial meetings and discussions, senior Sesame Workshop staff and local experts and gatekeepers must decide if and what they will coproduce. An attempt to develop an Italian version of *Sesame Street* ended at this stage because potential partners did not think young children should be watching television at all. If they decide to move forward, Sesame Workshop and its partners attempt to align their interests by constructing value in relationship to the project and the process of coproducing it. In general, "value" means whether partners view coproduction as offering something of worth, utility, or importance. The meaning of "value," however, varies by local context and is multi-faceted. For Palestinians, value meant building their local capacity in media and television production. For South Africans, it meant developing a curriculum that addressed the HIV/AIDS crisis.

Alignment of interests is also multi-faceted and can vary across a variety of different dimensions, including the alignment of goals, strategies, desired outcomes, budgetary priorities, etc. Aligning interests, however, does not necessarily mean that interests must be identical or shared. Rather, interests can be different, but cannot conflict in ways that prevent each side from identifying value in the process and/or outcomes of engaging in coproduction.

The process by which interests are aligned involves disassembly, which I define here as breaking down the essential characteristics of the cultural product (e.g. form, content, structure), the rules governing it, and its relationship to the environment it is entering. New York staff disassemble the essential values and qualities of *Sesame Street* and of Sesame Workshop. Partners must evaluate whether these are compatible with their own values, and within their own environment. They are unlikely to accept a product whole cloth or create a hybrid form, unless they view it as having value and resonance at the local level.

Breaking down these components into their smallest parts allows Sesame Workshop and partners to put options on the table, and to build from those small units possibilities for new and unforeseen common ground. Disassembly is, therefore, much more extensive than translation. But New York staff and partners must also overcome challenges, including how to divide and share resources, how to deal with moral landmines and high-level values, and how to set the rules for their own partnership and interactions, including managing conflict.

At this stage, Sesame Workshop and its partners engage in myriad interactions to communicate their own goals, expectations, preferences, beliefs, and values. And they must decide if they can accept each others' bottom line demands. If they cannot align their interests *and* construct value in relationship to the cultural product, the process ends.

Reconstitution: Exchanging Cultural Knowledge to Customize

Once New York staff and partners have aligned their interests and agree to move forward, the cultural product moves from being imagined to becoming real, concrete, and producible. After disassembling *Sesame Street*, they must put it back together, or reconstitute it, but in a new and hybrid form. The process they use to reconstitute *Sesame Street* as a hybrid is customization, which means modifying it to meet local needs and goals using both essential elements of *Sesame Street* provided by New York staff and essential elements of the local culture, provided by partners.[11] In order for a team of New York staff and partners—all creative and technical experts—to create a local *Sesame Street* program, they must begin to exchange knowledge and construct collective meanings in order to customize *Sesame Street*.

Coproduction requires an exchange of different kinds of resources, including various forms of partners' knowledge about culture and networks, and Sesame Workshop's technical knowledge of all that is needed to create the program. Different kinds of knowledge are exchanged and utilized, including knowledge of local needs, values, and access to local gatekeepers, brokers, experts, and networks. Only partners have these resources. Knowledge exchange occurs when one partner provides information/insight that the other does not possess. That knowledge becomes a resource in the course of negotiation when it is asymmetrical (meaning when only one team possesses it), and is perceived as being valuable and essential to coproduction. Knowledge exchange involves deeply relational work that exposes variations in how New York staff and partners conceptualize ideas related to the cultural product—including childhood, gender equality, education, humor—and to the collective process of creating it together, which involves discussions of autonomy, accountability, quality, etc.

Customization is important for many reasons, as will be discussed in detail in later chapters. It reveals the importance of meaning making, particularly for innovations viewed as having *potential* value if they are transformed to suit local needs. Customization facilitates local acceptance, increasing the likelihood of success and impact, and outcome optimization. And finally, customization can strengthen organizational relationships and build trust. For partners, having their needs and goals prioritized sends a strong signal that their knowledge is valued.

---

[11] Although local adaptation is also used in the diffusion literature, I use the term customization for ease and because I think it also connotes the possibility of a more extensive transformation of a cultural product; whereas local adaptation suggests an addition to or subtraction from the original product, customization suggests direct changes to the original product itself.

Dissemination: Exchanging Cultural Knowledge to Build Alliances

Throughout the coproduction process, Sesame Workshop needs to build alliances with a range of potential stakeholders—including the local private sector, NGOs, civil society organizations, local elites, and state actors—that help them move with little friction into new locales. The process by which this occurs involves dissemination, as partners share knowledge about local gatekeepers, brokers, and experts, and about how to identify potential allies, particularly with governments, NGOs, and broadcasters who then facilitate this spread. Building alliances and networks is critical to garnering support for local programs and spreading them among diverse constituencies. Effective alliances help legitimize *Sesame Street* projects, provide New York staff and partners cover when problems or conflicts arise, and allow for more effective scaling and sustainability of projects.

Although the process of dissemination culminates with *Sesame Street* programs and community outreach projects reaching local audiences, many of the alliances that make this possible are initiated in earlier stages of coproduction. Chapter 6, therefore, also tracks alliance-building that occurs during disassembly and reconstitution—when New York staff, partners in charge of community outreach, and local brokers devise alliance-building strategies that will enable them to spread the newly constructed program to local audiences and users during the final process of dissemination.

As New York staff and partners engage these processes of disassembly, reconstitution, and dissemination, they also engage practices of flexibility, trust, and mutual learning (as also outlined in Table 1.1). They nurture flexibility by their willingness to disassemble and "thickly" customize and adapt programs, nurture trust by valuing each others' resources and knowledge, and nurture mutual learning by recognizing the limitations of their own knowledge and committing to learn from each other. They are also willing to engage and manage tension that inevitably arises—reflecting on and learning from mistakes is built into their collaborative process. These practices allow them to manage conflicts and navigate the cultural and political obstacles they confront, and to engage in diagnosis and repair of potential problems as they arise at different moments in the process of coproduction.

My framework lays the foundation for understanding transnational interaction in relationship to cultural coproduction, using the case of *Sesame Street*. The analytical purchase of this framework will depend on its usefulness to other scholars applying it in different contexts and with different cases. We can imagine, however, that the framework could be useful for examining cases of cultural coproduction across a variety of fields, from the arts and media to advertising, and public health and human rights campaigns, among others. It could also serve as a guide for practitioners in organizations who want to engage in transnational work and/or build transnational teams.

Sesame Street: Creating Cultural Friction

I return, then, to the question of what makes *Sesame Street* unique. In this book, I suggest that what makes *Sesame Street* unique is not the nature of Sesame Workshop—the organization that creates it—or the fact that it is *not* created for profit. What makes it unique is its relationship to the local environment and how this creates "cultural friction." In her highly influential book *Friction: An Ethnography of Global Connection*, Anna Lowenhaupt Tsing introduced the concept of "friction" to describe social interactions in a globalizing world. She writes, "A wheel turns because of its encounter with the surface of the road; spinning in the air it goes nowhere. Rubbing two sticks together produces heat and light; one stick alone is just a stick. [...] Friction reminds us that heterogeneous and unequal encounters can lead to new arrangements of culture and power" (2005:5).

Tsing's idea of friction—which is now a concept that has been embraced by scholars across a wide range of disciplines—helps us understand how cultural friction can be generated when a product challenges or destabilizes certain aspects of its target audience's local environment. I suggest that friction is not an inherent feature of the cultural product. Rather, friction inheres in the *relationship* between the product and the environment. The more a cultural product challenges aspects of the local environment, the more friction is generated in the encounter. *Normative friction* occurs when a cultural product confronts pre-existing cultural and moral frameworks, and *relational friction* occurs when a cultural product challenges pre-existing social arrangements. The relationship between a cultural product and the local environment, in turn, shapes the way originators, distributors, local partners, target users, and local audiences localize products in different contexts.[12]

Sesame Street programs generate both normative and relational friction, making it necessary for New York staff and partners not only to construct value and build alliances, but also to customize the cultural product together. A central contribution of this book therefore lies in its focus on transnational organizational relationships, which is absent in much of the literature on diffusion.

---

[12] These ideas of normative and relational friction were first developed with Isabel Jijon in a paper titled "Theorizing "Cultural Friction": Or, How Norms, Technologies, Media, and Commodities Spread."

Organizations Are Key to Moving Complex Hybrid Cultural Products Around the World

The nature of the complex knowledge that must be shared and exchanged in order to create a complex hybrid cultural product like *Sesame Street* means that relationships among organizations in different countries are central to the story of how *Sesame Street* is able to replicate itself from Beijing to São Paulo. Indeed, the spread of *Sesame Street* requires significant interaction among organizational partners. Running throughout this book is therefore a more general argument about the role transnational organizational relationships play in the creation and diffusion of a complex hybrid cultural product such as *Sesame Street*.

Sesame Workshop lacks local knowledge and is completely dependent on local partners to share it. Partners are protective of their knowledge, but willing to share it in order to engage with a cultural innovation that represents universality and has a global reach. Thus, Sesame Workshop and its partners each benefit from a local program's simultaneous universality and particularity. But what can be particular and what becomes universal is not predetermined, and varies by country. Indeed, it is through a complex process of negotiation that these decisions are made and that hybrid cultural products are created. In this book, I will take readers through this process, revealing the nature of hidden interactions that are usually taken for granted as cultural products travel around the world. Because *Sesame Street* programs are so complex, they require complex negotiations across a myriad of organizations at local and transnational levels. And it is through this iterative process of organizational negotiation that innovations are constructed and, like *Sesame Street*, generate paths toward universality and particularity simultaneously.

The Value of Studying Sesame Street from an Organizational Perspective

The vast majority of research on *Sesame Street* focuses on the program's educational curriculum and impact, both in the US and around the world. There are a handful of studies that examine local *Sesame Street* programs, though not from an organizational perspective. Sara Lederman (2012) adroitly analyzes India's *Galli Galli Sim Sim* and its effects on political debate. Helle Strangaard Jensen's (2023) excellent historical study examines Sesame Workshop's efforts to market and spread *Sesame Street* to European countries in the late 1960s and early 1970s. Her work, which raises important critiques of

Sesame Workshop and the spread of local *Sesame Street* programs, provides an important foundation for understanding why a model of coproduction was developed and where it falls short. Naomi A. Moland's (2020) insightful examination of the Nigerian program called *Sesame Square* centers on the challenges of using children's television to promote multicultural education and peace, particularly in fragile states with segregated populations and ongoing conflict. And Yael Warshel (2021) offers a compelling audience reception study to gauge how both children and their parents received and decoded peace messaging in the joint Israeli/Palestinian *Sesame Street* program.

I am aware of no studies that actually examine Sesame Workshop as an organization, centered on how New York staff and partners function as a transnational team. An analysis of Sesame Workshop's coproduction process spanning multiple countries and using data gathered in real time on the ground was, until now, yet to be written. Why is it important that we examine Sesame Workshop and the way it creates programs with its global partners? And what can we learn from studying *Sesame Street* from an organizational perspective?

First, looking at how Sesame Workshop and its partners negotiate between global and local tensions illuminates how organizations in general engage in transnational collaboration and teambuilding. We know little about how they build collective goals, manage conflicts, and navigate the cultural and political minefields they confront as they work together to produce a hybrid cultural product. We therefore do not adequately understand the dynamics of transnational teambuilding as they relate to constructing and disseminating these hybrid cultural products. The lessons from Sesame Workshop and its partners can therefore be applied to a range of other hybrid cultural products. NGOs engaged in creating public service campaigns, corporations creating innovative products, and social movement activists moving strategic repertoires (such as nonviolent resistance) to other countries can all learn from the work that Sesame Workshop and its partners engage in.

Second, examining the relationships between Sesame Workshop and its partners can reveal possibilities for building more equitable relationships between organizations in low- and high-income countries. Sesame Workshop's model is unlike the vast majority of US organizations that engage in collaborative work in other countries. As I will describe in more detail in the next chapter, Sesame Workshop's model is based on creating a local team of experts that chooses the themes and curricula for its program, and writes and produces the program. This is very different from the dominant model, which is for development organizations to send Americans to live and work in other countries.

Of course, the relationships between Sesame Workshop and its partners *are not* devoid of power asymmetries and inequalities—they certainly are, and this will be discussed in later chapters. But partners have much more autonomy and input than the majority of collaborators who work with US development organizations. An analysis of how Sesame Workshop builds relationships with partners that are characterized by trust and equity, and where it falls short in building those relationships, can be extremely useful for other organizations as they strategize how to build their own. And, perhaps most importantly, it helps us to evaluate whether equitable collaborations are more or less likely to generate successful or optimal outcomes.

Research Strategy: Seven Years Traveling the Longest Street in the World

There are many aspects of *Sesame Street* that make it an interesting and compelling case to study. Sesame Workshop and its partners coproduce *Sesame Street* in multiple countries, which allows for analyses of internal variation and cross-country comparisons. Local programs are currently being aired in over twenty countries. In addition, Sesame Workshop engages in development or community "outreach" projects with local partners—including governments, NGOs, and other civil society organizations—that prioritize the UN's Millennium Development Goals, from literacy and health to environmental stewardship. They also address controversial topics, including gender and social equality, and respect for racial/ethnic and religious differences in conflict zones such as Kosovo, South Africa, Israel/Palestine, and Northern Ireland. And finally, studying the international spread of *Sesame Street* allows me to engage a cultural product that embodies values and goals that are meaningful to people in partner countries and therefore potentially controversial.

In 2007, when I began the research for this book, there were many decisions to be made. Primary among them was what programs would I study, and how would I study them? It was important to examine more than one program so that I could generalize beyond one case. Given that a core question of the book centers on how organizations in the US and low-income countries collaborate to create a hybrid cultural product, I chose to only study programs in low- and middle-income countries. This eliminated some of Sesame Workshop's most popular and longstanding programs in countries such as Germany (*Sesamstrasse*), the Netherlands (*Sesamstraat*), and newer programs, such as in Northern Ireland (*Sesame Tree*).

Since 2000, the vast majority of new local Sesame Workshop programs have been created in low- and middle-income countries, including: Bangladesh, Brazil, China, Egypt, India, Indonesia, Jordan, Nigeria, Palestine, South Africa, and Tanzania. According to New York staff, this is the result of a conscious effort by Sesame Workshop leadership to focus on areas where educational needs are high, and where opportunities, capacity, and funding are available. I chose programs that provided religious, ethnic, and linguistic variation, differences in educational history and infrastructure, and variation in relationship to the US.

I ultimately chose to study programs within four regions of the world: Latin America, the Middle East, Africa, and South Asia. Within those regions, I chose programs that offered interesting variations. In Latin America, I chose the longstanding program *Plaza Sésamo* in Mexico, which was updated for a pan-Latin American audience and included Sesame Workshop partners in Mexico, Colombia, and Puerto Rico. I also chose an iconic program, *Vila Sésamo*, that was revived in Brazil in 2008. In the Middle East, I chose Palestine (*Sharaʾa Simsim*) and Jordan (*Hikayat Simsim*), and included Israel, a high-income country (*Rechov Sumsum*), because Israel had been involved in joint programs focused on mutual respect and understanding goals with Palestine and Jordan (*Rechov Sumsum/Sharaʾa Simsim* and *Sesame Stories*).

I included *Iftah Ya Simsim*, a program produced among the six nations of the Gulf Cooperation Council (herein the Gulf States): Bahrain, Kuwait, Oman, Qatar, Saudi Arabia, and United Arab Emirates (UAE). Including this case is particularly important because it allowed me to observe interactions among New York staff and potential partners who had not yet committed to participating in a local *Sesame Street* program. These and Israel are the only high-income countries in my sample. Similarly, I chose the Nigeria program (*Sesame Square*) because it was new, and I was able to attend the first meetings at which decisions were made about the future content of the program. In Africa, I also chose the South African program *Takalani Sesame*, which in many ways focused on post-apartheid reconciliation. In South Asia, I chose India (*Galli Galli Sim Sim*) and Bangladesh (*Sisimpur*). India is an important case because in 2009, Sesame Workshop created Sesame Workshop India, the first subsidiary and local office in a foreign country. In 2013, Sesame Workshop launched another subsidiary in Bangladesh. Figure 1.1 provides a visual of the cases I chose around the world. The map includes country names and local *Sesame Street* program names.

To understand why people all over the world adapt and adopt local versions of *Sesame Street* required me to be present and observe what was actually

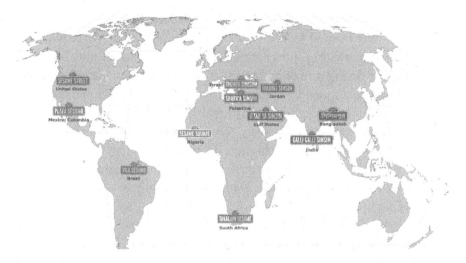

Figure 1.1 Cases around the world

occurring between Sesame Workshop and its partners. How do they relate to each other in real time? What kinds of conflicts arise, and how are they resolved? It also required me to sit down with Sesame Workshop staff and partners and ask them to reflect on their experiences—often for hours at a time. Memories needed to be gently prodded, and documents locked away in files needed to be consulted to verify dates and places. Intensive observational or ethnographic fieldwork and in-depth interviews in multiple countries were therefore necessary to answer the questions posed in this book. A more detailed discussion of my methods can be found in Appendix I.

Access was critical, and in 2007, then Sesame Workshop President/CEO Gary Knell gave me full access to the organization, both in its New York headquarters and to partners around the world. Under his leadership, it was common for researchers to be given access to the organization and to its data. He and key staff members welcomed results that were critical and would allow Sesame Workshop to improve its strategies and practices.

My fieldwork spanned seven years. It began in Sesame Workshop's New York office in 2007, where I took on the role of participant observer and made multiple research trips to attend key staff and research meetings, strategy sessions, conference calls, and visits with partners. Each of these research trips generally lasted two to five days. This was made easier because I was at Harvard at the time and could travel quickly and easily from Cambridge to New York by train. While in New York, I interviewed New York staff involved in coproduction, including multiple representatives from each of the content, production, and research teams. I interviewed New York staff in key leadership positions from at least one core division of Sesame Workshop (e.g. international, marketing, international education, research and outreach, etc.) who had decision-making power, and those who interacted regularly with partners (see Appendix I, Table A.1 for New York staff's job titles).

Intensive ethnographic fieldwork in multiple countries was necessary to understand the dynamics between New York staff and partners, and to observe the processes by which coproduction occurs. Between 2008 and 2011, I traveled with New York staff to Mexico, Colombia, Puerto Rico, Israel, Palestine, Jordan, and Nigeria to observe and participate in a variety of events, including meetings, seminars, workshops, and training sessions (see Appendix I, Table A.3). I also observed meetings between New York staff, partners, local broadcasters, NGO representatives, government officials, funders, journalists, and researchers. I took extensive field notes during each trip.

I also observed meetings and training sessions held in NY with local partners (see Appendix I, Table A.3). These included a three-day event in December 2012 introducing potential partners of *Iftah Ya Simsim*, a program among the Gulf States, to Sesame Workshop.[13] And it included a 2013 writing workshop held for eight days to train *Iftah Ya Simsim's* newly selected writers. In addition to my observations in various countries, I interviewed a sample of Sesame Workshop's current and past partners in Brazil, Mexico, Colombia, Israel, Palestine, Jordan, India, Nigeria, and the Gulf States using a purposeful sampling approach (Seidman 2012). I also interviewed broadcasting, sponsorship, NGO, government, and funding partners involved in local programs and outreach projects (see Appendix I, Table A.2 for international partners' job titles). After each event with New York staff concluded, I generally remained in the country to interview partners for up to two weeks. The data includes 140 in-depth interviews with New York staff and current and past Sesame Workshop partners around the world gathered over seven years from 2007 to 2014. Between 2021 and 2024, I conducted approximately twenty additional interviews primarily to learn about any changes that had occurred since I left the field. This data served mainly to write the epilogue. Interviews lasted between one and seven hours and were recorded and professionally transcribed. Interviews totaled over 200 hours, and their transcripts

---

[13] On December 14, 2012, during the event, we heard the tragic news of the shooting at Sandy Hook Elementary School that took the lives of 26 people, including 20 children. New York staff, and partners from across the Middle East—whose work was devoted to children—and I, sat in stunned silence as the grief and sadness washed over us. It is not possible to think of that afternoon at Sesame Workshop, without remembering and honoring the children and families whose lives were shattered by such inexplicable and senseless violence.

generated over 3,500 single-spaced pages of text. In the data presented in this book, I edited quotations for clarity and brevity.

I did not code data with any preconceptions about what I might find. Rather, I relied on an inductive and iterative approach and only explored themes that emerged organically from my analyses (see Miles and Huberman 1994; Glaser and Strauss 2009). I first read all interview transcripts on printed paper copies (kept in three-ring binders by country) and made coding notes on them. I then reread all the transcripts two additional times, each time modifying and adding to the initial set of codes. I created a final coding dictionary with 316 individual codes (see Appendix I for more details on codes). I trained three Harvard PhD students to code the data with Atlas.ti, checked the robustness and reliability of the coding among them, and modified some codes a final time. They completed coding interviews in approximately four months.

The process of building my framework using the coded qualitative data involved recognizing patterns that emerged in how New York staff and partners described their interactions while creating local programs together. I was initially surprised that partners wanted more interaction with and less autonomy from New York staff. When I began the research, I expected the opposite to be true. As I went back and forth between my data and the literature, I saw that their interactions involved aligning interests, mitigating asymmetrical power dynamics, facilitating mutual learning, and building trust. I realized the unique theoretical contribution emerging revolved around how transnational teams create hybrid cultural products together. Thinking about and delineating the process they engaged in led me to the concept of coproduction as a process of relationship building.

How This Book Is Unique

This book is unique not simply because its subject—the process of creating multiple local versions of *Sesame Street* across the globe—has not been examined before. Its approach is also unexpected because it enters the debate on culture and globalization from an organizational perspective, devoting significant analysis to the relationship between organizations involved in constructing a hybrid cultural product. This focus is rare among books on diffusion and localization; it therefore makes a significant contribution to scholarship across these fields.

The book is also distinctive because it relies on rich observation and interview data gathered in and from seventeen countries over seven years to track the *process* by which decisions are made about how *Sesame Street* is locally adapted. It is one of the only diffusion or localization studies to use observational data to track how actors make decisions about cultural adaptation in real time, illuminating how actors define and think about cultural authenticity and change, how they weigh and attribute value, and formulate and prioritize concessions and bottom-line demands. Examining relationships between organizational partners offers scholars new ways to conceptually map complex negotiations and relational dynamics, revealing what has previously been unobservable—the negotiations that precede adoption or rejection of cultural products and that shape localization. The Sesame Workshop case also shows how local partners negotiate the adoption of global cultural products, combining global influences with local specificity, and resulting in a product and process that simultaneously promotes universality and particularity. By focusing not only on the product created, but also on the process organizational partners engage in, this book offers a useful framework for understanding diffusion and hybridization processes more generally across a variety of organizations.

Finally, this book is unique because it provides a compelling new framework for understanding the factors that constrain *and* spark adopters' resistance to cultural globalization—it considers agency in localization and diffusion processes. While critics of world society approaches rightly suggest that diffusion processes can reflect the imposition and dominance of Western values, practices, and products, excavating the interactions brings to light adopters' sources of leverage, influence, and autonomy. The book reveals the often-hidden sources of leverage that partners in low-income countries have.

The Book Organization and Chapters Ahead

The story of how local *Sesame Street* programs are created and spread around the world unfolds in eight chapters and an epilogue. Chapter 2 begins with a vignette about why Sesame Workshop developed a coproduction model. It then discusses the organization's history, the Sesame model in the US, and its relationship to local *Sesame Street* programs around the world. Partners who create a local *Sesame Street* program replicate the content-production-research model developed for the US program by working as a local team of experts that chooses the themes and curricula, community outreach projects, and writes and produces the program. Although they must promote key values in their programs, including nonviolence, tolerance, and respect, and are subject to certain restrictions and oversight, partners have tremendous freedom to adapt their programs. The chapter explains the process of creating a new program from conception to launch, and details the international variation in relationship to content and curricula, funding, relationships to governments and civil society organizations, and sustainability.

While Chapter 2 provides a broad overview of Sesame Workshop's coproduction process, Chapter 3 centers on how the process of coproduction begins as Sesame Workshop and its partners attempt to align their interests by constructing value in relationship to *Sesame Street* and the process of coproducing it. To do so, they engage a process of disassembly that involves breaking down what is essential to *Sesame Street* (e.g. form, content, structure), the rules governing it, and its relationship to the environment it is entering. At this stage, Sesame Workshop and its partners engage in numerous discussions to communicate their own goals, expectations, preferences, beliefs, and values. They must also determine whether they can accept each others' non-negotiable demands. Ultimately, this process enables the transnational team to coproduce a program that is both universal and particular, and varies by country. The chapter includes examples of disassembly from various local *Sesame Street* programs.

Chapter 4 examines how Sesame Workshop and its partners customize *Sesame Street* in various countries around the world. Coproduction continues as they engage in a process of reconstituting or putting together a new and distinctive version of *Sesame Street* that resonates with local audiences. During this process, New York staff and partners with technical and creative skills engage in reconstituting *Sesame Street*, transforming an imagined program into a real one that meets local needs and goals. They must also construct collective representations and meanings between New York staff and partners, who do not share them. The chapter includes examples of customization from various local *Sesame Street* programs.

Chapter 5 examines how Sesame Workshop and its partners conceptualize and utilize programs as vehicles for social change, and how their social change goals intersect and collide. It also highlights how norms that are highly contested—particularly around gender and racial/ethnic and religious equality—gain local acceptance and legitimacy, particularly in places where there is potentially strong opposition. The chapter explores how Sesame Workshop pushes cultural boundaries, relying on the expert knowledge of key partners who act as cultural brokers. Brokers navigate complex issues and create alliances with key local actors who help to activate norms such as gender equality that are often already present—at least at some level—locally. Cultural brokers can therefore be powerful facilitators of norm acceptance and internalization. The chapter includes examples of how New York staff and local partners push cultural boundaries with various local *Sesame Street* programs.

Chapter 6 focuses on how building alliances allows Sesame Workshop and its partners to coproduce and disseminate the program. During this stage in the coproduction process, a new *Sesame Street* program exists and must be disseminated and received by external audiences in a new locale. This means programs are aired, and outreach projects are launched in local communities. The core group of people involved shifts to New York staff, partners in charge of outreach, and local brokers who leverage networks and alliances with governments, NGOs, and broadcasters. Building alliances and networks is, therefore, critical to garnering support for local programs and spreading them among diverse constituencies and broad audiences. The chapter includes examples of dissemination and alliance-building from various local *Sesame Street* programs.

Chapter 7 examines conflicts between New York staff and partners and how they are managed and resolved. It examines the nature of their relationships, including power dynamics and differentials, levels of control and autonomy, and the nature of collaborative work and interactions. The chapter foregrounds how Sesame Workshop's control over intellectual property rights, including those created by its partners, significantly shapes the nature of their relationship. And yet, it reveals a perhaps ironic twist: partners from all over the world explained how they want to produce the best work possible, and how stronger connections to New York staff, more training and on-site visits, and more resources would improve the quality of their programs and outreach projects. The chapter details the nature of conflicts—particularly over humor, autonomy, modeling safety, and includes examples from various local *Sesame Street* programs.

In the concluding chapter, I reiterate the key findings in the book: that Sesame Workshop's secret sauce for creating a hybrid cultural product with partners is coproduction. In order to coproduce, partners from different cultures who do not share collective representations must create them together. They do so by constructing value to align their interests, and exchanging complex cultural knowledge to customize the product and build alliances to support and spread it. The final chapter, then, situates the case of *Sesame Street* within broader debates about power and agency in the global arena and highlights the inherent and inevitable contradictions that emerge in relationship to translation, local adaptation, and diffusion processes. The chapter concludes by demonstrating how an analysis of *Sesame Street* programs has implications for a broad swathe of cultural products that move around the world and the organizations that move them.

Finally, an epilogue (Chapter 9) utilizes data I gathered more recently to detail changes that have occurred since I left the field. It includes discussion of the effects of economic challenges and reorganization, changing technologies and consumption patterns, and globalization and competition, on the Sesame model and Sesame Workshop's relationships with partners.

2

Universality and Particularity

Variation and the Sesame Model

I exited the metro station at Etiopia and made my way toward a leafy middle-class neighborhood in Colonia Narvarte, known for its famous artists, writers, and revolutionaries, including Che Guevara, who lived here before leaving for Cuba in 1956. I arrived in front of the Spanish colonial and was greeted warmly by Antonio Federico Weingartshofer y del Sordo, or "Fritz" as his friends and colleagues called him. Fritz was a well-known filmmaker in Latin America, and I was here to interview him because he had been involved with the Mexican program *Plaza Sésamo* in various capacities for over two decades. He was one of the guardians of *Plaza Sésamo's* institutional memory, and it was he who explained to me why Sesame Workshop embarked on a coproduction model in the early 1970s after early dubbing disasters in Mexico.

As we sat in his studio and I sipped chamomile tea on this unseasonably chilly September morning, Fritz explained that in the early 1970s, very few Mexican children had access to preschool education: "The conditions of preschool children, from the ages of 4 to 6 years old, were much more serious than now. At that time, there were probably no more than 20 percent of children who had a school. The rest of the children, the other 80 percent, did not have any kind of preschool education whatsoever."[1] As in the US, the problem was even more severe for poor and minority—particularly indigenous—children in Mexico.

At the same time, the context for importing a US cultural product such as *Sesame Street* was not ideal. US-Mexican relations were at a simmer. President Luis Echeverría sought to build stronger ties with other developing nations in Latin America and resist US domination in the region. A dispute over water from the Colorado River further intensified US-Mexico tensions. Despite this political climate, there was interest in both countries to develop a program centered in Mexico City.

---

[1] Personal Interview, Mexico City: 9/3/08.

Sesame Street Around the World. Tamara Kay, Oxford University Press. © Oxford University Press (2025).
DOI: 10.1093/9780190844325.003.0002

As Fritz explained, however, the first version of *Plaza Sésamo* that aired in Mexico had a significant amount of dubbed content from the domestic version of *Sesame Street*. It therefore generated controversy and lacked key government support: "That first adaptation did not function because at that time, the Mexican Secretary of Public Education did not like the concepts that would drive the program. They were not what they wanted. It was a contradiction because they were not resolving it. Eighty percent of the children in Mexico did not have a school to go to. So, it seemed that it was more of a political gesture. It was a bit absurd."[2] Strong public opposition and criticism of the program also emerged, particularly in leftist circles. Fritz explained that some of the dubbed segments triggered fears of US imperialism:

Many of the Muppet segments that were made were made in a classroom environment. So, the students and the teacher were Muppets. But the American flag was in the classroom just like the classrooms in the United States. That is absolutely logical because it was a product made for the United States. When you bring the product to Mexico, you dub it, and there is an American flag in the classroom—that would cause strong resistance.[3]

Fritz also described critiques that emerged about US consumerism:

If you're going to count four things, then you can count four cookies, or you can count four apples. Because they had this character, Cookie Monster, they would use graham crackers to teach how to count numbers. The public was arguing that there was subliminal advertising occurring so that these products would be introduced to Mexican children.[4]

There was also concern that children would learn more easily and effectively if they were taught in the context of their own physical environment and cultural context. In the dubbed *Sesame Street* segments, all kinds of objects—from doorknobs to shoes—were easily recognizable to Mexican children (and their parents) as not Mexican, as Fritz explained:

Within poor and middle class families, those cookies did not exist. When you had to count, you would count with soda bottle caps or with everyday things. Also, the way that the US middle class looks is different from the way that the Mexican

[2] Personal Interview, Mexico City: 9/3/08.
[3] Personal Interview, Mexico City: 9/3/08.
[4] Personal Interview, Mexico City: 9/3/08.

middle class looks. The tables, the tablecloths, the curtains, everything had a reality that did not correspond with Mexican reality.[5]

This early experience in Mexico signaled to Sesame Workshop leadership that simply dubbing this unique children's television program could present problems around the world. According to Fritz:

> What I can tell you is that when Sesame Workshop came for the first time, they thought that it could be just like other programs with Spanish translation and dubbing. Nevertheless, it did face very strong resistance. That helped Sesame Workshop to realize that there were some aspects that could not be exported directly.[6]

The experience in Mexico, however, was not unique. Soon after it aired in the US in 1969, a variety of producers approached Sesame Workshop to rebroadcast the program in each of their countries. Creator Joan Ganz Cooney and her team in New York had not expected the interest, as she explained: "To be frank, I was really surprised, because we thought we were creating the quintessential American show. We thought the Muppets were quintessentially American, and it turns out they're the most international characters ever created."[7]

The Development of Sesame Workshop's Coproduction Model

Because Sesame Workshop did not have a policy for how the program could be adapted, the result was a hodgepodge of different approaches. In Japan, it was used as a vehicle to teach English, so it aired unedited. The Israelis added commentary in Hebrew to certain scenes, and other countries dubbed portions into local languages such as Papiamento in Curaçao (Gettas 1990:56). In 1970, Germany aired a dubbed version of *Sesame Street*, and in 1971, producers began to include segments that reinforced the national educational curriculum (Gettas 1990:57). The television program that was beamed into households around the world was therefore slightly different in each country. As in Mexico, partners repeatedly voiced concern about how local government officials and audiences would react to the program and emphasized the importance of local adaptation.

---

[5] Personal Interview, Mexico City: 9/3/08.
[6] Personal Interview, Mexico City: 9/3/08.
[7] Quoted in the film The World According to Sesame Street, 2006.

Sesame Workshop leadership realized that the lack of a coherent international licensing policy could lead to inconsistencies and problems. So, in the fall of 1969, they created an international division to manage Sesame Workshop's international licensing (Gettas 1990:56). They worked with Sesame Workshop's research and domestic production teams to create licensing guidelines that required local programs to be broadcast commercial free, meet the highest production standards, reflect local culture, values and traditions, and be approved by local educational experts in consultation with Sesame Workshop (Gettas 1990:57). Joan Ganz Cooney also hired former CBS executive Michael Dann to sell *Sesame Street* in various forms to broadcasters in other countries.

As a result of the failure of early dubbed versions, and to avert future political disasters, Sesame Workshop developed a coproduction model in the 1970s that prioritized localization. Mexico, Germany, and Brazil were the first three countries to develop programs in the early 1970s under the new guidelines. Like *Sesame Street*, a local program is a product that develops from a Western educational philosophy and is created using a standard curriculum and a replicable educational model. Partners who embark on creating a local program replicate the content-production-research model developed for the US program by working as a local team of experts. Those in charge of educational content include experts in education, child development and psychology, medicine, public health, and many others. Those involved with production include writers, directors, producers, artists and animators, musicians, and puppeteers. Research on the program's effectiveness is conducted by scholars who measure and analyze the program's educational outcomes.

Local teams choose the themes and curricula for their programs and outreach projects, and they write and produce the program. Sesame Workshop does not send US staff to live and work in-country. There are rare instances in which a key New York staff member will be in-country for a few months during critical periods when extra assistance is needed, or when requested by partners. Partners are paired with their counterparts in the New York office, who provide technical assistance and oversight. Each program, for example, has a local producer and a New York producer. Each also has a local educational specialist who is paired with an educational specialist in New York. Local teams are organized in different ways in different countries. In some countries, a production company is chosen that also hires the creative team. In others, Sesame Workshop hires and pays the creative team directly.

In the early 1970s, when that model emerged, Sesame Workshop staff saw it as an experiment, one that was malleable and dynamic. There was a lot of uncertainty about how the coproduction process would develop, and whether it would succeed and become institutionalized within Sesame Workshop. That uncertainty is part of the early history of local *Sesame Street* programs. The New York staff who were involved with early programs, therefore, did not consistently record or document their activities.

Piecing together the details of the initial emergence of local programs is therefore quite challenging because little documentation exists. Few remain at Sesame Workshop from that era, and those I was able to track down could not recollect dates and details with certainty. Dr. Charlotte Cole, Sesame Workshop's former Senior Vice President of Global Education, confirmed the difficulty of piecing together the early history of local programs. She described how in order to verify dates for her own research, she had tried to hunt down original contracts between Sesame Workshop and its partners stored in Sesame Workshop's New York office. She was not able to find all of them, nor to confirm if those she did find were the final versions. And contracts did not reveal critical data such as the names of all participants and partners, production schedules, final expenditures, and air dates. As she explained, "The model itself was trying to be fluid so uncertainty is part of the story of its evolution."[8]

The Process of Initiating and Funding a Local Program

There are currently local *Sesame Street* programs being aired in over twenty countries. During the past fifty years, these programs have been initiated in a variety of ways. Most commonly, Sesame Workshop receives a request from a person in-country, or a funder offers financial support to create a project in a particular country. New York staff then conduct a feasibility study to determine if there is a sufficient media infrastructure, expertise, and potential support in that country. If there is, they conduct a needs assessment, assemble a local team, raise funds, and build relationships with government ministries and officials.

Producing a season of *Sesame Street* in the US is expensive, generally costing $16 to $18 million per season of twenty-six episodes.[9] In 2015, a production deal between Sesame Workshop and HBO increased the number of episodes to thirty-five at about $25 million per season.[10] Producing one

---

[8] Personal communication on November 8, 2017.
[9] https://slate.com/business/2012/01/does-sesame-street-lose-money.html
[10] https://www.hollywoodreporter.com/news/general-news/sesame-street-gets-funding-how-it-went-broke-1183032/

season of a local *Sesame Street* program generally costs less, but local production expenses vary, as do the number of episodes and the length and format of each episode. The most significant factor in terms of cost is how much local content is produced. Local content costs more to produce than dubbing segments from what is referred to as Sesame Workshop's library. The library is a repository (now fully digitized) of US and international segments that can easily be dubbed and repurposed for use in local programs. Animation and Muppet segments, which are easier to dub, are overrepresented in the library compared to studio segments with US actors. The library segments that are chosen generally have few US symbols or references, such as the US flag or English words.

Partners have access to the library and can choose library segments to supplement locally produced material. And partners' content is also shared in the library. Segments from programs all over the world have therefore been used in the US version of *Sesame Street*. Both New York staff and partners most commonly use international content from the library to teach children about other parts of the world. These are often live-action segments that highlight cultural events or holidays, or a child's first day at school in a given country.

In low- and middle-income countries, local *Sesame Street* programs are usually initially funded with grants and financial contributions from foundations, NGOs, and philanthropic organizations. In many of those countries, including Afghanistan, Bangladesh, Egypt, Indonesia, Jordan, Kosovo, Nigeria, Pakistan, South Africa, and Tanzania, projects were initially funded, at least in part, by the US Agency for International Development (USAID), an independent agency of the US federal government that supported its foreign policy goals and geopolitical interests by administering development and disaster aid around the world. USAID has a long history of rewarding US allies and has been accused of favoring and promoting certain parties and groups in various countries, and punishing others (such as Palestinians). USAID grants generally did not cover all costs and were used in combination with other funding sources. USAID limited its funding to five years, and its financial contributions were therefore generally considered seed money.[11]

From a new program's inception, Sesame Workshop and its partners seek permanent funding sources to provide support for future seasons, often from broadcasters, governments, and corporations. When a program is sustainably funded, Sesame Workshop receives a licensing fee for use of its brand, characters, and content.

---

[11] Within a month of taking office in January 2025, the 47th president and his administration began dismantling and defunding USAID.

Broadcasters generally pay licensing or other fees to air programs. Sesame Workshop's executives begin the process of securing a broadcaster in the early stages of development. They generally have tried to guarantee that both domestic and local versions of *Sesame Street* are accessible to all children, regardless of their family's resources. To this end, Sesame Workshop historically broadcast *Sesame Street* on public television stations supported by government funding, without commercials. Sesame Workshop has tried to replicate this model internationally, with limited success. In high-income countries that have strong state-supported public television broadcasters, such as Germany and the Netherlands, programs are aired commercial-free to all children with access to terrestrial (meaning non-cable and non-satellite-based) television. Some low-income countries air programs on state-owned television stations. As will be discussed in later chapters, however, this can present challenges in countries such as Bangladesh, where the political party in power wields tremendous control over access to broadcast privileges.

Large and middle-income countries such as Brazil often have irregular broadcast coverage, with large swaths or regions of the country unable to receive certain broadcast channels. And in some countries, high production costs make broadcasting on public stations—which also have to pay licensing fees to Sesame Workshop—prohibitive. Sesame Workshop has therefore experimented with hybrid broadcasting arrangements. In India, for example, Turner Broadcasting paid the production costs of *Galli Galli Sim Sim* and aired it on its satellite channel. As part of its contract with Sesame Workshop, however, Turner Broadcasting allowed the program to be broadcast on India's public television station. Ironically, Sesame Workshop modeled its contract with HBO for the domestic broadcast of *Sesame Street*—which allows public broadcasters to air the program six months after it is premiered on HBO—on its unique arrangement with Turner Broadcasting in India.

The most vexing problem Sesame Workshop and its partners face is garnering long-term support so that local programs can be sustainable. Because of funding issues, few programs, however, are in constant production. Most go through periods when no new seasons are being produced because funding is not available. German and Dutch programs are the only ones that produced new content every year, and both are in high-income countries and are funded primarily by public broadcasters. Programs in low-income countries go in and out of production frequently. This creates a plethora of problems, not the least of which is the loss of well-trained and talented partners who quickly find employment with other organizations when there is a lull in production. Partners who have worked on local *Sesame Street* programs are often in high demand: their skills are unique and scarce in countries with emerging communications and media industries. Capacity building is one of Sesame Workshop's explicit goals in creating programs, particularly in low-income countries. It includes training in production techniques, animation, puppetry, script writing, and evaluative research.

Organizational Structure of Partnerships

The financial and organizational arrangements with partners vary, often reflecting the local programs' funding source. Partners in Germany, the Netherlands, and Israel, for example, pay licensing fees to Sesame Workshop and must follow licensing agreements that stipulate rules for the use of the brand. In India, the organizational structure is quite complex. Sesame Workshop created Sesame Workshop PLC, a local office in India and a 100 percent subsidiary of Sesame Workshop, and Sesame Workshop India Trust, a grant and donor-driven non-profit with an Indian board. Its registration as a trust in India allows it, under Indian law, to engage in educational outreach, advocacy, and policy. *Sesame Schoolhouse* is a for-profit, fully owned by Sesame Workshop PLC, that generates revenue from its school business and products. Financial subsidization and content sharing, however, occur across all three entities.

In the Gulf States, *Iftah Ya Simsim* was structured as a joint venture, specifically a "public/private sector partnership"[12] between the founding sponsor Mubadala Development Company, a state-owned investment vehicle for the Abu Dhabi government, which provided capital for operations and content production to the Abu Dhabi Educational Media Trust, which together with Sesame Workshop established Bidaya Media, a company founded to produce *Iftah Ya Simsim*. As these examples show, the nature and structure of Sesame Workshop's organizational arrangements with its partners, like the local programs themselves, must also be adapted to meet the needs of the unique political and economic environments in which they are embedded.

Building Transnational Teams

Sesame Workshop's ability to engage in coproduction depends on building transnational teams of New York staff and partners—all of whom must be willing to engage in mutual learning and manage conflict productively. They must also share some basic values, including a commitment

---

[12] https://www.tradearabia.com/news/edu_182091.html

to education, nonviolence, and racial/ethnic and gender equity. Teams that shared these values were particularly critical to programs focused on conflict and post-conflict zones, for which financial contributions from initial funders were contingent on prioritizing mutual respect and understanding messages. These funders included the United Nations Development Program and the United Nations Children's Fund (UNICEF) (Kosovo), the American Ireland Fund, the International Fund for Ireland, and the Northern Ireland Fund for Reconciliation (Northern Ireland), the Revson Foundation, European Union, Ford Foundation, and the Dutch government (Israel/Palestine).

The process of finding partners for each program begins after a feasibility study is completed and funding for an initial season is secured. Sesame Workshop then puts together not only the production team but also a local educational content and evaluation team. Dr. Charlotte Cole, Sesame Workshop's former Senior Vice President of Global Education, explained the process by which she and her team found local partners, beginning with a fact-finding trip:

> What was really interesting is we would usually go and do a fact-finding trip. And before the fact-finding trip, we would've identified a few key people to visit. And then what would happen is as you're engaged with the typical people that sort of surface and you start to have a conversation, then certain names start to surface and percolate. And then you start to hear these names multiple times, and then you go to those people, and then those people mention people. And, yeah, it is kind of a snowball.[13]

From this fact-finding trip, a core group of possible partners emerges, including members of the local educational content and evaluation team. In most cases, Sesame Workshop chooses a director of educational content who holds a PhD or a master's degree, and supporting staff members usually have a B.A. degree. In most cases, the partners in these positions speak English, and many have lived, worked, or studied in the US or Europe.

This director's primary job is to put together a curriculum for the program. This process begins with the director creating a preliminary list of curricular goals in consultation with her local team and Sesame Workshop educational specialists in New York. During this initial stage, Sesame Workshop tries to identify key areas of need in a country, controversial issues, and different perspectives on how to address them. To this end, Sesame Workshop often commissions experts in the country to write white papers on a given topic and

---

[13] Phone interview: 4/28/15.

then runs a workshop with them to consider and discuss the issues the papers raise. Topics have included gender, health and sanitation, and best practices for teaching Arabic across the Gulf States. Dr. Charlotte Cole described the process:

> We asked very specific questions. It was everything from what's the situation for boys and girls in education, family life, religiously? What are key goals? How can Sesame, in your mind, speak to them? And the papers would lay out a basic case. And then, often we would have a whole seminar just focused on that one paper. And the professor—usually a professor—or the expert, would give sort of a verbal presentation of the paper, and then people could ask questions and things. That's what helped shape some of it. So there was a whole process. Frankly, I would use these as a way to kind of find good people. You could get a sense of the kind of contributions somebody would make. And so a lot of times, the people that wrote these papers stayed with the project for its whole course.[14]

What is learned from the white papers and the workshop provides a foundation for a curriculum seminar in the country that lasts for one to three days. The purpose of the seminar is to get feedback on the preliminary curricular goals and garner ideas for how to address and achieve them. Curriculum seminars are usually repeated before the beginning of a new season, particularly if there has been a lull in production. Sesame Workshop and its partners invite stakeholders from across a wide spectrum of society, including teachers and experts in education, child development, health, psychology, linguistics, and other related fields. Other invited stakeholders vary by country and have included prominent environmentalists, feminists, scientists, artists, and children's book writers. Dr. Cole, who was in charge of putting together Sesame Workshop's curriculum seminars for over two decades, explained how she tried to ensure a diverse group of participants:

> One of the things that I was always trying to do was not just go to the usual suspects in education. So obviously those people were invited, but then we also tried to expand upon what we were calling education, so that we were bringing in anybody who was doing kind of innovative things with kids or parents or something related to kids. So, you know, you might have a museum curator, a children's book writer, somebody who's doing an outdoor program or a sports program or some kind of creative arts endeavor with kids. Or, you know, maybe it's a human rights person that was speaking with street kids or other concerns around kids, social work or

[14] Phone interview: 4/28/15.

something like that. So that we weren't just getting kind of, curricular advice. We were getting a much more holistic orientation to what children's learning needed to be.[15]

Dr. Cole also discussed how she tried to foster a diversity of opinions, particularly around difficult topics:

> I tried very hard—this was sometimes controversial—but I did try very hard to get people that might disagree with each other because I wanted the curriculum seminars to have some kind of controversy. Controversy might be the wrong word—but a dynamic discussion. And that we could get the most out of listening to people dispute different approaches. There were times where some of the discussions were kind of heated, but, you know, that was really helpful. That could be really, really helpful.[16]

During the seminar, participants discuss the preliminary curricular goals and whether any should be added or removed. They confer about new trends in educational research and practice. And perhaps most importantly, they identify potential curricular areas that could be problematic and develop strategies for how to address them effectively. Former Sesame Workshop producer Nadine Zylstra explained that members of the production team also attend the curriculum seminar: "And certainly creatively, it's incredibly exciting to suddenly hear an academic talk about what a child needs to learn about the environment. And to take that information and to start thinking about what you would do creatively to send that message is wonderful."[17]

The curriculum seminar is not meant to resolve all issues. Rather, as Zylstra explained, it is meant to bring together the people who "represent the greatest thinkers in those issues in that country," and lay the groundwork for creating a final curriculum for the program: "And out of that seminar, Dr. Cole and her group write a curriculum document which we then use, really, as the cornerstone of our educational messages."[18] According to Zylstra, the production team then usually has a series of "creative brainstorm" sessions to "say these are some of the primary issues, what do we do with them?"[19]

The details of the curriculum document are fine-tuned yet again during an educational content seminar that brings together partners on local educational content and evaluation teams with their New York counterparts.

---

[15] Phone interview: 4/28/15.
[16] Phone interview: 4/28/15.
[17] Personal interview, New York: 1/14/08.
[18] Personal interview, New York: 1/14/08.
[19] Personal interview, New York: 1/14/08.

Traditionally, this happens in New York as part of an extensive training of the entire team. The writing team, production team, puppeteers, and other creative partners visit the studio in Queens where *Sesame Street* is filmed, the Henson Company workshop in Manhattan, and meet with their counterparts in Sesame Workshop's Broadway offices. It is during this seminar that the local educational content and evaluation team, in consultation with their New York counterparts, develops the goals and themes of the program, with the final curriculum document as a foundation.

Variation in Format and Style

In addition to choosing the goals and themes of their program, partners also choose its location and title. The location is the place or setting where most of the action occurs during the scenes with actors and Muppet characters. Producers of *Sesame Street* located action for the US version on an urban street in an effort to promote inclusivity and diversity; it would be easier to include poor and minority children, they reasoned, on an urban street. Many partners have also strategically chosen settings to reflect diversity. In Mexico, *Plaza Sésamo* is centered in an urban plaza; in India, *Galli Galli Sim Sim* takes place in an urban alley; and in Indonesia, *Jalan Sesama*—which means "street for all" in Indonesian—is set on an urban street.

Sesame Workshop requests that partners use some reference to *Sesame* in their titles, and those that reference physical spaces are preferred, such as *Sesame Square* (Nigeria), *Sesame World* (Egypt), *Sesame Tree* (Northern Ireland), and *Sesame Street* (France, Portugal, Israel, Kosovo, Germany). Not all partners, however, choose titles that reference places. The Jordanians chose Sesame Stories (*Hikayat Simsim*); the South Africans dubbed their program Be Happy, Sesame (*Takalani Sesame*), Gulf State partners call their program Open Sesame (*Iftah Ya Simsim*), and a program created in the United Kingdom was called *Play with Me Sesame*. Sesame Workshop provides brand guidelines, which offer guidance that allows partners to more easily customize local programs while ensuring global brand identity. Other than preferences for its title and logo, Sesame Workshop does not require a particular format, length, or characters for a local program. Partners are not even required to use puppets created by the Jim Henson Company (i.e. Sesame Muppets[20])—an iconic element of the US program, although most partners choose to use them. Partners in Spain, the original 1970s Brazilian program *Vila Sésamo*,

---

[20] The term "Muppets" is trademarked by The Walt Disney Company, which allows Sesame Workshop to use the term in relationship to certain characters that appear on *Sesame Street*.

the 1980s program among the Gulf States *Iftah Ya Simsim*, and most recently, Pakistan (*Sim Sim Hamara*), for example, decided to create their own puppets. The number and type of Muppets a program creates depend on funding. The most expensive is a full-body Muppet that requires the performer to wear the puppet. During production, a performer using a full body Muppet— such as Caroll Spinney, who played Big Bird—are provided an assistant, or "wrangler" who helps put on and take off and care for the Muppet. Full body Muppets in programs include Abelardo (a large parrot in *Plaza Sésamo*), Samson (a bear in the German *Sesamstrasse*), Boombah (a lion in India's *Galli Galli Sim Sim*), Mosche (a meerkat in South Africa's *Takalani Sesame*), and Nimnim (a green creature in Egypt's *Alam Simsim*).

Partners can also choose smaller sack (also called hand) puppets, such as Cookie Monster, that are generally operated by two performers—the principal puppeteer operates the Muppet's head and mouth and left hand. The second puppeteer usually operates their right hand and can take over both hands in scenes that require it. South Africa's Zikwe and Mexico's Pancho, and Israel's Moshe Oofnik, a brown grouch, are all sack puppets. Some of the most iconic Muppets in the US version of *Sesame Street* and around the world are rod (also called hand-rod) puppets, including Elmo and South Africa's Kami. Rod puppets are usually smaller than sack puppets, and are operated by one puppeteer who uses her dominant hand to operate the head and mouth, and the other to manipulate rods that are attached to the Muppet's hands.

Partners that use Henson Muppets choose from among humanoid characters, monsters and various creatures, and animal characters—of diverse colors, textures, and features. Partners often use their puppets, including Muppets, to reflect their culture and national identity. Bangladesh's *Sisimpur* includes Halum, a Bengal tiger, and Shiku, a jackal. In Indonesia's *Jalan Sesama*, Tantan is an orangutan, and China's *Zhima Jie* features Lily, a tiger. Financial resources also dictate the number of Muppets that partners can create. While the Palestinian, Jordanian, and Brazilian programs each introduced two Muppets, India's program featured ten Muppet characters.

Partners, in consultation with Sesame Workshop staff, also decide the length and style of their format. From its premiere on PBS in 1969 until 2016, *Sesame Street* aired 60-minute episodes each season. The number of episodes per season varied (due to funding) from a high of over 145 to a low of 26. When *Sesame Street* moved to HBO in 2016 for its 46th season, Sesame Workshop changed to a 30-minute episode format and created 35 episodes. The original US version of *Sesame Street* utilized a magazine format, meaning a series of short segments of different kinds—animation, live-action, in-studio with actors and Muppets—usually connected by a theme such as a word or concept (such as hibernation) that is developed throughout an individual episode. The magazine format was developed in response to research suggesting small children had difficulty focusing for long amounts of time on a continuous story. The magazine format, like commercials, used short segments that allowed children to shift focus with each new segment. The format also allowed producers to easily and flexibly incorporate curricular elements in the program.

The format of local programs varies widely around the world and is often dictated by budget limitations. Episodes generally run for 15–30 minutes rather than the 60 minutes allotted to *Sesame Street* for most of its history. Because it is expensive to create original local content, "blocks" created as stand-alone inserts for the US *Sesame Street* and programs (such as "Global Grover" or "Bert and Ernie's Great Adventures" segments) or material from Sesame Workshop's library are combined with locally-produced content. A 30-minute program could therefore have a significant amount of US content. Sesame Workshop staff informally refer to the "Cadillac" model as one in which programs have significant local content, including a new set, characters, and scripts. In contrast, the "wrap-around" model means that local content is wrapped around or interspersed with blocks of Sesame library content.

The belief that the magazine format was best for capturing and sustaining children's attention continued for decades and became associated with *Sesame Street*. Many partners have also utilized the magazine format in their programs, although in shorter 15–30 minute timeslots. The format is flexible, making it effective for either Cadillac or wrap-around programs. There are partners, however, who have chosen not to use the magazine format. The Northern Ireland team chose a more narrative format centered on a group of creatures living in the Sesame Tree. Each 15-minute episode begins with children asking the tree's inhabitants to answer a question, such as "Why do we have to share?" The episode proceeds to answer the question from a variety of perspectives, utilizing live-action, animation, and studio segments, including material from the Sesame library.

It is not uncommon for Sesame Workshop and its partners to experiment with and then change the format of their local programs. A variety of factors can result in format changes, from funding to ratings, among many others. Sashwati Banerjee, the former director of Sesame Workshop India, explained the various iterations of *Galli Galli Sim Sim*, the Indian program:

When we started, we really did what we called the classical format. It was very magazine-y. It was very classic *Sesame Street*. We did 65 episodes for season one and season two. And then, we were doing what they call a wave research, so I think the first wave of the research showed that children weren't very used to the magazine format, but they were used to a much more narrative style. So I think season two, we tried to link the segments together, and to use less segments within one show. And then Turner said, "We really need 100 percent original production here." So we used no library materials. So in season three we cut down the number of episodes we would produce because we weren't using library segments anymore. We went into a block format.[21]

Although formats used in different countries have varied over the years, one element remains constant in all local *Sesame Street* programs: the content must be educational.

In many countries where families do not have access to television, partners use other platforms such as radio, digital technologies, and apps to transmit content. In India, for example, families with television access can watch *Galli Galli Sim Sim* either on a satellite channel or on a local public channel. A *Sesame Street* radio program is also available in rural areas and those in which radio is popular. The program is transmitted through a community radio system, and other content is available on cell phones. In rural areas in Bangladesh, partners worked with the NGO Save the Children to equip rickshaws with televisions, DVD players, and generators, and train workers to facilitate community viewing events. In India, similar mobile community viewing programs were set up in urban areas, where rickshaws could operate without electricity using bioscopes.

Variation in Curricular Goals

Sesame Workshop's partners use the flexibility of the format and style to create an aesthetic that represents and reflects their cultural sensibilities and national identity. The most critical component of creating a locally adapted version of *Sesame Street*, however, is the content, in particular, its curricular goals and messages. Although they must promote key values in their programs—including nonviolence, tolerance and respect, and gender equality—and are subject to certain restrictions and oversight, partners have tremendous freedom to adapt a program's content and curriculum. The primary requirement for partners is that the program is educational

---

[21] Personal interview, New York: 12/3/12.

and is based on a sound educational curriculum developed by local experts. Sesame Workshop's former President and CEO, Gary Knell, described the model:

> This was the opposite of sort of the McDonald's hamburger approach where every hamburger tastes the same from Bangalore to Boston. This was not about taking American values and dumping them in country X. It's quite the opposite under a certain sort of global framework which we roughly put under the UN millennium goals. It's all about trying to transfer the technology and know-how, and to try to translate that in a local context. I like to say we help design the kitchen, and our local partners decide what to cook for dinner.[22]

The curricula that partners develop for their programs vary, but generally replicate Sesame Workshop's whole child curriculum that is divided into three broad categories: cognitive learning (literacy, numeracy), socio-emotional learning (mutual respect and understanding), and physical well-being (health and wellness, such as nutrition, personal hygiene, safety). The flexibility of the Sesame Workshop model allows partners to include curricular goals to address specific needs in their countries. Curricula can be revised or recreated for each new season of production. Generally, local educational teams make decisions in consultation with New York staff and local experts. For example, the Palestinians focused on boys' self-esteem and empowerment during their first season. Teams from Afghanistan, India, Egypt, and Bangladesh prioritized girls' education and school attendance. And during *Plaza Sésamo's* first seasons, Mexican educators highlighted problem-solving and reasoning goals, which they argued were not prioritized across Latin America (Gettas 1990). Table 2.1 provides a summary of the educational objectives for *Galli Galli Sim Sim*, which contains a section on "harmonising diversity."

Although there is a lot of convergence in curricular goals across countries, particularly around literacy and numeracy, there is significant divergence in pedagogy and approach. Research suggests that all children go through key stages of development at similar times. For example, at about a year, most children begin to walk. Although children all over the world reach these milestones at similar times, culture can influence how emergent abilities are expressed (Cole and Lee 2016:19). As Rogoff (2003) famously observed, in some cultures, once children are physically able to hold and manipulate a large object, they are taught to use a machete safely.

---

[22] Personal interview, Cambridge: 11/14/07.

Table 2.1 Summary of Educational Objectives for *Galli Galli Sim Sim*

Summary of Educational Objectives for Galli Galli Sim Sim				
I. Cognition (Stimulating and Enriching Mental Functions)	**II. Emotion (Caring, Sharing, and Nurturing)**	**III. Physical Well-Being (Body Care and Safety)**	**IV. Social Relations (Independence and Interdependence)**	**V. Culture (Harmonising Diversity)**
A. Joyful Learning 1. Relating Formal and Informal Learning 2. Learning for Skill Building 3. Exploring and Inventing 4. Learning with Others **B. Literacy and Communication** 1. Reading and Learning Hindi 2. Teaching the English Language 3. Writing Fundamentals 4. Exposure to Multiple Languages 5. Library 6. Computer Awareness **C. Mathematics** 1. Number Sense 2. Number Operations 3. Measurement and Estimation 4. Everyday Experiences of Numbers 5. Geometric Forms **D. Intuition & Methods of Science** 1. Understanding Children's Notions of Natural Phenomena 2. Living Things 3. Our World 4. Biological Diversity and Interdependence of Species 5. Ecology **E. Thinking and Reasoning** 1. Observation and Learning through Senses 2. Visual Discrimination 3. Asking Questions 4. Listening 5. Auditory Discrimination 6. Classification 7. Problem Solving 8. Planning 9. Predicting 10. Cause and Effect 11. Guessing from Clues 12. Remembering 13. Imagining **F. Creativity** 1. Curiosity and Wonder 2. Art, Dance and Music	**A. Emotions** 1. Recognizing and Labeling Emotions **B. Coping with Emotion** 1. Empathy and Sympathy 2. Overcoming Obstacles and Coping with Failure 3. Task Persistence 4. Self Esteem and Confidence 5. Dealing with Sorrow, Grief and Trauma 6. Optimism 7. Taking Responsibility for Mistakes	**A. Hygiene and Health Care** 1. Health and Well-Being 2. Illness and Disease 3. Nutrition 4. Healthy Habits 5. Good Hygiene and Care of the Body 6. Exercise and Yoga **B. Safety** 1. Traffic Safety 2. Safety at Home and in the Neighborhood 3. Protecting from Natural Dangers and Disasters	**A. Social Interaction** 1. Basic Interactions 2. Friendship 3. Playing and Thinking 4. Conflict Resolution 5. Cooperation, Healthy Competition and Good Sportsmanship 6. Helping 7. Sharing 8. Turn Taking 9. Entering Social Groups 10. Adult-Child Relations and Negotiation **B. Common Property and Civic Responsibility** 1. Common Property 2. Proper Disposal of Waste 3. Caring for Community Facilities and Spaces 4. Role Models **C. Group Relations** 1. Social Units: Family and Community 2. Occupations and Respect for Labour 3. Gender Roles and Equity **D. Understanding Variation in Ability** 1. Possible Ranges in Ability 2. Self-Worth 3. Varying Needs 4. Group Festivity for the Challenged 5. Barrier Free Environment	**A. Culture and the Arts** 1. Learning about Culture 2. Appreciating the Arts 3. Recognizing Different Forms of Art **B. Understanding Diversity and Ethnic Variability** 1. Appreciating Differences 2. Ethnicity 3. Language 4. Festivals **C. Bridging Diversity, Forging Unity** 1. Folklore 2. Folktales and Songs 3. Common Moments 4. Common Celebrations **D. Regional and Geographic Variation** 1. Multiplicity of Customs **E. Religious Plurality** 1. Multiplicity of Faiths 2. Places of Worship and Festivity **F. Unifying Symbols** 1. National Symbols and Identity

Although children learn to read at roughly similar ages, how they are taught to read varies by country and language. English-speaking children are taught to read phonetically, sounding out words letter by letter, and to recognize and memorize exceptions (such as the "ough" sound in rough). Children who speak Spanish, in contrast, learn to recognize consonant-vowel clusters (ma, me, mi, mo, mu) and put them together to form words (as in be-bi-da). In Bangla, there are 26 letters that vary minimally by a dot or line and are therefore easily confused. Children are taught to recognize these slight variations by using drills (Cole and Lee 2016:96). The variation in how languages are taught, therefore, reflects differences in the languages and alphabets themselves.

Local partners not only choose their own curricular goals, but they also decide the best and most appropriate ways to incorporate those goals into their programs. A segment reflecting the curricular goal of promoting school attendance may be depicted in very different ways around the world. In Colombia, it might highlight children of different ages learning together in a one-room schoolhouse, while in China, it may focus on children of the same age learning in a large urban school classroom (Cole and Lee 2016).

By far the most challenging aspect of creating a local program is seamlessly integrating the curricular goals in each segment with the production goals of making each segment entertaining, engaging, and funny. In the many training sessions and workshops I observed, by far the greatest source of partners' expressed frustration was the process of learning and mastering this curricular-entertainment integration. It is objectively quite difficult for artists to incorporate educational content into their work, and for educators to learn the language and nuances of television production. During a meeting to train Jordanian directors, a New York staffer explained the "marriage" between educational and creative content that is the hallmark of *Sesame Street*, as recorded in field notes:

> The thing that differentiates a *Sesame* show from any other kind of children's television show is that it's a very rich mix of the creative which is entertaining—the fun—but it has to have a backbone. And that backbone is educational value. It's the goal. Right? So it isn't just about entertaining kids. It's not Teletubbies—which has its own virtue and its own value, but it's a very different kind of format than this. This isn't just a fun story. This has to have some educational value. And that's what makes it unique. And It really is a marriage between those two things.[23]

In many countries, there is little original children's television programming, which means few people are trained and skilled in writing and producing for children. As Sashwati Banerjee explained:

> It's not like India doesn't have great writers. You can find great script writers. But they are not used to writing for children. There's no children's programming in India. The children's programming in India traditionally has been, "Oh, let's do a fairy tale. Okay. Let's do good and bad and evil and all of that stuff"—not this kind of programming. So how do you then get a bunch of people who are not ever used

[23] Field notes, Amman: 3/1/09.

to writing to this and expect them to turn out a fantastically cutting edge product in an environment where you're competing with all sorts of big things?[24]

The answer is through a lot of training and mentoring. Sesame Workshop holds a writer's workshop for each new program, and generally for each new season. The intensive workshop is usually held in the partner country and generally lasts from three days to a week. In attendance are local partners, including the local writers and their chosen head writer, an educational content specialist, and a producer. They are joined by an experienced writer for the domestic *Sesame Street*, the Sesame Workshop producer assigned to the program, and an educational specialist. The workshop usually begins with a discussion of the basics of writing for children in the context of Sesame Workshop's model, the program's curriculum and goals, and local storytelling traditions that could be useful for local writers to tap into. Sesame Workshop staff show many clips from *Sesame Street* and local programs around the world to serve as examples, bring Muppets to demonstrate their capabilities and limitations (sometimes puppeteers from the US and other countries participate), and share previous scripts.

After the Sesame Workshop staff teach the local writers how to develop ideas and write scripts for *Sesame Street*, the local writers write a series of draft scripts (usually in teams). A significant amount of time is then devoted to a critique of those scripts, during which Sesame Workshop staff offer feedback and guidance, and the entire group collectively discusses ways to improve each script. These feedback sessions usually focus on how to better connect curricular goals to entertaining plots and narratives, how to infuse the scenes with humor, and how to write in ways that engage children and co-viewing parents and caregivers. During my fieldwork, it was not uncommon for local writers to express their frustration with the writing process during the workshop, and for Sesame Workshop staff to explain to them that developing the skill takes time—as it also did for writers of the original US version of *Sesame Street*.

A few partners also noted that cultural differences in writing and the prevalence of other artistic traditions generate challenges to creating a local program that are difficult to overcome. As Sashwati Banerjee explained:

Many countries around the world, particularly in the Global South, it's damn difficult to do it because that's not how culturally we operate. Because there is no capacity, and even if you try and build that capacity, it takes a completely different

---

[24] Personal interview, New York: 12/3/12.

cultural context to understand that. Popular culture is very defined by films in India, by Bollywood. To produce a really entertaining show, which is intellectually entertaining, where writing is a craft, and you can get into the granularity of that craft and understand how the craft has made a great show, that's missing. Yeah, you can get great production values. You can teach people how to shoot with a Muppet. You can tell directors, "Eyes on screen." You can teach people to do a three-camera setup. You can tell writers, "Here's a plethora of *Sesame Street* to choose from, but we want you to culturally contextualize it in your language." And it just breaks down.

When I asked Banerjee to clarify whether she thinks it doesn't work, or that it just takes a lot of time, she quickly responded: "I think it takes time."[25]

On various occasions, I overheard Sesame Workshop staff members explain to partners that the production quality of *Sesame Street* is so high in the US—making it appear to be effortless—because many of the core producers, writers, educators, and puppeteers have worked together for decades. Because landing a position on *Sesame Street* is such a desirable job, there is little turnover. The US team was able to hone this new educational/entertainment medium over decades, not months. Moreover, by creating a successful children's educational program, Sesame Workshop helped build a media infrastructure in the US for skilled talent, which makes replacing the small number of employees who do leave easier. During a meeting at Kibbutz Almog, an Israeli partner expressed concern about turnover, as recorded in field notes: "We don't know if we'll have funding or not, if we're going to do another season. The last time we launched was 2006. We're already in the beginning of 2009. That's quite some time to be hanging around waiting for another gig."[26]

Sesame and International Development: Local Outreach Projects

Sesame Workshop's work extends far beyond creating television programs. It also includes community outreach projects with local partners—including governments, NGOs, and other civil society organizations—that focus on literacy and health, environmental stewardship, and social equality and religious tolerance. Sesame Workshop works with governments and organizations to develop and distribute free outreach materials (books,

---

[25] Personal interview, New York: 12/3/12.
[26] Field notes, Almog Junction, Israel: 1/13/09.

educational games, and parents' guides, etc.) that reinforce partners' curricular goals, particularly in areas where children do not have access to television.

Outreach has been a critical (though often unrecognized) component of the US *Sesame Street* for decades. During its first seasons on air, Sesame Workshop created *View, Do, Read,* a guide that explained to families and caregivers the educational messages of the program and provided suggestions to build on them at home.[27] Sesame Workshop also collaborated with the National Women, Infants, Children (WIC) Association to create a healthy eating and physical activity curriculum that was distributed to over 10,000 local clinics. To create *Talk, Listen, Connect,* an outreach project focused on helping children in military families deal with the deployment, injuries, and the death of family members, Sesame Workshop teamed up with various military agencies and organizations. The project includes videos, storybooks, and workbooks that help children and their families deal with the challenges of military service.

Like Sesame Workshop's domestic outreach projects, those outside the US also address local needs, usually of underserved populations and communities. Outreach projects are, therefore, quite diverse. In Bangladesh, for example, New York staff and partners created an outreach project focused on oral hygiene. Partnering with Unilever, they outfitted a bus as a mobile dental clinic. The Denti-Bus traveled the streets of Dhaka, offering free dental screenings, toothbrushes, and educational materials about dental care and effective tooth brushing skills for parents and caregivers. Sesame Workshop partnered with the NGO Malaria No More in Tanzania on a project to educate children about malaria. The campaign sought to distribute insecticide-treated bed nets to all Tanzanian children under five and educational materials on how to use them, via public service announcements, storybooks, and posters.

Sesame Workshop and its local partners in Colombia worked with local NGOs and the World Heart Federation on a *Healthy Habits for Life* outreach project to address the dual problems of obesity and malnutrition in the region. A grant from the Bill & Melinda Gates Foundation in 2013 enabled Sesame Workshop to develop a "behavior-change program that empowers children to prevent illnesses related to water, sanitation, and hygiene (WASH)"[28] with partners in India, Bangladesh, and Nigeria called "Cleaner, Healthier, Happier." They developed a new Muppet named Raya as the vehicle and global ambassador for the project and its educational messaging. The current

---

[27] For information on this and other US outreach projects see: http://www.sesameworkshop.org/what-we-do/our-initiatives/domestic-outreach/

[28] https://sesameworkshop.org/our-work/what-we-do/wash/

program is a global campaign called WASH UP!, in collaboration with World Vision. It includes the creation and distribution of outreach materials—storybooks, games, teacher training materials, and videos featuring Raya and Elmo—to children, caregivers, and teachers in 18 countries.

In 2016, at the first World Humanitarian Summit, Sesame Workshop and the International Rescue Committee (IRC) announced "a new partnership to help children and their families living in crisis … to develop, disseminate, and test multi-media educational resources and programs aimed at young refugees."[29] The Bernard Van Leer and Open Society foundations provided early financing support to the project. In December 2017, Sesame Workshop and IRC, and their humanitarian initiative to educate children affected by conflict and crisis, won a $100 million grant from the MacArthur Foundation.

Outreach projects are conceived and developed collaboratively by New York staff and partners. As will be discussed in more detail in later chapters, the success of outreach projects depends primarily on partners, who have the local knowledge and networks necessary to initiate, plan, and carry out collaborative projects with governments and NGOs.

Research

Sesame Workshop's model prioritizes various types of research at multiple stages in the content development and production processes. Feasibility studies compile information on a country's media infrastructure, skilled workforce, and potential support to determine if a local program is likely to be viable. Formative research tests an audience's receptiveness to content, from themes and messaging to set designs. For example, in Mexico, partners used focus groups to determine which set—traditional or modern—should be used for *Plaza Sésamo*. Sesame Workshop also commissions independent research to assess whether programs are perceived as local. They generally are.

Evaluative research tests the effectiveness of the content of programs and outreach projects, and measures and analyzes educational outcomes. During a meeting to train Jordanian directors, a New York staffer explained the intensive research that goes into each scene, as captured in field notes:

> Every segment is so, so intensely researched. And they do a little bit of formative research, which is trying to see what parts of the segment worked, what part needs to be changed. And if it needs to be changed, they go back and change it. I mean

[29] https://sesameworkshop.org/about-us/press-room/sesame-workshop-and-international-rescue-committee-announce-new/

from the script, all the way through to the final cut is researched and researched and backed up and looked at from a content perspective and looked at from an educational, and then looked at from an entertaining perspective.[30]

Research on outreach projects generally focuses on the range of their distribution, accessibility, and ease of use to parents and caregivers, and the effectiveness of curricula and messaging. Focus groups, interviews, and surveys are often used to gather information in order to develop outreach materials, test them before distribution so that modifications can be made, and evaluate them once they are disseminated.

Although Sesame Workshop research staff conduct some evaluative research, large studies of outcomes of programs and projects are generally conducted by outside independent research firms. To test the educational impact of Bangladesh's *Sisimpur*—including whether viewers scored higher on literacy and numeracy tests than nonviewers—Sesame Workshop commissioned the Dhaka-based firm Associates for Community and Population Research to conduct a large-scale longitudinal assessment. Two Boston University faculty members found a positive impact of *Sisimpur* on the child-rearing attitudes of caregivers and teachers in rural areas (Kibria and Jain 2009). In 2009, researchers at the Centre for Effective Education at Queen's University Belfast carried out a longitudinal study of the effects of viewing Northern Ireland's *Sesame Tree* on young children's attitudes and awareness. Similar research was conducted for the Kosovo and Israeli-Palestinian programs.

Sesame Workshop, its partners, and particularly their funders are also interested in the television ratings of programs. Ratings data vary in reliability across and within countries, often making it difficult to gauge accurate viewership. The quality of rating data can also vary widely within countries; in particular regions, data collection can be difficult to obtain. As in the US, ratings matter as a measure of the program's popularity and relevance. Although Sesame Workshop has always used ratings data, it has become more problematic as the number of children's programs with which *Sesame Street* must compete has exploded over the years, on both terrestrial and cable/satellite channels. In 1990, there were two television programs for preschool-age children—*Sesame Street* and *Mr. Rogers Neighborhood*. By 2009, there were forty-seven. The majority of children's programming in the US and around the world is purely entertainment. Children's programs are quite profitable. Nickelodeon's *SpongeBob SquarePants* and *Dora*

---

[30] Field notes, Amman: 3/1/09.

the Explorer have each generated total gross revenue of almost $15 billion. Some of these programs include educational messages and goals, forming what some have dubbed "edutainment" programs. Very few programs, however, are centered on or rooted in an educational curriculum, as is *Sesame Street*.

Big Bird's Chinese Cousin

This chapter focuses on the model and processes Sesame Workshop utilizes to construct local versions of *Sesame Street* with its partners around the world. Sesame Workshop's goal is to infuse the essence of the program—its educational mandate, inclusive messages, and humor—with local nuance and meaning. Capturing the spirit of *Sesame Street* while transforming it so that it resonates with a local audience is no small task. But what if local partners actually prefer to adopt core elements without transforming them?

This is what happened when Big Bird went to China in 1983. New York staff visited Asia to introduce Big Bird to the Chinese public and to meet with Chinese producers about possible collaborations. Four years later, in 1987, a television special featured Big Bird on Central China Television. Following these appearances, Big Bird became wildly popular in China, so much so that in 1997, when Sesame Workshop began the process of developing a Chinese program with Shanghai TV called *Zhima Jie*, Chinese partners insisted that they wanted Big Bird as one of the show's primary characters. New York staff explained that they could create their own local characters. "No," they insisted, "We want Big Bird." Ultimately, Chinese partners developed a new character who became the focal point of *Zhima Jie*, named Da Niao, who looks exactly like Big Bird—because he is Big Bird's cousin. And Da Niao, like his US cousin, is extremely popular in China.

Given its history and culture, it is perhaps unexpected that Big Bird—a US cultural icon—became beloved in China. And yet, the fact that Chinese audiences adored him, Chinese producers wanted to adopt him whole cloth, and *Zhima Jie* has a character who is an exact replica of Big Bird raises compelling questions about how partners make decisions about whether and how to combine global influences with local specificity. The process they engage in with New York staff results in a hybrid cultural product that is both universal and particular to a given environment. And yet that same process produces different results in countries all around the world. We now turn to an analysis of how *Sesame Street's* universalism and particularity are produced on the ground between transnational organizational partners.

3

Disassembling *Sesame Street*

Constructing Value to Align Interests

The mood in Sesame Workshop's offices on Wednesday, December 12, 2012 was electric. The eighth-floor event space was bustling; staff were running around preparing equipment and materials while visitors gathered around an enormous buffet breakfast, laughing and chatting. It was a big day—the first of a three-day workshop with partners from the Gulf States program *Iftah Ya Simsim*. Some of the participants had already officially signed on as partners, but others were here to learn about *Sesame Street* and its coproduction process in order to decide if they would participate in *Iftah* or not. New York staff would also decide who among them to work with on the program. Sesame Workshop had invited key partners from around the world to participate and give presentations as a "Sesame Workshop Support Unit," including: Dr. Cairo Arafat, the former Education and Research Director of Palestine's *Shara'a Simsim*, who would take on that role for *Iftah*; Sashwati Banerjee, the Founding Managing Director of Sesame Workshop India; and Amr Koura, the executive producer of the Egyptian program *Alam Simsim*.

I asked a few support staff if they needed any help, and went to speak with Banerjee, who I had already interviewed. She greeted me warmly and then told me she had flown in early for a Sesame Workshop board meeting the day before. Robert Knežević, then Senior Vice President of Sesame Street International, asked everyone to take a seat. He then began the meeting by introducing each member of the Gulf States team. Soon after he introduced the Sesame Workshop Support Unit, explaining that it had existed in other programs but not officially, and this would be the first official support team.[1] He introduced Amr Koura with a handshake and a hug, and asked him to say a few words. Koura addressed the guests:

I got involved in Sesame Workshop fourteen years ago, and from the first day when I met Robert, Robert told me this project will change your life. I laughed him off because I had been in production for thirty years and nothing had ever changed my

---

[1] The conversations that follow were recorded in field notes in New York on December 12, 2012.

Sesame Street Around the World. Tamara Kay, Oxford University Press. © Oxford University Press (2025).
DOI: 10.1093/9780190844325.003.0003

life. But Sesame changed my life. I no longer am a producer to make money. I have a noble mission. I now have a mission in life. It's to change the lives of children in my country. It is important in this trip to ask questions. The ability to speak our minds about what's culturally relevant to us but not necessarily to them. I know you might be thinking, "Well, I don't know these Americans. What do they think of us?" If you're embarrassed to ask them, ask us. They allow us to ask questions. But fourteen years from now we'll be celebrating what you did for the countries of your region.

The next to address the guests was Sherrie Westin, then Sesame Workshop's Executive Vice President and Chief Marketing Officer, who explained the delicate balancing act they would have to accomplish: "We don't want to impose American values. Children learn best in the context of their own cultures. But with any great brand there have to be certain attributes. We want *Iftah* to be uniquely Arabic but we also want people to recognize *Sesame*. So the goal is to translate it into each culture. This requires a give-and-take. You have leeway, you need to make sure it's local." Dr. Charlotte Cole followed Westin with a discussion of culture. She said that cultural specificity was important and proceeded to tell the story of how the Norwegian team decided to show the live birth of a baby on their program. "We wouldn't do that here in the US and I imagine not in the Gulf States," she said. I looked around the room and many of the guests were shaking their heads no.

Dr. Cole, who has a Ph.D. in education from Harvard, has an easy rapport with people, and partners frequently expressed to me how much they liked and respected her. I had the opportunity to see her in action many times. She is a straightforward but thoughtful communicator and has an uncanny ability to gauge people's emotions, drawing them out and putting them at ease. And this day was no different. After her presentation, guests expressed concerns about working with New York staff, about power asymmetries, and their decision-making power. Amr Koura began the conversation by asking her a question about control and autonomy:

KOURA: Who has the final—I don't want to say power—but the final say?

DR. COLE: It's okay to say power.

UAE POTENTIAL PARTNER #1: Well initial say?

UAE POTENTIAL PARTNER #2: Who gets to say yes or no? I'm not worried about the easy stuff, but more worried about the controversial stuff.

KNEŽEVIĆ: You'll figure it out (joking. Everyone laughs).

DR. COLE: In the end you have to produce something so you can't not make a decision. Diplomats can talk and not make decisions. Producers have to make decisions but doing it on the basis of information and expertise, sound information, will result in the best educational effect. And we're not the educational police, we help people understand there's always a way to do it. … It's a dance.

[later in conversation]

KOURA: One thing to say in Charlotte's favor is that there is a dance. They are always respectful of your opinion and don't force something on you that you don't believe.

POTENTIAL PARTNER FROM UAE: That's comforting.

This exchange reveals a tremendous amount about how New York staff and partners not only figure out in real time what the essence of *Sesame Street* is, but also how they will coproduce it together. And, in doing so, as Sesame Workshop's Vice President of Brand Strategy explained a bit later in the meeting, partners are expected to protect Sesame's brand:

> Many people are skeptical of brands. But our brand is gold. People trust us. You can decide what's funny for you, what's heartfelt for you, and you execute it for your part of the world. So you create an Arabic version of that—these same things through a cultural lens. And we get it right, and we get it wrong. You will be stewards of the value of the brand, protectors of the values of that brand.

New York staff view partners as brand stewards because Sesame Workshop is a unique organization—a nonprofit with a very powerful brand.

As I observed this and the other interactions during the workshop, and similar ones all over the world, I realized that what Sesame Workshop and its partners are engaged in goes far beyond a simple translation of *Sesame Street* into other cultures. They are involved in a process of coproduction by which they take apart or disassemble *Sesame Street*, and then put it back together again in a new way, or reconstitute it, for each local program they create. In the above exchanges, New York staff and partners not only disassemble the product, but also the *process* of co-creating it—including the nature of the relationships they will construct and the norms governing them. The exchange also shows how they develop practices that nurture trust; by acknowledging and encouraging discussion of their power asymmetries, New York staff sent a strong signal that they see their role as helping partners achieve their aims. By inviting current partners to share their experiences with potential partners, New York staff also signaled that mutual learning and honest exchange were essential organizational practices. This chapter focuses on the earliest stage in the process of coproduction, as Sesame Workshop and its partners attempt to align their interests by constructing value in relationship to the cultural product and the process of creating it together.

Introducing and Setting the Terms of Coproduction

I heard a version of Sherrie Westin's introduction to coproducing *Sesame Street* articulated by New York staffers at every meeting with new partners I attended over the course of seven years. At a content and format ideas meeting with new and returning members of the Jordanian team to plan a new season of *Hikayat Simsim*, a New York staffer explained:

> I just want to say it's really an honor to be here. We're here to support you. We're here to offer whatever experience we have. But this is your project. And it's for you to make the decisions. We're here to help you better understand the *Sesame* brand, that you probably know very well, but we're not here to impose. We're here to just support, and throw out ideas on how to make it better.[2]

From their first interactions with partners, New York staff emphasize the collaborative dynamics they want to nurture.

Unsurprisingly, many partners do not take this at face value and are skeptical of how they will be treated. During the first educational content seminar in Nigeria, partners worried about how they would build relationships with New York staff, and how equitable and respectful those relationships would be. A Nigerian writer, for example, revealed to me that prior to the educational content seminar, she was ambivalent about participating and worried whether New York staff would be racist:

> I definitely was concerned. I said this: are they going to be the typical Americans that come to Nigeria, and as far as I'm concerned, are racist? I worked at Sheraton, for example, and left because the racism was really bad. You know, a customer complained about the potatoes and said, "What do you expect, they're Nigerian potatoes." Things like that, you know. And so that was sort of in the back of my mind. I was hoping that they were not that kind of people. I was thinking that they just may be, but let's see. So I was expecting that when we wanted to do certain things they may be like, we have to do it this way, or we have to do it this way because it's *Sesame Street*. Yes, it's called *Sesame Street Nigeria*[3] but certain things we need to do.[4]

---

[2] Field notes, Amman: 2/26/09.
[3] This interview occurred before the program was officially named. Due to copyright issues, the Nigerians could not use their preferred name, *Wazobia Sesame* ("wa", "zo" and "bia" each means "come" in Yoruba, Hausa and Igbo respectively) but instead opted for *Sesame Square*.
[4] Personal interview, Abuja: 10/30/09.

She explained that during the seminar, New York staff's stated commitment to mutual learning and respect convinced her to sign onto the project:

> So I was pleasantly surprised and very happy that it was not like that. It was more the way I would have wanted it to be where everybody's part of it and we all have a say. And they kept on saying that "advice is for life" which means I will keep on asking you as Nigerians what exactly it is that you think your children need. So that, you know, is very, very important and a very vital part of the whole thing for me. That really got me even more interested than I was before I came.[5]

As this experience reveals, partners distinguish between the words and actions of New York staff and measure their level of comfort with respect to their actions.

For many partners, being cautious about engaging with Sesame Workshop is a normal response to uncertainty. Dr. Cole explained that she welcomes the skepticism of potential partners:

> And I think when we're first engaging with our partners, I actually think that it's important for them to have a healthy skepticism about us. Because we're saying one thing and the question is, are we going to live up to what we say? And they should be questioning it because we're saying something that's pretty extreme. We're saying we have this framework, you use it and tell us what you want to do. But oh, by the way, you have to still kind of fit our brand and it's a very tricky kind of thing that we're suggesting. So if they were just kind of like, okay, great, I think we would have the wrong partners. So you want people who are going to challenge it and bring their own sensibilities to the table. And the only way they do that is by kind of asking questions and kind of well you said this, but we're doing this, so what does that really mean?[6]

For Dr. Cole, skepticism is a positive signal that potential partners are willing to seriously engage and invest in the process of coproduction.

Given my own skepticism about how willingly partners collaborated with New York staff, I included a question during each interview intended to gauge their desire to engage in coproduction with Sesame Workshop. I asked them: "If you were given money to do a completely new and original children's program instead of *Sesame Street*, would you do it? Why or why not?" Again, I assumed that behind closed doors, a good number of partners would readily admit a preference to create their own original children's television

---

[5] Personal interview, Abuja:10/30/09.
[6] Personal interview, New York: 1/17/08.

program. Most did not. Of a sample of 28 partners, 23 said they preferred to coproduce *Sesame Street*, one said both, and four preferred to produce something else—one of whom said they would produce using what they learned from *Sesame Street*.

In fact, some partners responded with surprise that I even asked the question. A common first response to the question was for partners to restate and clarify my question: "You mean *not* create *Sesame Street*?" Partners repeatedly emphasized quality and values when explaining their answer to this question:

> They know the right and wrong. They've been researching. So I think their experience is more value than going and doing it on my own from scratch and just go ahead and try to do my own experience. Now I would go with them because they've been Sesame for forty years, and every single child loves Sesame. Me too as well. So I think no, I would go with Sesame. I would go 100 percent.[7]

A Nigerian partner explained her reasoning for engaging in coproduction: "So to me it's super fantastic doing something that's really universal—except Nigerian content with an international standard—I think, there's nothing better than that."[8] This kind of response from partners that linked the universal and the particular was incredibly consistent. At one point, after interviewing the Jordanian producer of *Hikayat Simsim*, who gave the same response, I began to have doubts. What if they did not trust me enough to reveal how they really felt? I decided to grill a New York producer, Naila Farouky, who was born in the US, raised in Cairo by Palestinian and Egyptian parents, and spoke fluent Arabic. One afternoon during a break at a writer's workshop for the Jordanian team at the Hyatt in Amman, I sat her down and asked, "Do you think they would want to produce something else if given the money?" She responded without hesitation, "No. Because they see it as their own, they really do."[9]

In many countries, well-educated partners with a lot of work experience are in high demand at NGOs and for-profit companies. They often have choices in terms of employment that less educated and experienced workers almost never have. A Nigerian partner explained that working with Sesame Workshop was a choice: "*Sesame Street* has always been concerned that I would disappear or run away or something like that. Because to be honest, I've gotten very good at being offered jobs that are almost twice what I'm

---

[7] Personal interview, Amman: 3/5/09.
[8] Personal interview, Abuja: 10/30/09.
[9] Field notes, Amman 2/27/09.

getting now—at Discovery Channel. I'm just telling you, if I don't want to do it, I've left a job before—and I didn't have anything waiting for me because I didn't believe in what they were doing. And it was very easy for me. So if I don't like what *Sesame Street* is doing, I would just leave."[10]

Partners frequently emphasized that working on a *Sesame Street* project allowed them to provide a balance to the less educational and low-quality television programming in their countries—which also inspired Joan Ganz Cooney to create *Sesame Street* in 1969. On our drive back from a studio visit to the *Sesame Street* set at Kaufman Astoria Studios in Queens during the *Iftah Ya Simsim* workshop in 2012, I ended up in a taxi with a few partners, including Dr. Ali Al Karni, the Director-General of the Arab Bureau of Education for the Gulf States. I asked him if he thought parents would be receptive to *Iftah Ya Simsim*. He replied, "Parents will be receptive. There's so much on television that is not good. *Sesame Street* is such high-quality and so intentional."[11] Another partner sharing the taxi with us added, "You never have an opportunity like this in the Arab world. It's an opportunity of a lifetime."[12] These conversations began to convince me that Amr Koura's motivation for engaging in coproduction with Sesame Workshop—to change the lives of children in Egypt—was shared by many other partners.

The gap between the opportunity to coproduce and the finished product, of course, is enormous. Although Sesame Workshop's secret sauce is its commitment to coproduction that involves engaging practices of flexibility, trust, and mutual learning, constructing relationships that allow partners to manage power asymmetries, misunderstandings, and conflict is much easier said than done. But those practices begin during the initial stages, during which partners' invaluable knowledge helps to alter the power differential with Sesame Workshop.

Taking Apart, or Disassembling Sesame Street

The process of coproduction begins as Sesame Workshop and its partners attempt to align their interests by constructing value in relationship to *Sesame Street* and the process of coproducing it. First, senior Sesame Workshop staff and local experts and gatekeepers must decide if and what they will coproduce. To do so, they engage in a process of disassembly that is much more

---

[10] Personal interview, Abuja: 10/30/09.
[11] Field notes, New York: 12/13/12.
[12] Field notes, New York: 12/13/12.

extensive than translation because it involves breaking down what is essential to the cultural product in terms of its form, content, structure, the rules governing it, and its relationship to the environment it is entering. Breaking down these components into their smallest parts allows Sesame Workshop and partners to put options on the table, and to build from those small units possibilities for new and unforeseen common ground.

Interactions are intense and numerous as New York staff and partners each communicate their own goals, expectations, preferences, beliefs, and values. They must decide if they can accept each others' bottom line demands. At this point, the cultural product is imagined, and interactions primarily involve Sesame Workshop breaking down what is essential or core to *Sesame Street* and articulating their non-negotiables: programs have to be educational, utilize a whole child curriculum, and promote key values of nonviolence, tolerance and respect, and equality and inclusion. In terms of content and form, almost all else is negotiable, including whether it will even be a television program—in Tanzania, a radio program was created.

Partners must decide whether they can agree to these terms. But they must also set their own and break down what is essential to a program in relationship to their local context, needs, and goals. Partners must evaluate whether these essential characteristics are compatible with the environment it is entering; they are unlikely to accept a product whole cloth or create a hybrid form, unless they view it as having value and resonance at the local level.

As we see in this chapter, aligning interests is key in this stage, but is possible *because* Sesame Workshop is willing to disassemble and encourage open discussion about what is negotiable and what is not—for Sesame Workshop *and* for partners. Knowledge exchange is interpersonal, and it is through interaction that differences in how they view the product and process of creating it emerge. This process of disassembly—over iterations of knowledge exchange and concession or consensus building—helps mitigate asymmetrical power dynamics, facilitates mutual learning, and builds trust. At this stage, they must align their interests *and* construct value in relationship to the cultural product in order for the process to continue.

Despite *Sesame Street's* global brand recognition, not all potential partners decide to coproduce. Discussions with two Palestinian teams ended with their initial refusal to participate in a joint Israeli-Palestinian program focused on mutual respect and understanding called *Rechov Sumsum/Shara'a Simsim*. Sesame Workshop also drew lines in the sand; they refused to coproduce a program in South Africa during the apartheid regime.

Palestine: The Value of Building Local Capacity

In 1993, after Israel and Palestine signed the Oslo Accords, the US-based Charles H. Revson Foundation, which funds medical and educational research and Jewish causes, offered initial funds to create a joint Israeli-Palestinian *Sesame Street* program in the wake of a fragile peace initiated by the Oslo Accords. The Revson Foundation had previously funded the Israeli program *Rechov Sumsum*. The main question, then, was whether Israeli and Palestinian partners and organizations in the region would be interested in cooperating on a local program together (Cole and Bernstein 2016:155).

In 1994, Sesame Workshop sent an exploratory team to meet with a politically diverse group of Israeli and Palestinian professionals, psychologists, and politicians to gauge interest (Cole and Bernstein 2016:155).[13] The Revson Foundation funded the trip. Dr. Cole wrote that the goal of the meetings was to answer three basic questions: "Is it important to teach children at a very young age to humanize the other? Is it an important idea? And finally, is it a feasible idea and, were there Israelis and Palestinians who would be willing to be involved in a Sesame Street project?" (Cole and Bernstein 2016:156).

Dr. Cole soon realized that Israelis and Palestinians agreed that the idea was *important*, but they also agreed that it was probably not *feasible* (Cole and Bernstein 2016:156). The Palestinian professionals thought a children's show would be unable to capture the harsh reality of their country inside the fictional bounds of a cheerful and fantastical children's television program, that the Israelis would dominate the production due to their advantageous position with more experience and infrastructure (Cole and Bernstein 2016:156). Moreover, the Israelis doubted that any Palestinian group would be willing to collaborate with them (Cole and Bernstein 2016:156).

Dr. Lewis Bernstein, Sesame Workshop's Executive Vice President of Education, Research, and Outreach, was a producer at the time who was charged with finding a local Palestinian partner. He approached the government-sponsored Palestinian Broadcasting Corporation, whose representatives told him that although they supported peace, they would not participate in the project. Many Palestinians opposed acts of "normalization," or friendly cooperation with Israelis before a peace agreement was put into place (Shapiro 2009).

---

[13] A research assistant, Audrey Lindemann, researched and wrote the original draft of the Israeli, Palestinian, and Jordanian program histories, some of which I incorporate and draw upon.

Daoud Kuttab, a renowned journalist and the founder of the nonprofit Jerusalem Film Institute, who was starting a private Palestinian television station, also initially refused to participate. He recalled that, at the time, he told Sesame Workshop executives: "We are looking for a divorce from the Israelis, not a marriage" (Shapiro 2009). Sitting in his home in Amman, Jordan, Kuttab explained his reasons to me:

> And I said to Lewis absolutely not. I was adamant against it. And I gave him very good reasons. I said look, we are about to set up our own Palestinian national station and it's going to be a very weak station, it will not have a lot of money. It will have very bad quality and all of a sudden you're going to come into the Palestinian TV station with a very high quality production of *Sesame Street* with Israelis and Palestinians? You are going to basically destroy the identity of that station. So instead of that identity coming up as a national identity, the first thing the people are going to see of high quality would be something Israeli-Palestinian. That would overshadow everything else. I just don't think it's appropriate.[14]

When Kuttab went back to his team, however, they had a very different reaction. They saw it as an opportunity to build a local media infrastructure and train young Palestinians. Kuttab described the meeting, which began with an engineer and amateur animator from Gaza exclaiming: "Daoud are you crazy? This is a chance in a lifetime for us to work with *Sesame Street* and you just turned it off? Let's do it. Okay, let's try to soften the blow, let's try to make it not the way they want it. But this is our chance, our artistic chance to do something with the best in the world."[15]

In this case, disassembly among various differently-positioned partners helped identify areas of value—specifically capacity-building and learning—that a key decisionmaker did not see. Kuttab described how he negotiated with Dr. Lewis Bernstein to increase the value of his team's participation:

> I went back to Lewis and I said it looks like we're willing to work but we have conditions. And I laid out three conditions. Condition one, we want a much bigger budget shifted from the production to the training. If we're going to do this and if for us the opportunity is a training opportunity, then you've got to give us more money to train people so that the next time around they will be self-sufficient. Second issue—we want to be totally in control of the Palestinian segments. And the third was—because they said we want to talk about mutual respect, mutual tolerance—I said look, we have different goals than what you've submitted.

---

[14] Personal interview, Amman: 2/28/09.
[15] Personal interview, Amman: 2/28/09.

Our number one goal is not about mutual respect between Israelis and Palestinians. Our number one goal is pride in our culture and identity. I want children to be proud of being Palestinian. Before I talk about Palestinians respecting Israelis, they should respect each other. And then after we do all this, then I'm okay with doing mutual respect between Palestinians and Israelis. Lewis said fine. All three conditions were accepted. They shifted $300,000 from production to training.[16]

Dr. Bernstein's recollection was similar, and he added that Sesame Workshop found additional funders so that the program was supported not only by the Revson Foundation, which offers grant programs in four areas, one of which is Jewish Life:

[It] was not the most comfortable position for the Palestinians, so we had to go and find other funders. We found the European Union, the Ford Foundation, and the Dutch government. We wanted to make sure that politically we were broadening the funding basket so that they could feel comfortable within that so that when the credits would roll they would feel okay with those credits.[17]

The Palestinian production company, Al-Quds University's Institute for Modern Media, led by Kuttab, decided to join the project with Israel Educational Television (IETV). These two teams agreed that there would be multiple versions of bilingual programming intended to reach both Israeli and Palestinian audiences. Two bilingual versions of the show would air, one in Hebrew with some Arabic, which would be seen in Israel and Palestine, with sixty episodes of twenty-seven minutes each. Another primarily Arabic version would be broadcast in Palestine, with twenty shows of fifteen minutes each (Miller 1998). The two bilingual versions and their different broadcasting locations were intended to be accessible to three groups: Jewish Israelis, Arab-Israeli citizens, and Palestinians (Warshel 2021:116).

Palestinians' ultimate decision to participate in a joint Israeli-Palestinian *Sesame Street* project hinged on their ability to negotiate what they considered to be a more valuable product *and* process—capacity building and control over local content—and then to align their interests with Sesame Workshop, which involved a shift in funding to achieve value. Moreover, in the Palestinian case, the process of constructing value occurred internally among the local team *and* externally with New York staff. Sesame Workshop's demonstration of real and substantive concessions early in the discussion was an important signal to partners that they would actually be valued

---

[16] Personal interview, Amman: 2/28/09.
[17] Personal interview, New York: 1/17/08.

and have a voice in the process, which helped build trust. Daoud Kuttab reflected on the success of the process of capacity building and learning: "And I'm proud. Almost everybody who trained there are working either with us or with other people in writing, in producing, in directing. So it went well."[18]

Kosovo: The Value of Understanding Ethnic Conflict

In Kosovo, negotiations over the terms of adoption were also critical and forced Sesame Workshop to reconsider what they had previously considered a core value—using the alphabet to teach literacy. During initial discussions, Sesame Workshop broke down what is essential to *Sesame Street*—in particular, teaching children to recognize letters. Partners explained critical dimensions of the local environment that would conflict with that Sesame Workshop core value: written text was wrapped up in deeply held cultural conflicts between Albanians and Serbians, who could not agree on a common alphabet (either Latin or Cyrillic). Partners thereby shared information essential to the program's success in the local market that would otherwise not have been evident to New York staff: parents would not want their children to view the alphabet of the "other." Basia Nikonorow, the New York producer for *Rruga Sesam/Ulica Sezam*, explained the dilemma:

> Well our basic approach on *Sesame* is that we address literacy through learning the letters. Well what do you do in a place where there's actually two alphabets going? In our discussion we came to the point that we can't do it through alphabet, this is also going to be one of these divisive things. Can we make a show without any alphabet in it? We had to get special permission and make a special presentation to our senior team because who would have a street sign—a show open—without text on it? We have no text when our show opens and for that very reason our street sign is not on the show—our brand, it's not there at the start. How did we go around it? We had kids' voices who shout out, "Rruga Sesam!"[19]

In addition to the language issue, partners explained to New York staff that parents would not allow their children to watch an ethnically integrated program. They therefore could not shoot scenes with children from each group playing together. Nikonorow emphasized the value of partners'

---

[18] Personal interview, Amman: 2/28/09.
[19] Personal interview, New York: 1/18/08.

warnings that parents would not allow their children to watch the program if Albanian and Serbian children were filmed together: "It's not realistic even though we really wanted to, to show an Albanian and Serbian kid playing together. It's just not realistic. You can't do that. They can't look like a fairy-tale and then kids would watch it and parents would encourage their kids not to watch it."[20]

Although the problem could have killed the project, New York staff and partners developed an innovative solution; they created a "visual dictionary" that featured children holding objects such as sunglasses and saying their corresponding words in different languages. Nikonorow explained how the team developed the new model:

> We had our funders who were saying we should be a show addressing a multi-ethnic society. We wanted to show a respect for kids of different ethnicities and highlight how different they are. There's no way to show a Serbian kid and an Albanian kid playing together, it just doesn't happen. And we decided, let's focus on our similarities, which seemed so basic. But yet, it was a giant realization to come to. And as a result we made a lot more segments which were montage segments where you had kids of different ethnicities and there was a song that unified it. We came up with this visual dictionary segment which was another way of kind of showing, look we all have a nose. I call it this in Albanian, I call it this in Turkish, I call it this in Serbian, and I call it this in Bosnian or in Roma. You know, I have a hand, you have a hand. And this is what my hand is called in my language. We're the same kids, right?[21]

This exchange reveals how far New York staff (as representatives of Sesame Workshop) were willing to go to reinterpret and expand their understanding of their own core values—in this case, literacy as a key component of the program—so that they could find new and unanticipated common ground with partners. They were flexible in what they conceded, reconsidered what would be a deal-breaker for them, and disassembled so they could reconstitute in a way that allowed them to align their interests with their partners. Of course, Sesame Workshop's flexibility was preceded by an arguably more critical one: the willingness of Serbian and Albanian partners to align their own interests and work together on the same team.

---

[20] Personal interview, New York: 1/18/08.
[21] Personal interview, New York: 1/18/08.

South Africa: Reassessing Value and Impact

The process of constructing value does not necessarily end after the first season of a *Sesame Street* program. For example, after the first season of *Takalani Sesame* aired in 2000, the partnership between Sesame Workshop, the South African Department of Education, and the state-owned South African Broadcasting Corporation faltered when the South Africans expressed concerns that the program was not groundbreaking enough. They gave Sesame Workshop an ultimatum: they would only continue as a partner if *Takalani Sesame* dealt with HIV/AIDS. A Sesame Workshop producer described the reaction in New York: "New York was freaked out. None, none of us were experts. The South African government was saying HIV didn't lead to AIDS so we would be going against the government. We struggled for a couple of months."[22]

The South Africans' strong position that *Takalani Sesame* include an HIV/AIDS curriculum divided New York staff. A writer for *Sesame Street* who helped train the South African writing team explained her initial trepidation and revealed how South African partners helped her understand why the HIV/AIDS curriculum was so valuable and necessary:

WRITER: Well there was a lot of controversy around the HIV/AIDS character and that took some time. I was against it at first. Yeah, I think a lot of people were. And I did not come around as soon as some people.

TK: What were your concerns?

WRITER: I was really worried that it would be too didactic. One of the reasons that I love my job is because I know that we're making kids laugh. And I thought, let the South African kids watch *Sesame Street* and have a laugh and leave them alone about AIDS right now. But the more I learned about it and the more devastating the numbers became, the more I realized it just wasn't even a conversation that I had the right to have anymore. It was something we needed to try.[23]

It is important to highlight that this writer listened to what partners needed, learned why they needed it, and changed her mind in response to their needs.

Sesame Workshop ultimately agreed to develop an HIV/AIDS educational curriculum with the South African team, but tailoring it to meet local needs proved to be quite difficult. Naila Farouky, who helped produce *Takalani Sesame*, revealed how difficult it was for South African educators, doctors, psychologists, and other experts, together with New York staff, to

---

[22] Personal interview, New York: 1/16/08.
[23] Personal interview, New York: 1/29/08.

develop the character that would ultimately be the vehicle for the HIV/AIDS educational curriculum. It took Sesame Workshop and South African partners four months to decide that she would be a female golden colored Muppet named Kami.

India: The Value of Sustainability

As in South Africa, Indian partners also reassessed the value of their collaboration with Sesame Workshop after the first season of *Galli Galli Sim Sim* had aired. But unlike their South African counterparts, they were not concerned with the value of the program—they already saw it as valuable. Rather, they wanted to construct more value for the brand in India by generating more revenue. That would make the brand and the work they were contributing to it more sustainable.

In 2009, Sesame Workshop created Sesame Workshop India, the first subsidiary and local office in a foreign country. Sashwati Banerjee, the Founding Managing Director of Sesame Workshop India, and her team developed a plan to generate a permanent revenue stream for their nonprofit work by creating a for-profit business called *Sesame Schoolhouse*—and they wanted to brand the preschools *Sesame Street* instead of the name of the preexisting television program *Galli Galli Sim Sim*. She explained the problem with the television program's name:

> On television, people don't mind a Hindi program. Because television, per se, culturally is Hindi. So *Galli Galli Sim Sim* on television is perfectly viable across the board. ... When it comes to buying a product, "galli" in India means – it does not even mean a street. It means literally an alley. Gallis are what is associated with slums in India.[24]

She explained the conflict that emerged immediately with New York staff when she suggested changing the name of the for-profit business:

> But see, now our preschools are not called *Galli Galli Sim Sim*. Our preschools are definitely called *Sesame Street*. And that, to us, was a very important positioning point. Because this is middle class India, where they're not going to send their kids to a *Galli Galli Sim Sim* school. They will send them to a *Sesame Street* school. So it's also leveraging the global brand. It's also knowing when to use the local brand and when to use the global brand. We had a big battle on this one, and then we had

---

[24] Personal interview, New York: 12/3/12.

to get our marketing team involved to resolve this because [New York staff] said, "There's no way you can do this," and I'm like, "There's no way you can't do this." And we did, and we've come up with a solution, so that's fine.[25]

The constraints that the Indian team confronted were not those that New York staff ever had to deal with—not only because Sesame Workshop owns the intellectual property of *Sesame Street* and can make autonomous decisions about it, but also because their program is not an adaptation; it is the original. And anything New York staff created would fall under the umbrella of the entire *Sesame Street* brand. Indian partners also faced a class structure and a consumer market with tremendous variation. When I asked Banerjee what her solution was, she explained the need for a dual brand strategy in India:

> The fact is that we do need a dual brand strategy in India. I think the big question was we didn't want to get into a situation where we were seen perceivably positioning *Galli Galli Sim Sim* as a brand that only extends to a mission-based, deprived population, and then *Sesame Street*, which is like this aspirational brand. So I think the strategy now is we'll brand everything as this umbrella, *Sesame Street*, and then we will house *Galli Galli Sim Sim* under that. And that, again, is a departure. I don't think they've done that anywhere else in the world.[26]

For partners in India, there was tremendous value in coming up with a viable solution to the challenge that most partners face—building sustainability for local Sesame projects. Aligning their interests with New York staff, therefore, centered on educating them about the nature of the Indian market and negotiating to generate value for them within it.

Aligning Interests with Government and Civil Society Experts and Gatekeepers

For Sesame Workshop, interests must also be aligned with high-level government and civil society experts and gatekeepers. Without these partners, Sesame Workshop could not even enter a country. Gatekeepers set their own ground rules, exchange information with Sesame Workshop about what local stakeholders want and can tolerate, and how the local culture works in ways that are relevant for the program to succeed with its audience. They help

[25] Personal interview, New York: 12/3/12.
[26] Personal interview, New York: 12/3/12.

Sesame Workshop and partners develop curricular goals that, if not properly implemented in the local context, could become contentious.

For example, I observed the first educational content seminar in Nigeria, where representatives from the Ministries of Education and Health weighed in, as did leading Nigerian writers, feminists, religious leaders, environmentalists, and academics, among many others. Stakeholders articulated the need for the program to conform to the national educational curriculum. They debated among themselves and with Sesame Workshop staff what languages would be used, how ethnic minorities would be depicted, how cultural and religious differences would be dealt with (particularly between Christians in the south and Muslims in the north), and how rural populations could be included. And they worried about how they would build relationships with New York staff, and how equitable and respectful those relationships would be.

The importance of building alliances with government and civil society organizations will be discussed in more detail in Chapter 6. But these alliances would not be possible at all if their interests were not aligned at the beginning stages of the process of coproduction.

Building Relationships: One Night in New York

After a long day of meetings and presentations, and the studio visit on December 13, 2012, participants of the *Iftah Ya Simsim* workshop were invited to the annual all-staff Sesame Workshop Holiday Celebration, which was being held at B.B. King Blues Club & Grill in Times Square. The food was abundant, and the dancing was nonstop; everyone seemed to be having a very, very good time. While many of the staff huddled over tables together, talking among themselves, the senior staff worked the room. Sesame Workshop President/CEO Mel Ming made his way around to talk to individual partners. Robert Knežević was chatting and hugging partners at his table. Eventually, he and I ended up near each other on the dance floor. "I think they'll do a great job," I yelled into his ear. He leaned in so I could hear him through the music, gestured in a wide circle with his hand, indicating everyone in the room, and said, "Tamara, this is a teambuilding exercise."

Many New York staff understood that at its core, the process of coproduction is about relationship building. During my travels with Sesame Workshop, I observed a plethora of interactions between New York staff and partners that were fundamentally focused on building rapport, respect, and trust. I witnessed skillful efforts to mitigate actual and potential conflicts, to correct misunderstandings, and to acknowledge each other's knowledge and skills. That does not mean all interactions were unproblematic or effortless. They were not.

But it does mean that both sides recognized that the strength of their relationship—like a good marriage—did not depend on a lack of conflict, but on how they managed and resolved it. Building rapport, respect, and trust would be even more critical for Sesame projects that tackled difficult and potentially contentious social issues, and for partners who wished to use *Sesame Street* as a vehicle for social change.

New York staff frequently reflected on how important seemingly small gestures are to help build trust with partners. Beatrice Chow, then Assistant Vice President of Strategic Communications, explained how the timing of phone calls demonstrates respect to partners:

> I mean, we try to speak to them regularly. And this is a small thing, but it's an important thing. We're working with people in many time zones. So in Indonesia, in India, we alternate who does the morning calls and who does the call in the evening at home. And I'm telling you, that makes a big difference. You don't want to be the one always on the phone at 10:30 at night. And that you're fair and you take turns? It's a good thing, It's a little thing about respect, a little thing about courtesy. But I think it makes a big difference.[27]

I also observed New York staff in real time in the New York office and around the world making efforts to recognize partners' birthdays, invite them to their homes, and create photo scrapbooks celebrating their shared work and memories together. And of course, partners always reciprocated these kinds of gestures when New York staff traveled to their countries.

Sesame Workshop's success *does not mean* the organization, the individuals within it, or its model are perfect. Coproduction is difficult, especially across cultural and linguistic divides. Indeed I observed, and both partners and New York staff informed me, of many Sesame Workshop mistakes and missteps (and some will be discussed at length in future chapters). What is distinctive about Sesame Workshop as an organization, however, is a general willingness to acknowledge, reflect upon, and course correct when mistakes occur.

The data in this section show that moments of give and take and flexibility build trust as partners realize Sesame Workshop is very willing to find agreeable common ground—even on core issues. And Sesame Workshop realizes partners are willing to do the same. Through transnational interaction, they

---

[27] Personal interview, New York: 1/18/08.

exchange knowledge and build consensus, which helps mitigate asymmetrical power dynamics and conflicts, and forges Sesame Workshop and its partners as allies. These numerous exchanges of knowledge become resources, helping align interests and construct value in relationship to not only the product itself, but also to the terms and process of creating it together. For hybrid cultural products like *Sesame Street*, whose value increases with local adaptation, those terms and processes are particularly critical, as the next chapter shows.

4

Reconstituting *Sesame Street*

Exchanging Cultural Knowledge to Customize

In December 2013, exactly a year after the initial workshop for potential *Iftah Ya Simsim* partners, the final team was in place and reconvened in New York for a week-long writing workshop to develop scripts for the new program. The mood, again, was electric. During one of the first sessions, Brett Pierce, who had written and produced for Sesame Workshop for decades, explained to partners that their first goal was to figure out what the soul of the program would be:

> But shows have kind of almost mission statements to them. They do have emotional cores around which everything kind of jumps off of. *Barney* was all about nurture, warm, love, everything is fine, everything is good, let's sing about it one more time. The challenge of *Sesame* is it has this whole child curriculum. *Sesame* has all these different elements. There's not an obvious natural core for *Sesame*, and that's a strength and a weakness of it. It doesn't kind of just land. You have to have your diverse themes. But that's not the soul. And one of the things that we want to do with *Iftah Ya Simsim* is find what the soul is—find what those pieces are.[1]

The soul of each *Sesame Street* program varies by its local context. Partners not only choose their own curricular goals, but they also decide the best and most appropriate ways to incorporate those goals into their programs. Once *Sesame Street* has been disassembled, it must be put back together again. It is not, however, reassembled in its former image. Rather, *Sesame Street* is reconstituted as a hybrid—an object with a wholly new form, generated by combining discrete objects previously existing in separate forms (Canclini 2005).

New York staff and partners recognize that they engage in a process of hybridization, as Dr. Cole described: "I think that we always are trying to have these productions be as based locally as we can and have our partner be kind of the front and center of the production. But in reality, it becomes

---

[1] Field notes, New York: 12/17/13.

Sesame Street Around the World. Tamara Kay, Oxford University Press. © Oxford University Press (2025).
DOI: 10.1093/9780190844325.003.0004

neither a local production nor an American production. It's a hybrid of sorts, because we're partnering."[2] Monica Toro, a Colombian partner, echoed this and elaborated: "The interesting thing about this is that when someone is working with someone else, it's not the sum of you and me. The product is a different thing. So I think this is a product that needs to be seen as a result of the interaction of the cultures."[3]

Partners consistently acknowledged that customization was critical to their decision to participate in a local *Sesame Street* program. Many even described how their colleagues initially refused to participate, reconsidering only after being reassured—and given evidence—that the program would be customized. Dr. Lewis Bernstein described the negative initial reaction of an Israeli official when he approached him to create a local program in the early 1980s:

I helped train the consortium of Arab Gulf States in 1979 when they first came in to do *Iftah Ya Simsim*, which was a cooperative venture to teach Modern Standard Arabic across borders.[4] And once we had done that we also said, why don't we make it available in Israel? And so I came to speak to the head of the Israel Educational Television. And he said, "Why would we want anything American? We have so much after the 1967 war that has changed so rapidly in our country. There's a co-colonization of Israel. We don't need anything American."[5]

Dr. Bernstein responded by touting the success of *Iftah Ya Simsim* and showing him film segments of how partners locally adapted it. He described the exchange: "And I said, fine, but maybe you should take a look at how your neighbors, one country down—Saudi Arabia, Kuwait—have used the show and made it their own. And after he saw it, he said, "I changed my mind.""[6]

When asked if potential partners frequently voice concerns about adopting a US cultural product, Naila Farouky, a producer from the Middle East who worked as a New York staffer, replied:

Always. They are not diplomatic when it comes to telling you that they don't want this to be Americanized. People are pretty straight forward. And the reason is because it's not about the money. It's a very very philosophical, ethical question for them. If you are importing some kind of subliminal shit from the US, we don't want it and we don't want to be a part of it. And to be fair, in many countries now

---

[2] Personal interview, New York: 1/17/08.
[3] Personal interview, Bogotá: 6/26/09.
[4] The original *Iftah Ya Simsim* program was produced in Kuwait in 1979.
[5] Personal interview, New York: 1/17/08.
[6] Personal interview, New York: 1/17/08.

especially, it's also very dangerous to be involved in something like that. And that's the thing, they just tell you straight out: if we are viewed or if we sell out and become this American franchise, then we're screwed.[7]

Senior New York staff are acutely aware of how critical customization is to partners. When I asked Dr. Cole how Sesame Workshop defines success, she explained: "If no one realizes it is a show that has its origins in the United States. If our role is invisible and it's seen as a local program."[8] To this end, Sesame Workshop commissions independent research not only to gauge every program's educational impact, but also to assess whether they are perceived as local. For example, an Egyptian consulting firm reported on the public perception of *Alam Simsim*:

> In focus groups, respondents strongly felt that *Alam Simsim* was an Egyptian production. One respondent felt that the program even promoted in children a sense of loyalty and commitment to the country. Although some respondents were aware that the program was modified from an American program, they felt that it had been "well-Arabized and Egyptianized" to suit Egyptian children. (*"Maybe an Astronaut" The Measurable Impact of Alam Simsim*, p. 33)

Like *Alam Simsim*, local *Sesame Street* programs are generally perceived as local by audiences in every location in which they are created.

Putting Together, or Reconstituting Sesame Street

As we saw in the previous chapter, coproduction begins as Sesame Workshop and its partners attempt to align their interests by constructing value in relationship to *Sesame Street* and the process of coproducing it. Coproduction continues as they engage in a process of reconstituting or putting together a new and distinctive version of *Sesame Street* that resonates with local audiences. During this reconstitution stage, the core group of actors shifts to New York staff and partners with technical and creative abilities, who must transform an imagined product into a real one. And this is not a simple task. It involves customizing or adapting *Sesame Street* to meet local needs and goals, and constructing collective meanings between coproducers who do not share them.

[7] Personal interview, New York: 1/16/08.
[8] Personal interview, New York: 1/17/08.

Through interaction, profound differences in how New York staff and partners conceptualize ideas related to *Sesame Street*, and the collaborative process it requires, are exposed. For example, they may not share collective meanings of childhood, humor, and quality, but through intensive and repeated interactions, they are able to build shared meanings for a hybrid program within which those differences can coexist.

As this chapter reveals, during this stage, New York staff and partners exchange different kinds of resources, including various forms of knowledge; Sesame Workshop offers financial resources for production, and technical knowledge. But the most crucial knowledge comes from partners who provide invaluable cultural resources that allow the entire team to create projects that address local needs in ways that are culturally appropriate. While they, too, bring technical knowledge and innovation, their deep knowledge of local needs, values, cultures, and access to local gatekeepers and brokers is essential. Customization cannot happen without them.

Indeed, partners infuse projects with meaning and provide subtleties of language, music, artistry, and humor. These are valuable resources that Sesame Workshop lacks and that only partners possess. Multiple and varied elements of *Sesame Street* must be customized, including the street or location itself, the characters, the curriculum, and the content. This process reveals how knowledge becomes a resource in the course of negotiation, particularly when it is asymmetrical, and is perceived as being valuable to successful outcomes. In this chapter, my goal is to make this process of meaning-making that facilitates customization—which happens behind the scenes—legible.

Customizing the Street

One of the first decisions partners make is where the action will take place; in other words, what kind of place is Sesame Street? As Nadine Zylstra asked her partners in Dhaka: "What is the vision of the street? Before we can decide who needs to be on the street, what is not just the street, but what is *Sisimpur*?"[9] Partners do not have to choose a street; they have chosen a plaza, a train station, a square, and even a tree as the center of their Sesame world.

---

[9] Quoted in the film The World According to Sesame Street, 2006.

The Gulf States: Customizing the Street to Reflect Values

Because partners have almost complete control over this decision, initial disagreements often occur within their local team, not between partners and New York staff. During the initial workshop for potential *Iftah Ya Simsim* partners in 2012, participants discussed with New York staff the difficulty of creating a program that would include multiple countries across the Middle East:

PARTICIPANT #1: They have the problem of who does this belong to? I feel for them, really. It's a tough job. How can they make it more generic—it involves six countries.

NEW YORK STAFF: We haven't had so many countries involved in one program before, but we have had different regions. And sometimes we have a hub like a train station.

When one potential partner suggested that the program could be centered in a shopping mall, another immediately rebuffed the idea, as recorded in field notes:[10]

PARTICIPANT #1: A mall—we all have that in common.

PARTICIPANT #2: That's very stereotypical and promoting consumerism, which we want to avoid.

This exchange occurred before a team was established, and yet it reveals how potential partners are already weighing and discerning how to best create a program that reflects the values they wish to promote.

In multiple countries, I observed New York staff engage new partners in exercises to help them come to an agreement on critical issues related to the location and soul of their program. These tools helped partners understand how to reconstitute the program according to their own vision. A year later, in 2013, the final *Iftah Ya Simsim* team was established and decided that the location would be a park where children enter through a gate. That December, they settled in for a long day of work in New York, and Brett Pierce asked them to get into two teams to answer key questions intended to move the discussion forward and facilitate decision-making:

We want it to kind of have its own *Iftah* core. So we gotta start looking for what that core is. Okay, so the first question is what is the internal logic of the show? Why are your characters there? Why does this place exist? The second one: what is the emotional tone of the show? Third thing: what do you want the kids to experience

---

[10] Field notes, New York: 12/12/12.

when the show is over? And then the fourth thing is the show open. It telegraphs what the show is—how does this thing start?[11]

As the two teams settled in to discuss these questions, their answers reflected a concept for their program rooted in a larger vision of how to positively impact the lives of children living across the Middle East.

Because values are often reflected through language, initial decisions about what language will be used on the street—particularly for programs intended for children in multiple regions or countries—can become contentious. After the first season of *Iftah Ya Simsim* was complete, I asked Brett Pierce, who served as consulting producer, what issue was most contentious among partners. He replied without hesitation:

> The big issue really had to do with the Arabic language, which is one of the most complex things in the world in terms of how words are written and how they're spoken. And you can have three experts in the room and they will all disagree on— you can't say that word that way, that is not classical Arabic. That piece of it was very, very difficult and challenging. ... Most of the live-action films were moved into voiceover where we could control the language. They did finally let us introduce certain accents of local kids from around the region just speaking the way they speak. But there was a lot of debate about that. So if there was a straightjacket on us culturally, it was around the language that we were showing when we had words on screen. We had somebody kind of supervising that at every moment.[12]

Because the program was centered on teaching children Modern Standard Arabic, New York staff were not in a position to make decisions on language issues. Those decisions had to be resolved among partners.

Palestine and Israel: Customizing with Crossover Segments in a Conflict Zone

How to positively impact the lives of Israeli and Palestinian children in a conflict zone was a daunting task for New York staff and partners. At a meeting in Haifa, and another in East Jerusalem in May 1995, and in Tiberias in November 1995, they worked on curricular goals that would have to address the needs of Jewish Israelis, Arab-Israeli citizens, and Palestinians (Cole and

---

[11] Field notes, New York: 12/17/13.
[12] Phone interview: 12/14/16.

Bernstein 2016:160). During these meetings of educators and artists, they discussed the future of their children. And yet, many of them had never been in a room with members of different groups before that day (Cole and Bernstein 2016:160). In the wake of violence that had occurred at the time, some New York staff had voiced concerns about convening the meeting at all (Cole and Bernstein 2016:160).

Clearly, the diverse urban neighborhood that US children enjoyed in their version of *Sesame Street* would not be viable for their Israeli and Palestinian counterparts. Multi-ethnic integration was not possible in a conflict zone. "We wanted to strike a balance between being grounded in reality," Palestinian producer Daoud Kuttab explained, "and at the same time being positive and forward looking."[13] Small steps needed to be taken. The participants decided to create two separate streets—one for each group—which featured authentic representations of Palestinian and Israeli culture filmed by members of the groups themselves (Cole, Bernstein 2016:161). A complete geographic integration of the communities simply would not have been realistic, and the producers knew this, as Kuttab articulated: "the political situation doesn't permit hugging and kissing when people are still dying. It is more credible to have a gradual build-up" (Miller 1998).[14]

One potential set idea was for a park to connect the two streets and serve as a place for cross-cultural gathering. Shared land, however, proved to be a hot-button issue. Daoud Kuttab explained, "We had to decide who owned the park, and we didn't want to create a border in the middle. It just produced more problems than solutions" (Cooper 1999). Eventually, it was decided that there would be crossover segments, featuring characters from the other team's program entering the opposite street—a digestible dose of tolerance.

The Muppets, like their creators, would express "mutual apprehension" about collaborating with their neighbors (Cooper 1999). When Haneen, a cheerful female monster from Palestine with orange fur and pink hair, meets the Israeli Kippi during a crossover segment, she is terrified; in turn, Dafi, an Israeli Muppet with purple pigtails, jumps in fear at the unfamiliar cock-a-doodle-doo of the Palestinian rooster Kareem (Cooper 1999). Other crossover segments occur when Kippi and Dafi are taken to *Shara'a Simsim* by Amal, an Arab-Israeli doctor character, to visit Dafi's Palestinian cousin, Adel (Cooper 1999). This type of customization increased the likelihood that parents would allow their children to watch the programs, and decreased the

---

[13] Found without page numbers at: https://www.jta.org/1999/02/12/lifestyle/behind-the-headlines-muppets-cross-the-street-to-join-israelis-palestinians
[14] Found without page numbers at: https://www.latimes.com/archives/la-xpm-1998-apr-01-ca-34706-story.html

possibility that missteps would jeopardize not only the programs, but also the relationship between the teams.

Customizing Characters

In addition to customizing the location and vision of *Sesame Street*, partners also customize characters on their local programs. As mentioned earlier, partners are not required to use Muppets created by the Jim Henson Company, which have a very unique and identifiable appearance. A majority of partners, however, choose to feature them.

Bangladesh: Customizing Characters to Reflect Local Puppetry Culture

During the content seminar in Dhaka, some members of the *Sisimpur* team, particularly those previously exposed to *Sesame Street*, wanted to incorporate Muppets into the program. Others were wary. Bangladesh has a strong cultural tradition of puppetry and of teaching children through traditional stories and songs. Nadine Zylstra explained to *Sesame Street's* creator, Joan Ganz Cooney, how she interpreted the Bangladeshi team's concerns and how she gauged their significance:

> Somewhere along the line, this team of people have identified the show as a way of defining their cultural identity in a way. It's a way of showing the world who they are and all the time they're saying we want the world to see what we can do. We want our kids to know how rich their heritage is. They have that as their guiding principle. So at one point Juise Haque who's the set designer—he's done a lot of work with puppets in Bangladesh—he was distressed that all our Muppets essentially have the same eyes—that they were these white orbs with the black dots. And I was new on the job and so I came rushing back to Henson, I said, "Why do they have all got the same eyes?" And they said well you know that's part of the focus and that's how kids find it. So I was pleased to have an answer.[15]

Chief creative advisor Mustafa Monwar, who expressed his trepidation earlier, wanted to use *Sisimpur* to share Bangladeshi culture with the world, and traditional rod puppets were a key element of that culture. As he explained: "This is a poor country, a developing country. But one thing we are very,

---

[15] Quoted in the film The World According to Sesame Street, 2006.

very proud—that is our literature, culture, song. So we want to keep those things. And in this world, the modern world, internationalism doesn't mean that you must copy a rich country. Internationalism means your best thing—your own country's best thing—when you can give it to the world, they will appreciate it."[16]

Sisimpur's team, then, had a difficult set of choices to make. Not only did they have to come to a consensus among themselves, but they also had to work with New York staff to develop a solution for how *Sisimpur* would be localized. Zylstra reveals how the situation was resolved:

> But the question lingered for me. I was thinking actually what they're trying to say is we have a history of puppetry that is our own and we don't want your puppets taking that away from us. And I thought that was a valid, valid point. So what we started talking about with them was about creating a space within the street that was a special space where traditional puppets could live.[17]

Ultimately, the Bangladeshi team decided to design their own Muppets—including Bengal tiger and jackal characters—and include traditional Bangladeshi rod puppets in *Sisimpur*. Together, New York staff and partners negotiated a unique plan to incorporate rod puppets by transitioning into "Ikri's World"—where traditional puppets live and where their stories are told through song—through the imagination of a blue monster Muppet named Ikri, who opens the segment.[18]

This experience in Bangladesh reveals how Sesame Workshop's organizational practices that prioritize flexibility allowed New York staff to diagnose and repair a potential problem before it thwarted their collaboration. But it also reveals the give-and-take on both sides; partners made key elements of the local context—and their concerns—legible to New York staff and worked with them to reconstitute the program with acceptable local inflections.

India: Customizing Characters to Reflect Local Diversity

The Indian team selected character names that intentionally attempted to obscure and minimize religious, ethnic, and caste identities. A writer for

---

[16] Quoted in the film The World According to Sesame Street, 2006.
[17] Quoted in the film The World According to Sesame Street, 2006.
[18] View a segment from Ikri's World starting at 4:07 at: https://www.youtube.com/watch?v=I9Qw tKaxS-c

Galli Galli Sim Sim explained how names were chosen for two characters: a girl humanoid Muppet named Chamki, and a male monster Muppet named Googly:

> The good thing about *Galli Galli Sim Sim* was that the characters' names were chosen such that one could not make out which region she or he is from, which religion, what caste, what ethnicity. For example, Chamki could be a Christian girl, a Muslim girl, a Hindu girl, a Sikh girl, whatever. Googly can be anything. So this was one thing that I actually liked about it that there's no religion, there's no caste, no region. They could be from anywhere. They could be anyone.[19]

This naming strategy allowed more viewers to identify with the characters because they lacked a specific identity. But it also reinforced the program's messages of diversity, inclusion, and equality.

Indian partners also ensured that the *Galli Galli Sim Sim* Radiophone Project, a community radio program that aired across large swathes of northern and central India, was appropriately localized. But in this case, localizing it did not mean making it less American and more Indian—it already was Indian. It meant making it resonate with people who spoke different dialects of Hindi across northern and central India. A writer explained: "Chamki will only talk in a specific manner, but she will not speak in a dialect which is specific to one community. In India, as you keep moving, the dialects change, the languages change, and the way you speak Hindi changes. So in Gurgaon, which is neighboring to Delhi, the way you speak Hindi is different from the way you speak Hindi in Delhi."[20]

It would be prohibitively expensive to hire voice actors to record each episode in every possible dialect. So the Indian team came up with an ingenious solution by using local disc jockeys (called radio jockeys in India) to serve as a bridge between each local community and the content that was not specific to that community. The writer described their strategy:

> We took this and we told the radio station, you are the top, and you are the tail to it. That's how we localized it. So they had a local radio jockey who introduced the program in her voice and said let me take you to where Chamki is today. So what happened immediately is that the listener said okay, this girl is from my community. She speaks my language. She's just taking me on a journey.[21]

---

[19] Personal interview, Delhi: 4/30/13.
[20] Personal interview, Delhi: 4/29/13.
[21] Personal interview, Delhi: 4/29/13.

This innovative way of localizing *Galli Galli Sim Sim* across northern and central India facilitated its acceptance, allowing it to resonate and spread not across the country, but across a particular region with linguistic variation.

Customizing the Curriculum

The foundation of *Sesame Street* is its educational curriculum, which is a required and essential element of all local programs. Partners have a significant amount of autonomy to choose and implement a curriculum that meets the needs of local children and audiences. They can also change or alter curricula from season to season if they choose. During my observations, partners often expressed concerns not with "Americanization," but with "Mexicanization" and "South Africanization." A Colombian partner, for example, expressed frustration that a DVD produced by Mexican partners and New York staff for Colombian children was not adequately localized: "But just to say the voice you hear in this DVD, it has a Mexican accent and has many Mexican words."[22] In reconstituting their programs, it was critical to distinguish themselves from regional counterparts.

During the content seminar in Abuja, a Nigerian advisor expressed concerns about using Kami, the HIV-positive Muppet created for South Africa's *Takalani Sesame*, in their program. She asked the Nigerian project director: "HIV/AIDS is a huge issue in South Africa, but it hasn't reached the same level in Nigeria. Did you check with folks in the different ethnic regions about it?" The latter replied: "Yes, we pilot tested it and it's okay."[23] As this example suggests, negotiations over customization often happen among local partners themselves in dialogues that are not North-South, but South-South.

South Africa: Customizing an HIV/AIDS Educational Curriculum for Impact

As mentioned in the last chapter, after completing the first season of *Takalani Sesame* in 2000, the South African team decided they would only continue with the program if they could address the HIV/AIDS crisis in an age-appropriate way on the program. At the time, one in eight South African

---

[22] Personal interview, Bogotá: 6/26/09.
[23] Field notes, Abuja: 10/29/09.

children had experienced the loss of a parent or caregiver to HIV/AIDS. And yet, South African President Thabo Mbeki notoriously denied that HIV caused AIDS and advocated the use of herbal remedies instead of antiretroviral drugs to treat it.

Once Sesame Workshop and the South African team decided to deal with HIV/AIDS in their second season of *Takalani Sesame*, South African educators, physicians, psychologists, and other experts, took the lead in developing a curriculum that ultimately included three educational objectives: 1) knowledge, centered on basic information, transmission, and standard precautions 2) attitudes, including humanization and destigmatization, and acceptance of and familiarity with the role of health care providers, and 3) skills, focused on coping with illness, open discussion, following a medicine regime, dealing with death and loss, and optimism. They also decided to choose a character who would serve as a vehicle for the HIV/AIDS curriculum. During a training workshop for Nigerian writers in Abuja, Naila Farouky, a New York producer on *Takalani Sesame,* described intense meetings between New York staff and South African partners as they debated different ideas for the character:

> The first idea was an actor with HIV. Problem was the person would never work again, so not a good option. Second idea was a real child with HIV. Problem was the child could and would die. Third idea was a humanoid puppet. The team worried that people would associate the humanoid with some racial group—if the puppet were purple would it be construed as black? Fourth idea was a monster puppet. But what would she look like? Fur would make her look like an animal. Don't want people to think they can get sick from monkeys or animals. Tried using orange fur and she looked sick. They cut her fur and changed the color. Fifth issue was what age she would be? Her age at first was seven. No child in this country with HIV will survive to seven. Then she was made to be five. Sixth issue was would she be a boy or girl? A girl would be better because there is a general myth that women spread HIV. But monogamous women in South Africa are getting it from men. Female HIV positive children aren't cared for as much.[24]

As noted earlier, developing the character took four months. The group ultimately agreed that the character would be a golden monster Muppet named Kami, whose name derives from a Setswana word that means acceptance, or "a welcoming."

Sesame Workshop's decision to help develop an HIV/AIDS curriculum in South Africa, however, was not without consequences for New York staff;

---

[24] Field notes, Abuja: 10/29/09.

when the news went public, Republican Congress members and conservative pundits threatened to pull PBS's funding (which aired *Sesame Street* in the US and contributed to its funding). The brouhaha died quickly after Sesame Workshop released a clip from *Takalani Sesame* in which Kami expresses her sadness that some children do not want to play with her because they think she will make them sick. Her friends reassure her that they know they will not get sick by being her friend. In 2003, UNICEF made Kami a global "Champion for Children." In this role, she has traveled the world making appearances with world leaders and celebrities, including with Whoopi Goldberg in 2002 to commemorate World AIDS Day at the UN, and in a 2006 UNICEF public service announcement about HIV/AIDS with former president Bill Clinton.

Nigeria: Customizing a Curriculum to Promote Values

One of the most interesting negotiations over customization in relationship to curricula and cultural change unfolded in real time during a writer's workshop in Nigeria. Partners expressed their desire to deal with corruption as a core theme in their curriculum. During the conversation, they shared knowledge about stereotypes they wanted to undermine, and New York staff shared knowledge about how to potentially accomplish that goal in their curriculum, as recorded in field notes:[25]

NIGERIAN TEAM MEMBER: We should deal with the corruption issue because the world and even many Nigerians think Nigeria is corrupt. And we want to teach our children that corruption is bad.

DR. COLE: Should it be anti-corruption or focusing on positive moral values? You have to think about how to present it to a child. Honesty and integrity are good. It could be something like healthy habits for life—people can rally around it. Or going green. What's a sexy way to say honesty and integrity? Maybe I'm totally off, and you can abandon it if you want, but people latch onto the word corruption and Nigeria, so you may want to redirect it.

NIGERIAN WRITER #1: How about "Do it Right"?

DR. COLE: That works well.

NIGERIAN TEAM MEMBER: How about "Yes I can, Going Green, Doing it Right"?

DR. COLE: YOU COULD USE A BUNCH OF "I's": "I can, I do it Right, I live here" [Everyone likes it]. Or what about "We can, We do it right, We live here"? [Everyone really likes that.]

NEW YORK PRODUCER: I love these themes!

---

[25] Field notes, Abuja:10/29/09.

NIGERIAN PRODUCER: They are great for kids to latch onto.

NIGERIAN WRITER #2: The government will love it.

DR. COLE: This way is a better focus than on corruption.

NIGERIAN WRITER #2: We're not mentioning a negative word. So we can say we're good.

DR. COLE TO NIGERIAN PROJECT DIRECTOR: It's up to you but you could reorient the curriculum to these three themes.

NIGERIAN PROJECT DIRECTOR REPLIES: It would help us when people say, "You're doing *Sesame Street*, but is it local?" [she pretends to respond to the hypothetical question]: Is it local? Yes. Why? Because We can and We do it right, and because We live here!

[Everyone laughs and expresses excitement.]

This exchange reveals *how* Sesame Workshop staff and partners construct collective meanings and representations. In their discussion, partners identify a locally resonant topic (corruption) and core shared values (honesty and integrity) to promote in their program. A senior New York staffer suggests a general way to communicate those specific values for children in the context of *Sesame Street* that could also apply to many different values: state the positive value rather than prohibit the negative value. She then offers a way to execute the message using themes. Partners embrace the concept, and *together* with New York staff, they experiment with different ways to articulate the themes. Through the exchange, they develop collective meanings about how to incorporate values that resonate locally using the *Sesame* approach of modeling positive messages for children.

Jordan: Customizing to Stimulate Change

In Jordan, partners customized their curriculum and outreach projects to include messages about road safety, which preliminary research showed was a huge problem impacting children. The Jordan Pioneers Content and Research Department surveyed around 100 Jordanian children in six public schools across the country, finding that, though many walked to school unaccompanied by an adult, over 80 percent could not identify the "do not walk" sign, and around 60 percent did not identify crosswalks as the proper place to cross a street.[26] The Jordanian team responded by making road safety a key curricular priority for its third season.[27] They partnered with the Global Road Safety Partnership to develop relevant educational content—fun

---

[26] https://en.ammonnews.net/article/5731
[27] https://www.grsproadsafety.org/hikayat-simsim-spreading-road-safety-awareness/

melodies with the lyrics "hold my hand" to demonstrate how adults and children should walk together, messages about looking both ways, precautions to take when playing near a road, and lessons about identifying signs and stoplight colors.[28]

Customizing Content

During my fieldwork, customization was most frequently discussed and negotiated in relationship to content for various kinds of segments. These discussions, then, usually centered on individual scripts. When New York staff conducted workshops and training sessions for new partners, particularly writers, they always emphasized the inherent tension between educational content and the creative, meaning the challenge of integrating the curricular goals in each segment, with the production goals of making each segment entertaining, engaging, and funny. During a workshop for new writers of *Hikayat Simsim*, Mathu Subramanian, a New York staffer with expertise in educational content, explained to the group that she and Reem Zada, her counterpart in Jordan, wanted to support the team's creativity as they guided them through the intricacies of meeting educational objectives from their curriculum document:

> And I also want to emphasize from the beginning that this shouldn't be an adversarial relationship between content and creative. The point is that content and creative work together to make the show better. When Reem is giving you ideas or I'm sending you script reviews, our job is not to make this segment be not funny or not entertaining. I mean kids learn when they're interested. So from a content perspective we want the scripts to be as funny and fun and silly as possible. So I just want to emphasize that we're there to support you. We're not there to stop you from creating things or being creative or silly.[29]

During these training sessions and workshops that I observed, New York staff helped new writers understand and learn the process of mastering this curricular-entertainment integration. In Mexico, at a writer's workshop, I participated in this process when writers seated at my table were given a curricular goal, "teach the concept of a triangle" to incorporate into an original script. The New York and Mexican educational experts leading this exercise reminded everyone that the segment had to be entertaining, not

---

[28] https://www.grsproadsafety.org/hikayat-simsim-spreading-road-safety-awareness/
[29] Field notes, Amman: 2/27/09.

didactic. The writers and I struggled to come up with a few ideas that were funny triangle lessons. It was an objectively quite difficult task for us all.

Because of the difficulty, writers' workshops generally front-load many examples at the beginning of sessions, and they are almost always visual—clips of segments from the US version of *Sesame Street*, or from other partners' local *Sesame Street* programs. During the writers' workshop in Jordan, before New York producer Naila Farouky introduced a segment, she emphasized the importance of customization:

> One of the things about many of the things we'll be showing you today is that they're produced in America for American kids. So already, when you're writing, you're coming from a completely different perspective and you're probably not going to like some of these ideas. But the point of us showing you these is to give you as many ideas as possible so that you can perfect them for Jordanian kids and for what you think, as a writer, is best for the show.[30]

She then explained that they were going to begin by focusing on how to teach new vocabulary words using a segment called "Word on the Street" from the US version of *Sesame Street*:

> I'm just going to go through some of these best practices for writing about vocabulary and the things that you can do in scripts to write about vocabulary. So from a content perspective, when you present vocabulary, the first thing that you want to do is introduce the words in a child friendly way. So you'll notice in the segment we're about to watch, the scenes are in a swimming pool. The other thing is to make them culturally relevant settings so places like a park or a swimming pool are places that American children are very familiar with and are just a part of childhood in America. The second thing is that these scripts communicate the meaning with lots of different cues—and this is a great place where you can inject humor. In the scene that we're about to see, the word is "squid" and there's a really great segment where the Muppet on the street asks the kids to move like a squid.[31]

Farouky then introduced the exercise to the new writers, highlighting how they were using words that Jordanian educators chose as important for Jordanian children to learn:

---

[30] Field notes, Amman: 2/27/09.
[31] Field notes, Amman: 2/27/09.

Reem actually has a list of words from the Ministry of Education here in Jordan, that the Ministry wants to emphasize during the school year. In the same way, in the US we got a list of words from schools that teachers felt were words that children should know. So in the writing exercise I picked out some words from the list that you need to emphasize to try and do these segments.[32]

As reflected in these interactions, the message that New York staff in this and other workshops emphasized repeatedly was that these skills were difficult and required practice.

New York staff also highlighted how educational content can be used to promote cultural values and traditions. During the workshop in Amman, a partner expressed his desire to expose Jordanian children to their cultural heritage: "We have a long history with the music, the tradition, with heritage—starting from the Bedouins in the country and the city. And so we can make a revival of this heritage in a creative way according to *Hikayat Simsim*, I believe."[33] A New York staffer responded immediately with an example of how to connect musical traditions to numeracy goals in the curriculum in a creative way. He suggested a segment between a monster Muppet named Juljul, who loves to fix things, and Jiddo Simsim (Grandpa Sesame, played by actor/musician Issa Sweidan):

If grandfather has a traditional instrument and he wants to show Juljul how it works and then Juljul wants to try, then maybe in order to make it simple for him he tells him just play like these five notes—like this. And then it's a way of telling kids about the number five, like, one, two, three, four, five. Do it again. So, he's learning about numbers, learning about rhythms, trying something new. But then, through the song, it's a way of also introducing the Jordanian culture in a very natural manner of this grandfather showing this kid character how this instrument works.[34]

The New York staffer's example of how to customize content not only responded to partners' desire to promote cultural values and traditions but also demonstrated to them how to incorporate multiple educational goals into one segment of their program.

At the directors meeting later in the week, a partner expressed his desire to focus on the relationship between a child and his grandmother, "Because

---

[32] Field notes, Amman: 2/27/09.
[33] Field notes, Amman: 2/28/09.
[34] Field notes, Amman: 2/28/09.

these kinds of relationships are kind of getting lost because the way we live our lives now. So I'm thinking of a segment about that idea—grandmas and the stories of grandmothers, and the relationship with the children."[35] Farouky responded by acknowledging and validating the concept, but also offered suggestions for how to make it work on film:

> So you know, for instance, like in our South Africa show, one of the things that kept coming up from the adults in the room is, "Oh, we want to highlight stories. You know, we're such a storytelling community and we want to continue oral tradi-tions." So we really also want to push a visual tradition because it's a TV show. And are you really going to do two minutes of a grandma of telling a story? You've got to be very interesting visually. So maybe this grandmother is a dancer.[36]

In this interaction, valuable knowledge was exchanged between partners and New York staff; partners shared their cultural knowledge, and Farouky val-idated that knowledge and vision. But she simultaneously offered her own valuable knowledge acquired through her years of experience as a producer and writer for Sesame Workshop. This interaction allowed New York staff and partners an opportunity to create shared meanings about how to integrate cul-tural values related to family into a segment that resonates on television for children.

During a meeting focused on content and format ideas, Khaled Haddad, the Executive Producer of *Hikayat Simsim*, expressed his desire to produce an alphabet song in Arabic for children across the Middle East:

> We had the Arabic literacy conference two years or three years ago. And one of those findings was that in Middle East we didn't have a good alphabet song. You have a [Singing] A, B, C, D, E. But in the Middle East we didn't have this song. So I'm thinking to create a song. Maybe Jordanian and the Palestinian and Egyptian, we can join forces together to produce an Arab alphabet song. And this alphabet song can be broadcast in all the satellite channels. And you can use our Jordanian, Palestinian, and Egyptian Muppets all together with the kids. So I have a vision. I'm planning to do this vision.[37]

His vision initiated a lively conversation during which partners had to educate New York staff about Arabic dialects across the Middle East.

---

[35] Field notes, Amman: 3/1/09.
[36] Field notes, Amman: 3/1/09.
[37] Field notes, Amman: 2/28/09.

Kosovo and Palestine: Customizing Segments in Conflict Zones

Although customizing content can result in entertaining exchanges about alphabets, it often involves confronting the difficult and painful realities that partners face, as Seipati Bulane-Hopa, the producer of *Takalani Sesame*, revealed about the experience of the South African team:

> When Sesame Workshop came to us, they came to us with an empty box, that had some specification. And we looked at this box and we had to fill it with content. And we felt that this was very challenging because the content that we've had in our history was a content of damage, of disruption, of distortion. And we were doing something that is a great phenomenon for all of us, which is the future.[38]

Bulane-Hopa suggests that although customization requires partners to actively engage distressing histories (and ongoing struggles), it also provides an opportunity for partners to create content that offers children alternative visions of their futures.

While New York staff can offer empathy and support for their partners who live in conflict zones, it is not possible for them to fully understand their partners' lived experiences of daily violence and the profound and myriad effects it has on their lives. Constructing shared meanings and representations is therefore incredibly challenging for New York staff and partners in conflict zones. Basia Nikonorow, the New York producer for *Rruga Sesam/Ulica Sezam* in Kosovo, described how a live action segment about children walking to school in the middle of the road at first worried her and other New York staff:

BN: This girl was in a rural setting in this little village. She was walking smack in the middle of the road. And at the beginning we were like, "Oh where's the sidewalk? There's no sidewalk. Oh, then she should be to the side of the road." And then from the landmine point of view, you're not supposed to step off of roads. So you'd think maybe she can walk on the grassy side next to the road. Well, with worries of there being landmines in places—especially in a rural area—then you wouldn't want to model a kid walking off of the road because if there was a landmine ....

TK: Because on the road, if there was a landmine, then it probably was already blown up.

BN: Right, because you've had cars going over it.

TK: So the safest place is the middle of the road.[39]

---

[38] Quoted in the film The World According to Sesame Street, 2006.
[39] Personal interview, New York: 1/18/08.

Nikonorow's example illuminates how New York staff and partners, who do not share collective meanings in relationship to places with conflict and ongoing violence, must exchange knowledge to build them. The exchange of this knowledge, however, involves a tremendous amount of work and emotional energy on the part of partners.

A compelling example of how collective meanings are forged across transnational cultural divides occurred during a workshop to train a new team of Palestinian writers in Amman, Jordan. I arrived with the New York staff in February 2009, a month after a cease-fire went into effect, ending the Israeli military operation "Cast Lead" in Gaza that lasted 22 days and killed over 1400 Palestinians and displaced over 60,000.[40] Intermittent violence continued, however. Unnerved, a New York head writer for *Sesame Street*, who would be training the Palestinian team, decided not to make the trip. Naila Farouky, who, in addition to producing local *Sesame Street* programs, had also written for them, took over that role in the workshop. It was in this context that we all sat in a conference room in the Amman Grand Hyatt (which suicide bombers attacked in 2005), to discuss script ideas for *Shara'a Simsim*.

The Palestinian head writer began the discussion by explaining an idea for a script offered by a new writer on the team who did not speak English. The head writer translated the script idea, which centered on two Muppets, as recorded in field notes:[41]

HEAD WRITER, TRANSLATING: He wants to deal with the violence in Gaza. So how he dealt with it is Kareem is on one side flying kites and celebrating International Peace Day and Haneen is actually on the other side in Gaza. And she's saying things are really bad here and the daycare is gone. She's saying I'm flying a dove towards you. Can you see it?

[THERE IS A LONG PAUSE]and then the New York writer asks: "What happened to the dove?"

HEAD WRITER: It got shot down. So I think he would really benefit from your input because as we saw, all the writers are new and they don't necessarily know what fits or what doesn't fit. And so that input really is important to them. And explain what can be done in a different way or what is more suitable.

NEW YORK WRITER: Think about the story. What's the goal?

NEW YORK STAFFER: More empathy, maybe?

---

[40] Fourteen Israelis were also killed during the operation. See: "Human Rights in Palestine and other Occupied Arab Territories: Report of the United Nations Fact-Finding Mission on the Gaza Conflict." United Nations Human Rights Council. September 25, 2009. Available at: https://documents.un.org/doc/undoc/gen/g09/158/66/pdf/g0915866.pdf

[41] Field notes, Amman: 2/25/09.

NEW YORK WRITER: But in terms of how you solve this problem, it's got to be something more positive because in the course of it you kill the dove. That kind of violence just cannot happen on this show. You can talk about it, about other places where it's happening and relate it to that, but it cannot actually happen.

HEAD WRITER, TRANSLATING FOR ANOTHER NEW WRITER: He suggests that Haneen and Kareem are making a kite on International Peace Day. And they have a friend from *Sesame Street* who's over in Gaza and they call each other. In the end they write her name on the kite and fly the kite to Gaza. What do you think about it?

NEW YORK STAFFER: So I think we don't want to shy away from these topics but it's important to pick sort of narrow ones. I think you can pick out parts like empathy, like what happens if you're missing your friend and you're worried about your friend. You can do a script on that.

In one of the few interactions I observed in which New York staff enforce a non-negotiable "rule"—in this case, no violence—they guide partners through a process of reconceptualizing the script around a socio-emotional learning goal (empathy, fear, grief). This allows partners to acknowledge the reality of the violence they face, but focuses on helping children deal with the emotions it causes. Practices of flexibility, trust, and mutual learning, on display in this interaction, allow New York staff and partners to more effectively exchange their knowledge. By pooling their different types of expertise to reassemble the product, they make it concrete—and, most importantly, producible.

The Israeli and Palestinian teams faced enormous customization challenges during the production of *Rechov Sumsum/Shara'a Simsim* in 1998. The Israeli version ended up featuring more Palestinian content, while the Palestinian version featured only a handful of Israeli segments (Shapiro 2009). This disparity resulted from, among other issues, the challenge of dubbing and adapting Israeli content. Layla Sayegh, who supervised day-to-day operations for the Palestinian program, explained that the team "tried to show only segments that didn't have anything recognizably Israeli in them," (Shapiro 2009) but that this was easier said than done. Many strong segments could not be used because they included Hebrew names and/or letters, as Sayegh explained: "the Israelis did one about recycling, and it was absolutely fantastic, but at the end, they showed a truck with Hebrew lettering" (Shapiro 2009). Daoud Kuttab echoed the problems that arose from sharing content that needed to be customized before it could air:

And so each story would have one of these fables dubbed into the local language and then you'd have your own program with two or three live action pieces that are exchanged. Again, this was a problem. So we basically found the ones that were the least politically problematic and we didn't want things that had Hebrew, either Hebrew wording or Hebrew spoken. And I mean Americans were saying look, you have to have some Hebrew because you're talking about tolerance. And I said, we can't. Our community will not accept. They'll throw eggs at us, they'll throw things worse. In the end, we did what we wanted, but it was a big fight.[42]

Ultimately, New York staff accepted and supported the decisions their Palestinian partners needed to make in order for the program to be accepted by the local population.

Kuttab was not exaggerating when he described the reactions of some Palestinians to the joint Israeli program. Palestinian partners, including writers, producers, and creators involved with the project, were often treated with little of the respect they aimed to cultivate; some Palestinians working at the television station harassed them for cooperating with Israelis (Shapiro 2009). The Institute for Modern Media was in a four story building on the campus of Al-Quds University, just outside the West Bank city of Ramallah. There, students sometimes cursed partners who worked on the program when they passed them in the hallways, insinuating they lacked loyalty to Palestine (Shapiro 2009). This was ironic given that many of the partners were outspoken defenders of Palestine, and some had been activists and suffered for that activism themselves (Shapiro 2009).

Stymied Coproduction: The Case of Brazil

A case in which the localization of a *Sesame Street* program was stymied strengthens the analysis in this book and affirms the critical role transnational organizational relationships play in these processes. Examining an unsuccessful case also addresses a significant limitation of quantitative research on diffusion—the problem of "survival bias."[43] Diffusion studies based on large datasets generally do not include data on cultural products that are not adopted, or that are adopted and then fail—these are unobservable. This presents a problem because variables that seem to have an effect on the adoption of a cultural product cannot be tested on products that fail to diffuse. My use of observational data, therefore, complements quantitative

---

[42] Personal interview, Amman: 2/28/09.
[43] Martin Ruef has a very similar point about research in organizational demography; most of it deals with only those organizations that have already survived the initial stages of development, which leads to biased results.

research by revealing the underlying processes that can stymie coproduction processes.

Both New York staff and Brazilian partners agreed that Brazil is a case of stymied coproduction. And among all cases, New York staff and partners rated it lowest in terms of the strength of their organizational relationship.[44] *Vila Sésamo* was the first local program to air in October 1972 and was a wild success, becoming iconic in Brazilian culture and even launching the career of Sônia Braga. *Vila Sésamo* ended production after two seasons due to lack of funding, but the original episodes were broadcast for years in Brazil.

In 2008, Sesame Workshop and the non-profit station TV Cultura launched a new version of *Vila Sésamo*. Convinced that *Sesame Street*'s past success in Brazil would enable them to raise money through licensing, Sesame Workshop used a new approach to enter the large and growing Brazilian market. TV Cultura contributed some funds, most of which came from advertising, and Sesame Workshop sold licensing rights to fund the project. Once the program aired and additional funds were raised, they intended to launch outreach projects.

With fewer resources up front, the program was limited and included significant US content. Despite extensive media coverage and publicity, *Vila Sésamo* failed to generate an audience. Its ratings were low, and production ended after one season. Data reveal that although *Vila Sésamo* faced stiff competition, its lack of success had more to do with issues related to micro-level mechanisms than with the market. Indeed, TV Cultura had great success with two other original Brazilian children's programs: *Castelo Rá-Tim-Bum* and *Cocoricó*, which former *Vila Sésamo* staff helped create and produce. But for Sesame Workshop's Brazilian partners, *Vila Sésamo* did not have enough value, was not sufficiently local, and did not create useful alliances or resources to justify continuing the program.

Lack of customization was a primary problem. In contrast to the original *Vila Sésamo*, most of the content was not locally produced. Because funds were limited, Sesame Workshop decided to use a 'wrap-around' format for the half hour program, meaning locally produced Brazilian segments were interspersed with US segments and content translated into Portuguese. According to partners, the hybrid version did not work: "We realized some of the American content wasn't that fun. And we would talk to each other,

---

[44] The ratings were based on two questions I asked each person I interviewed, on a scale of 1 to 5: How would you rate your experience working with your partners (in New York/in other country)? How would you think your partners would rate their experience working with you?

but [people in New York] wouldn't consider editing it."[45] Partners negotiated more local content, but it was not enough, as the producer explained: "Even this, we fought for it. Because the proposal was to have like three minutes of local content. Five minutes. Then we have fifteen."[46] Although partners stressed that New York staff encouraged them to adapt the program, the format did not allow for it, and ultimately, the program did not read as locally authentic, as a Brazilian producer explained:

> I don't think Brazilians see it as a Brazilian show. You know, I think children relate more to a Brazilian show. And I don't think Sesame, and *Vila Sésamo*, were seen as absolutely Brazilian. I think it's seen by a mixture of different things. We had a wraparound show. And the cartoons weren't Brazilian. The wrap-around was Brazilian, but we didn't have any actor, human actor in the show.[47]

This lack of customization was particularly problematic in a country such as Brazil, where a prior and fully customized version of the program had existed, was beloved, and could always be compared to the new version.

Partners also revealed other mistakes New York staff made that undermined the success of the new iteration of *Vila Sésamo*. Sesame Workshop's decision to delay the development of outreach projects until after the program was established on the air meant the local team had nothing of value to show potential sponsors or allies. A partner recounted a conversation with a senior New York staffer in which the partner criticized Sesame Workshop's lack of a plan and strategy for Brazil:

> I told him, you came to Brazil two years ago with a project—with a contract with TV Cultura to produce your show. You didn't have an outreach project in Brazil. You didn't check our educational problems, our traffic problems, our nutrition problems. You didn't get information about the country to develop something for our needs. You just want to come here and get money from media for sponsored projects. That's what happened to us. So he said, "We have to go and listen to the needs of the country and then create together something." And I said, "Yes, but you are saying this, but you didn't do the homework for Brazil. You did it for India, for Africa, for Egypt. But not for Brazil." He said, "Yeah, you are right." And I said: "You're not offering anything educational. You went to TV Cultura and didn't talk to any other NGO, government, anything, like you did in other countries. You came to Brazil as an adventure."[48]

[45] Personal interview, São Paulo: 6/19/09.
[46] Personal interview, São Paulo: 6/19/09.
[47] Personal interview, São Paulo: 6/19/09.
[48] Personal inteview, São Paulo: 6/18/09.

The partner explained that when he asked New York staff to send him outreach materials, such as the "Healthy Habits for Life" curriculum, they were not adapted for Brazil:

> We have a different culture in Brazil, with food and everything. It's simple. What's the main food in Brazil? Rice, beans and salad and beef. And all the projects that we get from Sesame are based on a different culture, an American culture. It's not a Brazilian habit. So I get all the booklets from Sesame, the recipes. Something that is not used here in Brazil. When I asked them to adapt something—Oh, it's too expensive for the educators to adapt this. So we have to adapt this in Brazil. So why am I going to pay for someone in Brazil to do this? I don't have to adapt something from *Sesame*. We can do it in Brazil with local nutritionists, local doctors. That's the difference.[49]

Without a viable outreach project, partners were unable to build alliances with Brazilian NGOs and key government ministries. There was nothing concrete to build alliances around, and no resources to exchange. Partners expressed frustration that the great potential for Sesame Workshop in Brazil was squandered, as one partner explained:

> And since the beginning, I told them: "Look, I've been in Brazil all my life. I was with Disney, and I have relationships, of course. Everybody does. So use me." And I told these people since the beginning: "I'm not telling you that I'm going to open the ruler's house for you, but I mean, some. Even if it's one contact—two, three people, two people because these people can open other doors, right? So why are you not using my relationships?" They couldn't care less. They couldn't care less, and now, they're struggling to get money. So that's very upsetting.[50]

When I queried the New York producer of *Vila Sésamo* about this critique, he immediately agreed with Brazilian partners' assessment of the problems and reflected on the mistakes Sesame Workshop made with Brazil:

> I think looking back if we all had a clearer picture of what we wanted to accomplish, I think a lot of that kind of struggle could have been minimized. That was the most huge learning experience for everyone. I think if we had a clearer concept, if we had a clearer map of what we wanted to do. I think sometimes we're eager to break into a particular country without really assessing what the needs are.[51]

[49] Personal inteview, São Paulo: 6/18/09.
[50] Personal interview, São Paulo: 6/15/09.
[51] Personal interview, New York: 7/10/08.

It was reassuring that Brazilian partners were willing to openly share their frustration and disappointment with me, and noteworthy that the producer in New York took full responsibility for the mistakes made by Sesame Workshop in Brazil. This kind of self-reflection was common within Sesame Workshop, although it is uncommon in many organizations.

The Brazilian case shows how critical customization is to coproduction; Sesame Workshop's failure to fully customize the new version of *Vila Sésamo* and its outreach materials affected partners' ability to develop viable outreach programs. But it also undermined their ability to build alliances with potential government and civil society allies. Indeed, this case illuminates how customization can grease the wheels for building alliances and networks, a topic we will turn to in Chapter 6.

It is evident in this chapter that partners' crucial knowledge allows them to mitigate some of the power disparities with New York staff. Of course, that differential remains, and power is always present; Palestinian writers could not break a fundamental Sesame rule regarding violence.

For hybrid cultural products such as *Sesame Street*, customizing not only affects local acceptance of the cultural product but also the strength of relationships among organizational partners. In the case of Brazil, Sesame Workshop's willingness to admit the mistakes it made and commit to rectifying them helped repair relationships with partners caused by lack of adequate customization. This explains why Sesame Workshop and the same Brazilian partners agreed to discuss coproducing a new season of *Vila Sésamo*. Without this kind of relationship, reconstituting *Sesame Street* would not be possible. Building rapport, respect, and trust is even more critical for *Sesame Street* projects that tackle difficult and potentially contentious social issues, and for partners who wish to use *Sesame Street* as a vehicle for social change.

5

Pushing Cultural Boundaries

Authenticity and Social Change

> I am Somebody! I am Somebody! I may be poor, But I am Somebody. I may be young, But I am Somebody. I may be on welfare, But I am Somebody. I may be small, But I am Somebody. I may have made mistakes, But I am Somebody. My clothes are different, My face is different, My hair is different, But I am Somebody. I am Black, Brown, or White. I speak a different language. But I must be respected, protected, never rejected. I am God's child! I am Somebody!

On May 9, 1972, Rev. Jesse Jackson appeared on *Sesame Street* and led a set filled with children of various ethnic and racial backgrounds in a call and response to the poem "I Am—Somebody" by civil rights activist and pastor Rev. William Holmes Borders, Sr.[1] Almost exactly two years before Jackson's appearance, the state of Mississippi banned the broadcast of *Sesame Street* because it had an interracial cast, as reported in the *New York Times*:

> The State Commission for Educational Television has vetoed the showing of "Sesame Street," regarded as one of the leading pre-school educational television series, on the state ETV system because of racial grounds. A member of the commission said, "Some of the members of the commission were very much opposed to showing the series because it uses a highly integrated cast of children." The same member who asked not to be identified said, "Mainly the commission members felt that Mississippi was not yet ready for it." (May 3, 1970, p. 54)

Fifty years later, the planet was in the grips of the global COVID-19 pandemic, and protests against police violence and racism erupted in the US, quickly spreading around the world. On June 6, 2020, Muppet characters Elmo and his father Louie appeared in a joint CNN/*Sesame Street* program titled *Coming Together: Standing Up to Racism*. The goal of the program was to help parents explain to their children the events unfolding around them. Elmo

---

[1] The segment can be viewed at: https://www.youtube.com/watch?v=tu0lNcrZjG8

Sesame Street Around the World. Tamara Kay, Oxford University Press. © Oxford University Press (2025). DOI: 10.1093/9780190844325.003.0005

asks his father about protesting and racism. Louie explains: "Not all streets are like *Sesame Street*. What we are seeing is people saying enough is enough. They want to end racism."[2]

For the creators of *Sesame Street*, the program, from the beginning, went far beyond literacy and numeracy. It was also an experiment in how to address and mitigate entrenched inequalities rooted in race, gender, and class. Research suggested that modeling prosocial values and diversity for children could have a significant impact. Joan Ganz Cooney, Lloyd Morrisett, and their original team, therefore, set the action on a diverse urban street. The primary cast included two married couples: one Latino and the other African-American. Over the years, the program featured Native American communities, an actress who is deaf, an actress who is blind, people who use wheelchairs, a Muppet character with autism, and another who is unhoused.

Undermining stereotypes and embracing and normalizing differences is a core and explicit goal of New York staff. During the *Iftah Ya Simsim* workshop in 2012, I observed Dr. Cole explain Sesame Workshop's values to partners: "Sesame has actually normalized the view that cultural diversity is good and normal." A New York producer was clear about Sesame Workshop's values: "We're socially progressive, we are. And we bring that to whatever show we're making."[3]

It is important to emphasize that my focus here is on how New York staff and partners coproduce local *Sesame Street* programs. Evaluating the effectiveness of efforts to change children's attitudes through media in general and *Sesame Street* projects in particular is beyond the scope of this book. But it is also imperative to note that research on children's exposure to positive messages suggests that it can change their attitudes (Mares and Woodard 2005; Strasburger, Jordan, and Donnerstein 2010). Scholars at Johns Hopkins University examined the effects of exposure to *Alam Simsim* on learning outcomes and gender attitudes. They found that children exposed to the program not only benefitted educationally, but also exhibited more gender-equitable attitudes (Rimal, Figueroa, and Storey 2013).

Research around the world on local *Sesame Street* programs also shows various positive outcomes in prosocial value attitudes among children in conflict and post-conflict zones who viewed them. Research by Larkin and colleagues at Queens University Belfast, showed that watching *Sesame Tree* was associated with "an increase in their willingness to be inclusive of others"

---

[2] The segment can be viewed at: https://www.boston.com/culture/national-news-2/2020/06/07/elmo-and-his-dad-discuss-protesting-and-racism-in-sesame-street-and-cnn-town-hall
[3] Field notes, New York: 1/14/08.

and "an increased interest in some of the cultural events associated with the other community" (Larkin et al. 2009:10). Cole and her colleagues found that exposure to *Rechov Sumsum/Shara'a Simsim* "was linked to an increase in children's use of both prosocial justifications to resolve conflicts and positive attributes to describe members of the other group." (Cole et al. 2003:1).

Research on the impact of programs in Kosovo showed that children who viewed *Rruga Sesam* or *Ulica Sezam* "were 74 percent more likely than children in the control condition to demonstrate positive attitudes towards children from different ethnic backgrounds" (Fluent Research, 2008). Taken together, all of this research suggests that efforts to activate various kinds of equality norms among children can be an important strategy to challenge bias and prejudice. There is also research, however, that suggests that *Sesame Street* projects have also fallen short of their goals of changing attitudes (see Moland 2020; Warshel 2021).

One of the most unexpected findings to emerge from my seven years traveling around the world to observe and interview partners was their desire to emulate how New York staff use *Sesame Street*, not only to reflect to children the positive aspects of their cultures, but also to stimulate particular kinds of cultural change. Israelis wanted to undermine negative stereotypes of Arabs, and along with Mexicans, to promote acceptance of people living with disabilities (both programs introduced characters who use wheelchairs). South Africans wanted to eliminate stigma for people living with HIV/AIDS, and Nigerians and Brazilians wanted to promote a culture of environmental responsibility.

Partners' interest in pushing cultural boundaries appeared early and often, as it did on the first day of the 2012 workshop for *Iftah Ya Simsim* in New York. During the first hour of the first session, a potential partner from the United Arab Emirates initiated a dialogue about how Sesame Workshop manages controversy:[4]

POTENTIAL PARTNER FROM UAE: When it comes to controversial issues when do you get advisors and research to give it the green light?

DR. COLE: Let me give you the example of South Africa. Educators let us know that you can't say you're an educational program in South Africa without addressing HIV. The Minister of Education was leading the way. He said we have the vehicle. And we had influential people in health, education, in the ministry who signed onto it, and it was coming from them. So key people would be behind it.

---

[4] Field notes, New York: 12/12/12.

POTENTIAL PARTNER FROM UAE: How do you know how much you can do?

DR. COLE: Maybe you never know. You can't be too afraid of everything but you have to do your homework. You build a network of folks, of experts so your choices are defensible.

The message from Sesame Workshop was to push cultural boundaries, but within acceptable limits. As Dr. Cole told participants that day: "If you can't get it broadcast, no one is watching it. So there's always the balance between pushing the envelope versus practical things on the ground."

But knowing how far to push the envelope on delicate and contentious issues is a valuable resource. Not every partner has the expert knowledge needed to make complex and yet subtle assessments about navigating cultural boundaries and identifying potential landmines. In this chapter, we explore how Sesame Workshop pushes cultural boundaries and how, in order to do this effectively, New York staff depend primarily on the expert knowledge of key partners who act as *cultural brokers*. Brokers navigate complex issues and create alliances with key local actors who help to activate norms such as gender equality that are often already present—at least at some level—locally. Cultural brokers can therefore be powerful facilitators of norm acceptance and internalization (Finnemore and Sikkink 1998).

The Critical Role of Cultural Brokers

Finding the right partners and choosing a highly functional transnational team is critical to effectively pushing cultural boundaries. It is the primary reason Sesame Workshop is able to push cultural boundaries in ways that rarely, if ever, fail or result in devastating missteps. As discussed in detail in Chapter 2, Sesame Workshop relies on a rigorous multi-stage process that begins with a feasibility study to ensure it will find the kind of partners and infrastructure it needs. The next step involves a fact-finding trip to find partners and select the director of educational content who puts together a curriculum for the local program. In consultation with her local team and Sesame Workshop educational specialists in New York, the director develops a preliminary list of curricular goals.

It is during this stage that Sesame Workshop actively tries to identify key areas of need in a country, controversial issues, and different perspectives on how to address them. Experts are then commissioned to write white papers on key topics, particularly those that may be controversial. Prominent Egyptian, Mexican, and Indian scholars, for example, wrote white papers on gender issues for each program (Rouchdy 1998; Platón and Lembert 1999; Capoor and Gade 2004).

A workshop is then held for the experts and educational content team to consider and discuss the issues the white papers raise. What is learned from the white papers and the workshop provides a foundation for a curriculum seminar in country for stakeholders across a wide spectrum of society. Participants provide feedback on the preliminary curricular goals and, perhaps most importantly, they identify potential curricular areas that could be problematic and develop strategies for how to address them appropriately and effectively. The details of the curriculum document are fine-tuned yet again during an educational content seminar that brings together final local educational content and evaluation team members with their New York counterparts.

This multi-stage process, a series of transnational meetings and knowledge-sharing sessions, ensures that there are many organizational fail-safes built into the process that allow opportunities for problems to be identified and corrected. The practice of engaging a wide range of experts and stakeholders also increases the likelihood that contentious issues are put on the table, addressed, and strategies for dealing with them are formulated. This process leaves very little room for surprises to emerge that would result in catastrophes or derail projects.

The process also allows Sesame Workshop to vet a plethora of potential partners. During multiple meetings and interactions, New York staff observe potential partners' strengths and weaknesses, including in relationship to their relevant knowledge and expertise, communication styles, interpersonal skills in group and collaborative settings, and leadership potential. They also get a feel for how potential partners communicate difficult issues, navigate and manage conflict, and advocate for their positions. And partners, of course, also have the opportunity to make these assessments about New York staff and, by extension, Sesame Workshop as an organization, before they commit to joining the transnational team.

Among Sesame Workshop's team for any given project is a handful of partners who have valuable knowledge about the local cultural context, and how far the envelope on delicate and contentious issues such as equality norms can be pushed. In some countries, these cultural brokers have formal advisory roles, and in others, their primary role may be producer, educational content specialist, among others, but they also bring expert knowledge—for example, on gender relations and equality—to the team. The majority of Sesame Workshop's cultural brokers work as educational content and curriculum experts and tend to be well-educated, middle-class, bilingual, and widely traveled—the epitome of "rooted cosmopolitans" (Tarrow 2005). Many are directors of educational content who hold doctoral or master's degrees.

Cultural brokers must determine how best to push for equality norms in ways that are acceptable to other Sesame Workshop partners, such as government agencies, NGOs, and other civil society organizations, and in ways that are appropriate for audiences of young children. Brokers are therefore skilled strategic social actors, meaning they "provide identities and cultural frames to motivate others" to cooperate (Fligstein 2001:105–6). As Fligstein explains, "The ability to engage others in collective action is a social skill that proves pivotal to the construction and reproduction of local social orders" (Fligstein 2001:106). Brokers use their social skills to determine how best to frame equality norms and push cultural boundaries in order to construct more equitable local contexts and motivate others to support them.

But cultural brokers also face significant challenges; gender equality norms, for example, may not be ubiquitous across a country or region due to local cultural differences or structural constraints. This is true in most countries, including in the US, where some states have more restrictive laws related to gender, sexuality, and reproductive health. Brokers, therefore, have to gauge the receptiveness of different populations to equality norms and adapt messages in ways that facilitate buy-in. Effective brokers, therefore, also know their limitations and when to seek input and advice on issues for which they lack knowledge or expertise—for example, on how to effectively navigate religious and gender issues in northern Muslim areas of Nigeria.

The data presented in this chapter show that Sesame Workshop's cultural brokers focus on incremental change—on the need to positively connect to cultural contexts first, and then to push cultural boundaries. Brokers must be embedded in social relations so that they can translate and adapt equality norms into the local context and access networks of support for the larger project of cultural transformation. But they must also be sufficiently autonomous such that they cannot be instrumentally manipulated by powerful state and civil society actors who would thwart that project. Autonomy and embeddedness allow them to detect and help activate equality norms that are already present—at least at some level and among key actors—locally.

The embedded and autonomous (see Evans 1995) cultural broker has tremendous power within Sesame Workshop because of her cultural and technical expertise and access to networks that would be difficult, if not impossible, for Sesame Workshop to penetrate and navigate. The limitations of Sesame Workshop's local knowledge increase the value of cultural brokers' resources. These resources help mitigate asymmetrical power dynamics between Sesame Workshop and partners. Indeed, brokers also have significant autonomy from Sesame Workshop to create educational programming that encourages equality norms in locations across the globe. The extraordinary politicization of gender and racial/ethnic equality in an era of globalization, epitomized by the clash between equality norms and opposition to them, presents compelling questions about how Sesame Workshop and its partners navigate the complexities of pushing cultural boundaries on these issues with local *Sesame Street* projects. It is to these questions that we now turn.

Translating and Adapting Equality Norms to the Local Context

In a hotel conference room in Amman, Jordan, on the first day of March 2009, New York staff gathered with Jordanian directors of *Hikayat Simsim* to discuss scripts for the upcoming season. Naila Farouky offered ideas for how to introduce diversity. She used an example of how the team from Egypt's *Alam Simsim* tackled the issue in relationship to Coptic Christians, who are considered an ethnic/religious minority in Egypt and have historically been subjected to discrimination and even violence:

> On *Alam Simsim* one of the main characters on the set is a Coptic grocer. We never once mentioned that he's Coptic but his name is Girgis. There's no way around it. He is Coptic. And the one way that we've established that kind of destigmatizing the fact that he's Coptic is that we broke down all stereotypes of what Egyptians have always said about Coptics by never once showing him to be any one of those stereotypes. And he, it turns out—in terms of the research that we've done on the show—is the most loved human character. And, maybe, kids have no idea that he's Coptic. Maybe they've never even thought about it. But that's the point.[5]

Farouky then explained how Jordanian partners could integrate diversity into their new season of *Hikayat Simsim*:

> You could do a live-action film with a kid and not have to mention that he was was Christian. Even your exposing a majority of your audience to a name that they may not be familiar with. And, it could increase a kind of acceptance and a receptiveness to something that's a little bit different. We can't all be Muslim you know. There has

---

[5] Field notes, Amman: 3/1/09.

to be something different. And we know that it exists. So we might as well show it. And it can be an implicit part of the film.[6]

Although Farouky's suggestion may seem innocuous, these decisions can be fraught with risks.

Egyptian partners' decision to include a Coptic Christian character on the program, for example, was contentious within their team. Dr. Cole explained the pushback the Executive Producer, Amr Koura, experienced, and how she backed him: "Amr Koura, the producer of *Alam Simsim*, is a hero for recognizing the need for a Coptic Christian character. It was difficult and he got a lot of flack for it. He did it on the advice of a very radical Egyptian activist—that was later jailed by Mubarak—who pushed inclusiveness. Some didn't want the activist on the team. I insisted he was on the team because I felt they should have his viewpoint."[7]

Although partners have the freedom to decide whether or not to incorporate social change goals in their *Sesame Street* projects, Sesame Workshop requires them to promote core values, including nonviolence, tolerance and respect, and kindness. A New York staffer offered more specific values that set Sesame Workshop apart:

To me, the essence is definitely I would say humanistic in the sense of being good to others, being mindful of others, being respectful of others, no matter what. We have certain no-no's that we absolutely won't tolerate. Like, you can't have a child be rude to another child, or you can't have people disrespecting others on the basis of any categorization. You promote empathy and tolerance and all the rest of that.[8]

How partners choose to promote these core values and the nature of their social change goals vary depending on the type of content and the local context. But the need to manage the potentially controversial nature of this work is ubiquitous across cultural contexts—as it is in the US.

The content that Sesame Workshop creates with its partners is centered on children's education, which is particularly important, meaningful, and potentially contentious for local populations. As a South African producer quipped: "No matter which way you look at it, education is political."[9] Partners, therefore, have to gauge the willingness of local populations to accept cultural change.

---

[6] Field notes, Amman: 3/1/09.
[7] Personal interview, New York: 12/14/12.
[8] Personal interview, New York: 1/15/08.
[9] Personal interview, New York: 1/14/08.

Undermining Stereotypes: Race, Ethnicity, and Language

As the example of Egypt's Coptic Christian character shows, one of the primary ways Sesame Workshop staff and partners promote equality norms is by undermining different kinds of stereotypes. I observed many instances where teams tried to walk a fine line by attempting to include differences, but not stereotype them. During a meeting of the Jordanian directors of *Hikayat Simsim*, Naila Farouky explained how difficult it is to utilize famous locations in live-action films and avoid romanticizing them:

> A lot of times you start to produce live-action films that are very—kind of like tourist pieces. You know so a trip to Petra or a trip to the pyramids. That's okay to do. It's not such a bad thing to do. So there is—there is space to be able to show something that is a little bit touristy that's, maybe, a little bit romanticized. But what you really want to do is to be able to show kids something that they can relate to, something that they can understand.[10]

Similarly, Dr. Cole explained to Nigerian partners how to avoid exoticizing in relationship to clothing, as recorded in field notes: "You don't want kids to think that everyone who lives in a given region dresses like this all the time. In a segment of a bowl dance in Mongolia the child is shown in normal clothing and then learning the dance, and then performing in fancy dress."[11]

But while in the New York office, I learned that New York staff do not always consistently practice what they teach. Dr. Cole described what happened when Egyptian partners visited the New York studio while the US team was filming a *Sesame Street* episode featuring Egypt:

> We were filming in the United States a piece that featured ancient Egyptians in a not very authentic context. And the Egyptians were in the studio and they were like, wait a second, you're telling us that things need to be authentic and you're filming this? And they were right. I think sometimes it's easier to see somebody else's stereotypes than to see your own. They happened to have a great sense of humor, but it certainly surfaced in multiple conversations. It came back to haunt us multiple times. And I think that was reasonable on their part. It's sort of like you've got to take what you give.[12]

---

[10] Field notes, Amman: 3/1/09.
[11] Field notes, Abuja: 10/28/09.
[12] Personal interview, New York: 1/17/08.

Although Egyptian partners challenged New York staff's inconsistencies, the interaction Dr. Cole describes also suggests that partners felt comfortable enough with New York staff to do so. And New York staff readily admitted that their partners were right.

Israel: Signaling Identity

At a research meeting in Tel Aviv, Jewish and Arab-Israeli partners struggled with how to depict Arab-Israeli characters so that children would recognize them, but not rely on stereotypes such as dress. A Jewish Israeli partner working on *Rechov Sumsum* asked an Arab-Israeli researcher for her advice on avoiding stereotypes, as recorded in field notes:[13]

> You discussed within the team the problem of not creating a stereotype by asking the question. And for us, it's the crucial question about do we create a stereotype? Or do we relate to a stereotype the kids still don't have? So I would like your recommendation for us when we're starting to think today about the way we portray Arabic children and Arabic families. What are the ten things that you would like us, yes, to portray that wouldn't seem to you eccentric, or old fashioned, or not characteristic? Because it's been the most problematic thing throughout all the previous seasons in Israel.

The researcher responded in Arabic, and a translator made sure we all understood what was being said: "Different foods. Different foods for the holidays. They're saying that Ramadan was not in the last program." Another Arab-Israeli researcher expanded upon this, speaking in English:

> You have to say rather than to represent. The main issue is that stereotypes always come up when you're trying to represent something visually. And you have to talk about it explicitly. It's not a shame to be Arabic. On the contrary, we should say my name. My name is Amir. I come from an Arabic country, just say it![14]

That evening, *Rechov Sumsum*'s Israeli producer and the Sesame Workshop country director overseeing Israeli projects met in a conference room to discuss the day's events. As I noted in my field notes, the former said: "The Arab researcher did not want the characters to wear traditional Arab dress. And the latter laughed that the Israeli team didn't want their character to wear a kippa either."[15]

A month later in Amman, the issue of stereotyping emerged again in relationship to including characters with physical challenges in *Hikayat Simsim*.

---

[13] Field notes, Tel Aviv: 1/13/09.
[14] Field notes, Tel Aviv: 1/13/09.
[15] Field notes, Tel Aviv: 1/13/09.

During the writer's workshop, Naila Farouky showed a live-action segment called "Word on the Street" from the US version of *Sesame Street*, in which Murray, a furry monster Muppet, introduces a word of the day to a group of children. She then unpacked it for the group, as recorded in field notes:[16]

> Did you notice when Reem was talking about doing disabilities, did you notice there was a child in a wheelchair? That's a great way to do disability. You didn't have to talk about the fact that she was in a wheelchair. She was just participating with all the other children, right?

A few days later, Farouky raised the issue again during a meeting of the directors:

> Another big thing we emphasize is when you're doing your live action is to include children with disabilities, but not to spotlight them. So you'll notice in the "Word on the Street" segment there was always a child in a wheelchair who Murray interviewed. We didn't talk about, oh, she's in a wheelchair. But she was there. So she was visually there.[17]

For New York staff, inclusion should be modeled for children. As Egypt's inclusion of a Coptic Christian character and Amr Koura's determination to do so suggest, there is some convergence across countries on how to model diversity for children. A discussion in Israel about how to include minority languages, however, raised some issues for partners and generated pushback.

Israel: Minority Languages
If education is political, language education—particularly in countries with many languages, spoken by minority communities—can be extremely contentious. In general, New York staff leave decisions about how best to teach language and what languages to incorporate into programs to partners. Dr. Cole explained that during seminars, she tried to get a lot of experts to weigh in so that issues came to the fore.

In January 2009, I was at Kibbutz Almog on the north shore of the Dead Sea, observing a heated discussion among a new group of Israeli writers about how to incorporate Arabic into *Rechov Sumsum*. The writers had just viewed a segment of "Word on the Street" in which Murray introduced a Spanish word of the day. When asked about the segment, an Israeli expert raised concerns

---

[16] Field notes, Amman: 2/27/09.
[17] Field notes, Amman: 3/1/09.

about how the segment introduced a minority language, as recorded in field notes:[18]

What happens here is that the child learns a little—a noun or two in Spanish through the English—and not because there was a negotiation with trying to understand Spanish as something that's whole. And I think we need to consider: what's the difference between giving children just a bunch of nouns in a foreign language, with which you can make no conversation or have any communication, or giving more language expressions and nouns so that, even at a very minimal level, you can talk to each other in one language? And not be playing the game of understanding the second language through the first language?

A New York staffer replied:

That's an important point, but I think it also depends on what the goal of what it is we're trying to do. For the purposes of what the goal here is—just to clarify, it's not about teaching Spanish—it's about introducing a familiarity with the concept that there is a language called Spanish, and this is what it can sound like, and that friends can speak Spanish just like they can speak English.[19]

Another Israeli partner pushed further, urging caution:

I understand the point that you're making, and [she] as well. But I also have a problem with the idea that a child is expected to absorb something about a minority language through the majority language. I think there's a lot of issues here that come into play, and just that you have to think about it very carefully.[20]

Finally, the Israeli expert reiterated her concerns:

I want to be very clear on this, Okay? I'm not saying that there's not a place for all that. I think we have to think very carefully about—and certainly with Hebrew and Arabic, and I think we can look at Spanish as well—about the message about minority and majority. It's there, it's absolutely there. And it's something that I think children unconsciously absorb in ways that we don't even begin to understand.[21]

---

[18] Field notes, Almog Junction, Israel: 1/14/09.
[19] Field notes, Almog Junction, Israel: 1/14/09.
[20] Field notes, Almog Junction, Israel: 1/14/09.
[21] Field notes, Almog Junction, Israel: 1/14/09.

This discussion provided the Israeli expert with an opportunity to raise concerns about how Arabic would be integrated into the program, and specifically how a minority language would be taught to Israeli children, many of whom are Arab-Israeli children.

Promoting Gender Equality Norms

Although Sesame Workshop does impose rules about gender equality messaging, it attempts to find local partners who share a commitment to the UN Millennium Development Goals, including gender equality. Dr. Cole, who as Sesame Workshop's Senior Vice President of Global Education, was responsible for creating local teams of educational experts that would choose curricula and content for local versions of *Sesame Street*, explained her experience finding partners committed to gender equality: "It was never really a hard sell that these programs should be promoting gender equity."[22] And, in many countries, there are ties between women's movements and local teams, with prominent feminists serving as cultural brokers. That partners often come to Sesame Workshop already committed to gender equality values is reflected in comments by a producer from the UAE who was considering whether to work on *Iftah Ya Simsim*. When asked what issues would be important to focus on, she immediately highlighted gender equality:

> I think it's very important to teach them ... power for the woman. The whole GCC is still far behind from the rest of the world in terms of where women have now recently slowly gained power in different work areas. At the same time, there are some countries like Saudi where the woman doesn't have a lot of flexibility, things like where it comes to driving issues or where the woman can come and go, things like that. Equality between men and women.[23]

This kind of prior commitment to gender equality greases the wheels for local programs to prioritize gender equality norms—Sesame Workshop does not have to convince partners to do so.

Although partners who serve as cultural brokers embrace gender equality norms, how to localize them is not predetermined, and varies around the world, as Dr. Cole explained of the views that emerged during meetings with potential partners:

> I think what people disputed was kind of how you translate gender equity, and there was very much a reaction to this kind of American vision of that. And they wanted to

---

[22] Phone interview: 4/28/15.
[23] Skype interview: 1/23/13.

be able to craft their own vision. I think there was a lot of discussion in many of the sessions that I was in about kind of the difference between the American feminist movement and what gender issues meant in other parts of the world. And there were a lot of people saying we don't want girls to be the same as boys, and equal rights doesn't mean boys and girls are the same.[24]

Many partners decide that the primary and most effective vehicle for transmitting gender equality norms are characters used in the program. Specifically, creating a strong female lead character who is charismatic, self-assured, active, and loves to learn both models positive messages about girls, and undermines negative or limiting female stereotypes. Dr. Marcella Lembert, the former educational content specialist for *Plaza Sésamo* who has a Ph.D. in educational psychology from Stanford, explained how she and her team decided to create a new female monster Muppet character in the early 1990s to undermine gender stereotypes:

We knew that we needed a female character. Since there is a big problem throughout Latin America concerning gender equality, we went ahead and created Lola. Even though Lola is a small pink girl Muppet, she was a very marvelous character that broke all stereotypes. She would basically do everything that a little girl supposedly doesn't do. The message that was trying to be sent through her was that a little girl can get on a bicycle, or climb trees, or play soccer. We also gave her characteristics of being a leader with a lot of autonomy and other characteristics to really transmit this idea that girls don't just go around crying with a doll in their hands. That is the typical stereotype that is in all Latin America.[25]

Strong female protagonists like Lola are now ubiquitous in *Sesame Street* programs all over the world—particularly in low- and middle-income countries such as Afghanistan, India, South Africa, Pakistan, Egypt, Palestine, Jordan, Nigeria, Brazil, Mexico, Bangladesh, and Indonesia. And although partners may not depict girls and boys as *the same*, all do focus on girls' equal access to educational and employment opportunities. In a segment from Egypt's *Alam Simsim*, Khokha, a female humanoid Muppet protagonist, enthusiastically sings:

My name is Khokha. My name is Khokha.
I am a young girl. I am a young girl.
Happy and proud.

---

[24] Phone interview: 4/28/15.
[25] Personal interview, Mexico City: 9/2/08.

When I grow up, I'll be a doctor.
I'll be a pilot, or a ship's captain.
Or, I could also be a lawyer.

In a similar segment from *Plaza Sésamo*, a young girl proclaims in her song that she wants to be a firefighter.

How female lead characters carry gender equality messages varies by country. In countries such as Bangladesh, Egypt, Afghanistan, and India, where girls' rates of school attendance are much lower, partners chose to foreground girls' education. Cultural brokers in Bangladesh addressed the stigma that girls who have never been to school face by creating a unique backstory for their female humanoid Muppet protagonist, Tuktuki. *Sisimpur's* lead female character comes from a low-income family and only recently started to go to school. Tuktuki not only undermines the stigma for girls who have not attended school; she also sends the subtle message that social change is possible—a girl is never too old to begin her education. South Africans chose the girl character Kami as a vehicle for both gender equality and HIV/AIDS messaging because a disproportionate number of South African women have the disease and are often ignored in their country. In Mexico, however, partners did not identify girls' access to education and school attendance as a significant problem.

Cultural brokers also signal gender equality messages by actively undermining traditional female *and male* gender roles. Although these messages also vary by country, cultural brokers commonly focus on inverting gender roles in the public and private spheres. In Mexico, for example, Dr. Lembert and her team depicted working women and men engaged in domestic roles, as she explained:

> We were the first program on television that sought to invert roles. For example, in the *Plaza Sésamo* of the 1990s, we would put a writer who was a father who stayed in his house and worked in his house, and a mother who would go out to teach classes at the university who would be out of her house. No one else had done this before. We would see the father setting the table and cooking with the children. This was something that you didn't see anywhere else. Latin America has always been a very male chauvinistic region in which the men don't stay at home, or don't cook, or don't set the table or don't sit down to read to their children. All these role inversions would be seen on *Plaza Sésamo*.[26]

---

[26] Personal interview, Mexico City: 9/2/08.

Similarly, in Jordan, at a meeting to discuss the curriculum for a new season of *Hikayat Simsim*, the cultural broker explained the importance of depicting the expansion of women's professional roles, as recorded in field notes: "And gender equity, especially to counteract gender stereotypes. Because now we have policewomen. Two years ago, you couldn't see them in the streets and the parks. Now, we have a traffic officer—a woman, a female officer. So it's also nice to counteract these gender stereotypes."[27] A partner on the Palestinian team described their efforts to invert gender roles and depict male characters as empathetic and able to express emotion, by introducing a new male character to carry these messages: "One of the things that we actually tried to change in the last season was the idea of the male as an authority figure. But for the children to see this guy, who was very nice and friendly and listened to them, was something that they liked."[28]

During the week-long workshop in New York for *Iftah Ya Simsim's* new writers in 2013, I observed how women writers from around the Middle East debated and chose the qualities for their female protagonist named Shams, and male protagonist named No'man. The male head writer for South Africa's *Takalani Sesame* advised and moderated the discussion, as recorded in field notes:[29]

IFTAH WRITER 1: Okay, [Shams] understands, she's organized, physically active. She's a leader, dramatic and graceful.

TAKALANI WRITER: I would wonder whether you want her to make her clumsy because [No'man is] a dancer and she's just sounds so ...

IFTAH WRITER 1: Uptight?

TAKALANI WRITER: I like the idea that he's graceful because it's unusual and it's unexpected and it's something to play with. And her, not necessarily clumsy, but that knees and elbows is a nice description.

IFTAH WRITER 2: But I wouldn't want to have a sketch being written that she's being really bossy and that she's told not to be bossy and it then becomes like other kids think that oh, I can't behave this way. I don't mind saying that she can be impatient. I just want it to be her weakness. I think she can be impatient. She can be talkative.

TAKALANI WRITER: So would you say that ... incredibly creative but talkative?

IFTAH WRITER 2: But talkative, and a little too talkative. . . . . Sometimes she has to like *[imitates a panting noise]* to keep going so then that's funny so it's . . . .

TAKALANI WRITER: So it becomes charming rather than negative.

IFTAH WRITER 2: Exactly, exactly, exactly, exactly.

---

[27] Field notes, Amman: 2/26/09.
[28] Personal interview, Ramallah: 3/4/09.
[29] Field notes, New York: 12/17/13.

As this exchange shows, the writers consciously tried to undermine gender stereotypes by creating a female protagonist who is smart, energetic, and a leader. They also inverted the typical gender roles so that the male protagonist is a graceful dancer, and the female protagonist is less coordinated. However, the writers also tried to balance or moderate qualities that, when associated with women and girls, are often interpreted in negative terms—bossy, talkative, impatient, finicky—so that the protagonist is not perceived negatively.

While at Kibbutz Almog in Israel for a new writer's workshop three months earlier, I observed a discussion of *Rechov Sumsum*'s female protagonist Avigail, a humanoid Muppet character. A male writer complained that the Israeli characters "are much less funny" than the US characters, and then began to criticize Avigail's personality. The women writers immediately and vigorously jumped in to defend the character, as this exchange, recorded in field notes, shows:[30]

MALE: Avigail is not funny and…

FEMALE #1: Avigail is funny, but she's cute-funny.

FEMALE #2: Yeah, exactly.

FEMALE #3: I agree.

MALE: She's whining. She's a whiny….

FEMALE #1: No, that's not true.

FEMALE #2: She's not whiny. Don't call her that.

FEMALE #3: That's a male point of view.

FEMALE #1: No, yeah, yeah.

FEMALE #2: Ask a woman point of view.

FEMALE #1: Yeah.

FEMALE #3: She's great.

This interaction epitomizes how certain negative qualities are often associated with females. The women writers' spontaneous and ardent support for Avigail not only made this visible, but also highlighted how female and male writers may have different points of view about "gendered" behavior that colors how they envision—and write for—their characters.

In India, Ghazal Javel, the puppeteer who performs the character Chamki, explained how undermining gender stereotypes required not only creating a strong female personality—a humanoid Muppet named Chamki—but also ensuring that other characters—in this case, a male Muppet monster

---

[30] Field notes, Almog Junction, Israel: 1/14/09.

character named Googly—interact with her in respectful ways that reinforce gender equality:

> You don't show Googly playing cricket and Chamki coming and saying, "Can I play cricket?" You actually show—Googly might be reading a book and Chamki says, "Come Googly, let's play cricket." You know? It's a positive reinforcement. I think that is the key … which has always been with *Sesame*. And that's what culturally we took it and sort of made our changes.[31]

Similarly, in the above-mentioned segment from Egypt that features Khohka singing about her aspirations as a girl, three male actors and two male Muppet characters serve as backup singers for Khohka, who enthusiastically echo her comments about being a proud girl.

Seeta Pai, then Sesame Workshop's Director of International Education, Research, and Outreach, pointed out the irony that strong female protagonists are more ubiquitous in *Sesame Street* programs around the world than in the US version of *Sesame Street*: "We—certainly even more in our international than I would say domestic *Sesame Street*—are very egalitarian in terms of girls and boys. Very strong female protagonists in all of our international shows. Something that the domestic *Sesame Street* only got a year ago with the introduction of Abby Cadabby."[32] This irony was not lost on partners, who also pointed it out to New York staff during a training session.

Pushing Cultural Boundaries

Partners not only understand how to positively connect to cultural contexts and frame gender equality norms, but also the nature of local resistance to them. Thus, in addition to translating and adapting gender equality norms, they must also accurately gauge the extent to which cultural boundaries can be pushed. Only partners know how to push cultural boundaries in ways that are likely to be effective and have a positive impact. Saed Andoni, a producer for Palestine's *Shara'a Simsim* was one among many partners who explained how promoting cultural change requires a delicate balancing act:

> You have to respect the culture. And you have to go within the culture and squeeze it, and do a little bit here, a little bit there. And to treat it in a respectful way because if you go against the culture, you will lose the public interest or the public faith. And

---

[31] Personal interview, Delhi: 5/3/13.
[32] Personal interview, New York: 1/15/08.

if you lose that, you will find yourself doing nothing, basically. You will find yourself like speaking to yourself. The program has to be acceptable for the parents in order to let their kids watch it, and be educated from it.[33]

Partners are explicit about their desire to create social change, as witnessed during the Palestinians' content seminar when Dr. Cairo Arafat, the educational content director, explained to her colleagues how they should try to stimulate social change using their program, as recorded in field notes:

What I'm trying to say is that maybe—in the shows, or how we produce it, or the new song that we have to introduce—it says that we are looking for a new way, that we are looking for change. We're not looking to hold on to just the past. I mean, maybe that's something that we also have to incorporate—that a lot of times because we always feel so uprooted, so unstable as a society, always conflict—that this sense of, we have to keep things as much as common, as basic, as possible. Maybe we need to introduce that idea into our show that's not always the case.[34]

Often, the first to be pushed is the local team itself. At the same seminar, the Palestinian producer asked Dr. Arafat if they should follow their previous curriculum centered on boys' self-esteem that dovetailed with the Ministry of Education curriculum. She responded, as recorded in field notes:

We don't have to just focus more on the boys, but maybe boys and girls. So I think on the boys issue it's still the same things where boys can have feelings, that boys can be productive, that boys share in the responsibility. Those same messages will be there. But maybe we don't have to make it so boy-oriented. It's boy and girl. Equality more is an issue.[35]

In response to her advocacy, the rest of the team agreed to expand the focus to include equity for girls.

Partners also face the challenge that gender equality norms may not be ubiquitous across a country or region due to local cultural differences or structural constraints. They therefore have to gauge the receptiveness of different populations to gender equality norms and adapt the messages in ways that facilitate buy-in. In India, Sashwati Banerjee, the Founding Managing Director of Sesame Workshop India, is a well-known feminist. She wanted to use the program to initiate changes in India for girls, as she explained: "I do

---

[33] Personal interview, Ramallah: 3/3/09.
[34] Field notes, Amman: 2/23/09.
[35] Field notes, Amman: 2/23/09.

believe that communication can be a powerful tool to look at social change. So having grown up in 1980s in India and going to college, you know, being part of the whole women's rights movement—being an activist really—I think, gave me a passion."[36]

Banerjee and her team decided to push girls' education in rural areas where girls are less likely to attend school, and where they have less access to television, by harnessing the power of local community radio stations, which are very popular and thrive across parts of rural India. They created a radio version of the television program *Galli Galli Sim Sim* that allows parents to call in and discuss the issues raised on the program. Banerjee described the effects of the radio program on one village where girls were not attending school:

> We see ourselves as a launch platform to look at other issues in the community. So they introduce the program and say, "We have this problem in our community. Let's now go to *Galli Galli Sim Sim* and see what they do." And then they come back and say, "Okay, you heard the program. Now I'm going to leave my phone lines open for you to call in." So children listen to it, but so are the parents, which is great. One village has decided that—because we promote girls' education and all of that—one village decided that the girls will take the cows herding in the morning, and that's why they miss school. So the village decided to do a pool herd. Basically they would pool all their cows together and appoint somebody to go and take it so that the girls could go to school.[37]

The outcome in this village depended on partners' understanding that people did not oppose girls' education; they needed a platform to address it and collectively create a solution.

In addition to low school attendance rates for girls, school segregation is more prevalent in rural than in urban areas in India. Banerjee and her team addressed this problem in 2009 when they developed a plan to generate a permanent revenue stream for their nonprofit work by creating a for-profit business called *Sesame Schoolhouse* that offers franchises for Sesame-branded preschools. They often face resistance from parents in rural areas who do not want to send their children to integrated schools. In a car on our way to visit a *Sesame Street* school in Uttar Pradesh, Sarika Dubey, a partner with a B.A. in education and a graduate degree in child development, explained how she respectfully but firmly pushes back when parents express resistance to integrated preschools:

---

[36] Personal interview, New York: 12/3/12.
[37] Personal interview, New York: 12/3/12.

In a smaller city, for them it was always boys separate and girls separate. In certain communities like Uttar Pradesh, where we are going now, there are teachers who would get into this because in these communities, the women are not treated as equals. In a small town in Kanpur the mothers are not coming in for admissions inquiries because they're not allowed to step out of their houses all by themselves. And only grandparents would come to inquire for boys' admissions. They will not come to inquire for girls' admissions. So these are the communities where we have to really push it—no, no, no this needs to be done, and then we give our reasons to the parents.[38]

When asked what she says to try to address parents' concerns and change their minds about gender integrated classrooms, Dubey explained:

We do address them. We do understand and we say that we respect what you're doing, but then you may want to visualize it again. We give them anecdotes that tomorrow when your child goes out into the society, he will not just be in a same-sex society, and there are a lot of things that you have to learn, in terms of dealing with the opposite sex. So if I say that I'm not doing this, I'm not really doing it the Sesame way. These are not something that is changing overnight, but we are progressing with time.[39]

This exchange with Dubey reveals how critical partners are to effectively challenging gender inequalities. Rather than trying to convince parents by focusing on the *rights* of girls to have an equal education—an argument likely to be made in the US—she highlights the benefits to all Indian children of learning how to flourish in an integrated society. It also illuminates how she is able to successfully navigate between Sesame Workshop and the local environment.

As the data show, building legitimacy for gender equality norms requires partners to constantly deploy their resources and knowledge in order to gauge the extent of the change for which they can advocate and the kinds of messages needed to support it. Although most partners may understand local norms in general terms, given their relatively privileged backgrounds, it would be impossible for them to understand the vast diversity within their countries, particularly in relationship to class, caste, race/ethnicity, language, religion, etc.

A successful partner, therefore, recognizes what she does not know and seeks input and advice on issues for which she lacks knowledge or expertise.

---

[38] Personal interview, Meerut, India: 5/2/13.
[39] Personal interview, Meerut, India: 5/2/13.

During a 2009 educational content seminar for *Sharaʼa Simsim* in Amman, Dr. Arafat explained to her colleagues the need for a diverse advisory board, as recorded in field notes:[40]

> I really wanted an advisory committee, and to ground our show. Because I think most of us probably represent five percent of the population in terms of education, in terms of all these things. And a lot of them haven't spent excessive amounts of times in the villages, in camps. It's still an outsider view, and I think sometimes when you have a broader team of people, then that gets through.

When asked how she creates messages that reflect diversity among Palestinians, Dr. Arafat explained how she consults with teachers across a wide spectrum of society:

> That's something that we were constantly trying to manipulate in such a way that we don't get skewered into one way or another. And I think that a lot of times with the scripts, I'll not only review them, but I'll take them and do a lot of sort of casual formative evaluation. I'll sit with groups of teachers, all of the curriculum documents with all levels of the society. So I really try to temper that kind of input with the local population with local teachers. It's the little kind of things that we have to always be careful of—we're sort of not seen as the elitist, none of us are seen as the elitist—in terms of that. And I think that that grounds the show, that's what's grounded the show.[41]

She described in detail, for example, how she navigates the contentious political terrain around head scarves within Palestine:

> It's the little kind of things that I feel that we have to always be careful of. It's certain things, like I know that I've pushed are simple things of saying we have to show women wearing head scarves. I mean, it's not demeaning for a woman to wear a head scarf. I mean, it's to show some without, some with, some wearing regular pants, I'm wearing a long dress. I mean, for me, if I can show a lady wearing a head scarf, and she's a doctor, that's fine. Sometimes, [someone here might say] "No, we wanted to show this kind, this is much more child friendly." And I say, no, children aren't afraid of women in head dress. I mean, they see it all the time, and it doesn't mean that this person doesn't laugh, doesn't joke, isn't friendly. So how do you make that kind of balance?[42]

---

[40] Field notes, Amman: 2/23/09.
[41] Personal interview, Ramallah: 3/4/09.
[42] Personal interview, Ramallah: 3/4/09.

Her decision to depict a diverse array of women wearing head scarves reflects a deep understanding of Palestinian culture.

Because many partners tend to be more educated, they rely on formal advisors with personal experience in or knowledge across class, racial, religious, and ethnic divides to help navigate cultural boundaries. The same is true for the US version of *Sesame Street*, which has enlisted the assistance of advisors across the country since its inception. During a workshop for new writers in Jordan, a New York staffer offered partners access to advisors: "If there's an issue that you really want to address but we don't have the content expertise to do it, we have the access to advisors both in the US and we can help you find advisors here in Jordan to help you figure out what the message should be and the best way to present it."[43]

The need for skilled cultural advisors and brokers unfolded in real time during Sesame Workshop's first educational content seminar in Nigeria. Ayobisi Osuntusa, the Nigerian project director, who was not an expert in local norms in Kano, the northern Muslim part of the country, chose an advisor from that area to consult with on potentially contentious issues, many of which involved gender norms. I observed how she explained (when asked by Naila Farouky) the role advisors would play on the team, and simultaneously illuminated for New York staff how building legitimacy in northern Muslim areas involved adhering to gender norms regarding women's appropriate dress, as recorded in field notes:[44]

FAROUKY: How are you envisioning advisors' role in the review process?

OSUNTUSA: We will give them the content map and then they will look at scripts and they will tell us what won't work in their areas, such as Kano.

NIGERIAN PARTNER: If you put something out in Kano and they don't like it – even if it's for *Sesame* – if they reject it and refuse it there's virtually nothing we can do about it after that.

OSUNTUSA: Our advisor in Kano knows what she's talking about. Two years ago I worked on a vaccination project for another NGO. They had a manual for teacher training that had a picture of a woman in a short skirt and just a slightly low neckline on the cover. And they had to make another cover for Kano state. They wouldn't accept it there.

This exchange also reveals how cultural variations *within* countries can be incredibly subtle, and how critical it is to adjust content in ways appropriate across various ethnic, racial, linguistic, religious, and other divides.

---

[43] Field notes, Amman: 2/27/09.
[44] Field notes, Abuja: 10/28/09.

Of course, cultural boundaries are often so subtle that even skilled advisors can fail to grasp their malleability. In Bangladesh, advisors warned that inverting gender roles by showing boys cooking on film would not be locally accepted, as Nadine Zylstra explained: "We'd been at this curriculum seminar, and we'd been asking the gender experts where is the line, how far can we push it beyond which the audience won't recognize it as plausible? And the gender expert had said, 'Look, you can't show boys cooking. Nobody's going to buy that boys are cooking.' So we were like okay."[45] And yet, something unexpected happened when local filmmakers trained adolescents in rural areas how to make short live-action films to document their experiences for *Sisimpur*:

> And then low and behold out of this rural filmmaker project, this one boy filmmaker makes this film that's all about these kids pretending to have a picnic. And they go and they have their picnic and they make a whole tent, but by the end there are these boys pretending to cook and serving, which is even more extreme in the Bangladesh context than cooking itself, but serving each other. And for me it was just this magical moment, which was like, wow, if you make space for that voice, you have pushed the gender line that even experts didn't think you could push. But in the most gentle, subtle, powerful way, without us being big brave Americans and saying, "Oh, you've got to show boys cooking—there we were, we'd pushed the line." And we hadn't pushed the line, the filmmakers had pushed the line. It was just a very powerful moment.[46]

This experience in Bangladesh suggests that gender norms are not always as fixed as even experienced advisors might perceive. Moreover, it shows how active creative processes—such as those nurtured by Sesame Workshop's rural filmmaker project—can actually reveal the vulnerabilities of seemingly entrenched gender norms, and perhaps help shift them.

The data above foreground the importance of partners' embeddedness in their society, which allows them to translate, locally adapt, and disseminate gender equality norms into a local context and assess how far cultural boundaries can be pushed. One of partners' most important roles is to identify and tap into pockets of support for gender equality norms among government and civil society elites, align Sesame Workshop's goals with theirs, and build alliances and networks that legitimize and promote gender equality.

[45] Personal interview, New York: 1/14/08.
[46] Personal interview, New York: 1/14/08.

Partners' autonomy facilitates this role because they are not dependent upon or beholden to powerful state and civil society actors. This allows partners to solicit support from those they believe can have a positive impact, rather than government elites who may simply be furthering their own agendas. Partners' relative autonomy also allows them to build alliances and networks of support for the larger projects that may be controversial, and to push back against interests that would thwart them.

Equality in a Conflict Zone: Mutual Respect and Understanding in Israel and Palestine

In addition to gender equality, Sesame Workshop has prioritized other socio-emotional goals in the US program and in programs all over the world, in particular, mutual respect and understanding goals centered on respect for racial/ethnic and religious differences. Curricula focused on these goals have been used in conflict and post-conflict zones, including Israel/Palestine, Kosovo, South Africa, and Northern Ireland. In recent years, Sesame Workshop has also initiated new projects in the Middle East, Myanmar, and Venezuela.

I interviewed New York staff who had worked on these projects, and partners in South Africa who also had worked on them. Although I did not observe these programs while they were in active production, I did include the case of Israel and Palestine in my research and made multiple trips to the region to observe meetings, workshops, and training sessions between New York staff and partners. While there, I also interviewed then current and former partners who worked on *Rechov Sumsum* (Israel), *Shara'a Simsim* (Palestine), *Hikayat Simsim* (Jordan), and the program produced between the Israelis and Palestinians, which later included Jordanians.

Coproducing the joint Israeli-Palestinian program *Rechov Sumsum/ Shara'a Simsim* was challenging in a plethora of ways, not least of which was the tumultuous political landscape whose fault lines shifted daily. Although the program was conceived in the wake of the Oslo Accords, by the time work began, tension and violence were building. It was difficult and even, at times, impossible for Israeli and Palestinian team members to meet due to the violence and discord that racked the region. Joint meetings were not only logistically challenging—requiring a delicate maneuvering around the complex array of travel check points, borders, and restrictions—but also psychologically taxing and potentially dangerous for the reputations of the project members: "[The project] was implemented against a harsh reality," Dr. Cole explained, "with major events, such as bus bombings, the assassination of the Israeli Prime Minister, the destruction of the Palestinian production facilities, any one of which could have led to the dissolution of the project" (Cole and Bernstein 2016:156). After the Israel Defense Forces destroyed the Palestinian team's studio at Al-Quds University, the Israelis offered to let them use their studio, as Daoud Kuttab explained:

> You have to remember that we had no studio, another problem obviously. So we had to use the Israeli studio. We brought our set, they didn't have the set, and so we literally had to film on video, measure the set, send it to them by mail or email and they would say okay to fit or not fit cause we brought this set with us.[47]

Israeli producer Dolly Wolbrum described how she insisted that the Palestinian truck carrying their set only be checked by authorities in Jerusalem, and not a second time when they arrived at the Israeli studio in Tel Aviv: "Over there, of course you check, but then after they pass, it took another two hours to come to the station."[48] Wolbrum explained that officials told her they would have to check the truck again at the studio entrance because the Palestinians could stop along the way. She assured them the Palestinians would not stop on their way to the studio, and requested that the truck not be checked again when they arrived. This gesture of consideration helped build trust and respect with the Palestinian team.

In 1996, when Benjamin Netanyahu, a conservative, was elected Israeli Prime Minister, some members of the Palestinian team decided they could no longer participate (Miller 1998). And the day before the Palestinian segments were to be filmed, a suicide bomber blew himself up in a Tel Aviv cafe, killing four Israelis (Miller 1998). Despite these challenges, Kuttab and Wolbrum insisted on moving forward. Wolbrum explained the urgency of the project: "it was very hard emotionally for both sides, but we felt we must do this despite the assassination and bombings, because this is what the show is all about" (Miller 1998). Dr. Cole noted, however, that it was the hardship presented by the situation, and the small triumphs in cooperation along the way, that encouraged Sesame Workshop to believe that their approach to "partnership dynamics that launch from and respect local context, needs, and sensibilities" was effective and worth the effort (Cole and Bernstein 2016:157).

Although the curriculum for *Rechov Sumsum/Shara'a Simsim* included literacy and numeracy and other standard educational goals, the Israeli/Palestinian program was unique because teaching tolerance was primary and prioritized in the curriculum. This concept was officially

---

[47] Personal interview, Amman: 2/28/09.
[48] Personal interview, Tel Aviv: 8/2/10.

termed "mutual respect," and included specifically "human diversity, commonality, and understanding" (Cole and Bernstein 2016:161). In a 1996 introduction to the project, Sesame Workshop wrote:

> While on the one hand the streets of Rechov Sumsum/Shara'a Simsim depict a fantasy place where we can go beyond our present reality, the images on the program must be presented in a manner that is true to the customs and beliefs of the cultural groups represented... We let children see that it is possible to break the barrier of fear that exists, to respect one another and even to develop friendships among each other (Sesame Workshop 1996, quoted in Cole and Bernstein 2016:163).

Producing segments focused on mutual respect proved to be difficult and politically loaded. Multiple partners mentioned one particular "crossover" scene where Israeli and Palestinian characters appear together in the same space, which caused criticism in Palestine. Producer Daoud Kuttab explained:

> There was another crossover that has caused us a lot of problems. The Israeli kid has a flat tire and the Palestinians come in and they say "Oh, what's your problem?" The tire is not working. Haneen says "Oh, I'll take care of it," and goes and gets a tire that is huge and she says will this work? And they say, no it's too big. And the whole learning objective is "big" and she goes "Oh, don't worry," and she goes and comes back with a tiny, tiny wheel like this. And they say no, it's too small. So she goes back again and gets the right size. And the kid rides off. And somebody wrote this piece that we were actually sort of justifying Israeli theft of land because they took the wheel. People went on and on about that particular segment.[49]

Naila Farouky echoed Kuttab's surprise that the segment was so problematic: "The research came back that the Palestinian viewers were so upset because all they got out of this was I can't believe the Palestinian Muppets had to give up another thing of their own for the Israelis. It was interesting because no one on either team had even thought of it. It never crossed our minds that people would see it as the Palestinians giving up something of their own to help the Israelis. It was so weird and they really had this very Holy Shit moment!"[50] Dr. Arafat also discussed the same segment during the 2012 meeting of potential partners for *Iftah Ya Simsim*, as recorded in field notes:[51]

> Dr. Arafat said that one of the stories was on helping. And it focused on a little Israeli boy that gets a flat tire. And the two Palestinian characters give their wheel to the

---

[49] Personal interview, Amman: 2/28/09.
[50] Personal interview, New York: 2/27/09.
[51] Field notes, New York: 12/12/12.

Israeli boy so he can get back. And people saw it as a political message. We give
everything to them and now we even give him the wheel to our bicycle.

That this story was referenced multiple times by partners highlights how
difficult it is to coproduce during an ongoing conflict.

The term "Palestinian state" was also particularly contentious. Palestinian
runner Majed Abu Marajil, who competed in the 1996 Olympics, was sched-
uled to appear on the show as a celebrity guest. A script draft noted that he
represented "the Palestinian state" (Miller 1998). Wolbrum knew this would
be problematic, as she explained to Kuttab: "I can't put 'Palestinian state' on
government television" (Miller 1998). Kuttab explained that there seemed to
be other issues with the segment that were not communicated directly to him
by the Israelis:

> And the script was that he would run on the beach and Haneen would say, "What's
> going on, why are you running?" And he says, "This is my job." And she's running
> with him and it's kind of a fun script. We were told—we never actually com-
> municated with the Israelis—but the Israelis told Lewis Bernstein that they were
> adamant against filming this…Although we never saw that when we met with the
> Israelis—they were quite nice and extremely lovely with us. So I don't know whether
> it was people on top, or the politicians, or whether it was in New York, but they were
> speaking on behalf of them and saying the Israelis wouldn't like it.[52]

As Kuttab reveals, it was not always clear to him who was making decisions,
which raised issues of transparency and communication with New York staff.

Certain elements, which were considered too political, had to be avoided
completely. Both Israeli and Palestinian team members agreed that there
could be no indicators of nationalism, such as flags. Other areas of contention required negotiation: Palestinians did not want Israeli characters to
wear yarmulkes, and Israelis did not want to see Muppets wearing kaffiyehs.
Wolbrum wanted to include Israeli soldiers on the show in order to personal-
ize them, making them appear accessible to the Palestinians who associated
them with fear (Cooper 1999). The Palestinians fervently disagreed with
the inclusion of soldiers in the show, and New York staff agreed with them
(Cooper 1999).

In 2003, as the Middle East emerged from a brutally tense start of the century, the second season of the project required changes. In 2000, the eruption
of the second intifada and then tensions after 9/11 made interactions between

---

[52] Field notes, Amman: 2/28/09.

Israeli and Palestinian characters in crossover segments unrealistic (Shapiro 2009). Thus, the spin-off series *Sesame Stories* was created, and it no longer featured friendly visits to neighboring streets. Jordan, having freshly crowned their first new King in over forty-six years, was extended an invitation to join the project.

Sesame Stories (Sippuray SumSum in Hebrew and *Hikayat SimSim* in Arabic for both Palestinian and Jordanian audiences) was the first program to air with segments made by and for Jordanians. The Israeli channel HOP!, the Palestinian Al-Quds Institute for Modern Media, and a Jordanian production company called Jordan Pioneers were in charge of production (Cole and Bernstein 2016:166). The three teams shared animated content but "independently managed and featured their own characters" (Cole and Bernstein 2016:166). Rather than employing "crossover" segments as the cooperative element, *Hikayat SimSim/Sippuray SumSum* used "parallel stories." This format focused less on cross-cultural contact between characters, and instead on giving viewers peeks into their neighbors' lives (Warshel 2009:117). Each version utilized approximately ten segments from the other versions, redubbed into Hebrew or Arabic (Shapiro 2009).

The objective of the parallel stories was cross-cultural exposure that defied the constant two-dimensional narrative of war and death. In a 2003 press release, Sesame Workshop stated:

> At a time when television and other media are transmitting difficult news, *Sesame Stories* will encourage children to appreciate similarities and differences in their own culture and others. *Sesame Stories* celebrates the diversity of the human experience and examines that diversity from within the child's own home and community, as well as in broader societal contexts (Sesame Workshop, 2003 quoted in Warshel 2009:117-118).

Through attempting to showcase the region's diversity, the format of *Hikayat SimSim/Sippuray SumSum* also acted as an equalizer, providing a unique scenario in which characters were portrayed as peers, not from vastly different socio-economic statuses or in competition with each other (Warshel 2009:119). Characters from five different groups were used: Arab-Israelis, Jewish-Israelis, Palestinians, Jordanians, and Americans. Each team created their own stories based on these characters, which the other teams featured on their own programs (Cole and Bernstein 2016:166). In 2006, as the ongoing conflict made the climate less and less suited to collaboration, the programs became increasingly independent. And ultimately, all three were transformed into stand-alone programs.

Embracing Culture and Stimulating Cultural Change

Partners that I met and observed all over the world repeatedly told me that they wanted to participate in a local version of *Sesame Street* to highlight the beauty and uniqueness of their culture. When I asked the Nigerian team what they wanted their program to convey about Nigerian culture for their children, one partner responded instantly:

> That it's beautiful, that it's rich. That Western culture isn't the be-all and end-all of a happy life. You can move back home, be very happy. I just want to say you don't have to move to America, live in America, or be American or have an American citizenship or have a British passport. Really, the green one isn't that bad. You find your little spot, be happy. Nigerian culture is so rich, so neat culturally, so many languages, it's so diverse and it should be embraced rather than shunned by some people.[53]

But partners also regularly articulated a desire to use the program to change certain elements of their culture—to squeeze it in ways that promote equality, inclusion, and tolerance. The intense politicization of diversity and inclusion related to race/ethnicity, gender, and religion in countries regardless of economic resources raises compelling questions about how norms and practices of equality sweep across the globe.

In this chapter, we have examined these processes at the micro-level to understand what partners do on the ground to negotiate between global and local tensions, and *how* they do it. Partners work to translate, adapt, and spread norms, particularly those that, like gender equality, are potentially contentious. Indeed, promoting gender equality norms among young children can be quite controversial. The data in this chapter show how critical partners are to the spread of equality norms. But they also reveal partners' strategic choice to focus on incremental change by first positively connecting to cultural contexts, and then pushing cultural boundaries.

The data also show that the success of partners, who have the difficult task of ensuring that equality messages are appropriately crafted for local cultural contexts, depends on both their embeddedness and autonomy in a given society—meaning partners must be embedded in social relations, which allows them to interpret and tailor equality norms to suit local settings, while at the same time, they must have enough autonomy to forge alliances and create supportive networks to advance the broader goal of

---

[53] Field notes, Abuja: 10/30/09.

cultural transformation. Cultural brokers in NGOs like Sesame Workshop can be powerful facilitators of change, not simply by presenting new ideas and norms, but rather, by facilitating the activation of existing equality norms that are already present to some degree among influential local actors—in the community.

The case of *Sesame Street* exposes how individuals *and* groups of people (at local, national, and transnational levels), in real time, articulate their motivations, weigh and attribute value, disentangle issues of authenticity and social change, and formulate and prioritize concessions and bottom-line demands for equality norms embedded in deeply held beliefs and values. The *Sesame Street* case also offers a critical lens through which to analyze and understand how partners build local acceptance and legitimacy for a broader institutionalization of equality norms by mobilizing constituencies and negotiating with local decision makers who weigh the costs and benefits of activating them. As the next chapter shows, their ability to do so depends on building networks and alliances with broadcasters, civil society organizations, and government officials in order to disseminate *Sesame Street*.

6

Disseminating *Sesame Street*

Exchanging Cultural Knowledge to Build Alliances

In March 2005, Sesame Workshop staff were eagerly awaiting the arrival of Bangladesh's Minister of Women and Children's Affairs at their New York office. The first season of *Sisimpur* had been completed, with a first episode focused on the April 14 Bangladeshi New Year festival. But Sesame Workshop and its partners in Bangladesh had an enormous problem: they still did not have a commitment from the government-run Bangladesh Television (BTV) to air the program. Weeks before, they had invited the minister to the set in Dhaka, hoping to gain her support. As Sean Love, *Sisimpur*'s New York-based project manager, explained: "This is really an opportunity for us to get the minister of Women and Children's Affairs solidly behind this project. They are not convinced yet that this is a totally Bangladeshi thing. You know, they see us as being an American company, and they're very sensitive to all these things."[1] The minister left the set in Dhaka without offering her endorsement.

The problem was political, as Sean Love explained: "We've hit a little bit of a roadblock in Bangladesh because the production company that we've chosen to work with has political associations that could be detrimental for the project. BTV represents the BNP, the Bangladesh Nationalist Party, which is currently in power. The principals of the company are considered to be opposition people in the Awami League."[2] Political tensions were particularly high because less than six months earlier, on August 21, 2004, terrorists attacked an anti-terrorism protest organized by the Awami League with grenades, killing twenty-four people and injuring three hundred. The terrorists had targeted Awami League President Sheikh Hasina, who was injured in the attack. Many Bangladeshis suspected that government officials in the BNP were involved.[3] As will be discussed later, choosing Nayantara Productions as a production partner created challenges for Sesame Workshop from day one. Now, in New York, the stakes could not be higher. Sesame Workshop staff pulled out

---

[1] Quoted in the film The World According to Sesame Street, 2006.
[2] Quoted in the film The World According to Sesame Street, 2006.
[3] In 2018, a special Bangladeshi court ruled that the government had been involved.

Sesame Street Around the World. Tamara Kay, Oxford University Press. © Oxford University Press (2025).
DOI: 10.1093/9780190844325.003.0006

all the stops, culminating in a meeting with Sesame Workshop's top brass, including President/CEO Gary Knell. At the end of the day, the minister committed to working with Sesame Workshop, and the program aired on BTV on April 21, 2005.

The uncertainty over *Sisimpur*'s broadcast highlights how important alliances and networks of support are to the process of coproducing and spreading *Sesame Street* programs around the world. Alliances must be built at every stage of the process. During the initial stages, alliances provide Sesame Workshop with legitimacy, access to gatekeepers, and key educational institutions and networks. Once a new *Sesame Street* program is created, it must be disseminated and received by external audiences in a new locale. This means programs are aired and outreach projects are launched in local communities. Alliances with broadcasters, NGOs, and government officials are critical at this stage in order to garner support for local *Sesame* programs and outreach projects and spread them among diverse constituencies and broad audiences.

The types of alliances and networks needed to disseminate *Sesame* projects vary depending on the type of content and the local context, and partners are essential to developing and nurturing them. During Sesame Workshop's 2012 meeting in New York for *Iftah Ya Simsim*, senior New York staff and then-current partners from around the Middle East explained how alliances—with local experts, civil society, and government officials—are essential to coproducing local *Sesame Street* programs. As Dr. Arafat explained to the group: "You need people who will back you—ministers of culture, education, the media, parents. Will you alone represent ten million Gulf children? No, you need to find people who will back you."[4] Alliances are not only essential to managing controversies but also to identifying potential minefields and laying the groundwork so that they do not explode.

In this chapter, we examine how and why Sesame Workshop and its partners build these alliances. Given the nature of Sesame Workshop's work, creating alliances with partners who share core values and are seen as legitimate by the local population is crucial. As discussed in previous chapters, Sesame Workshop does so by assembling a broad swath of civil society actors at a series of initial meetings in each country to discuss issues that may be problematic and by identifying experts to help navigate them. The alliances built during earlier stages are therefore essential to success in later stages, as Cooper Wright, the former New York project director for South

[4] Field notes, New York: 12/12/12.

Africa's *Takalani Sesame*, explained regarding Sesame Workshop's decision to coproduce after the apartheid regime ended:

> It really, really is important who is your first contact in a country—like I used to call the godmother, the godfather of the project. And all projects have these. Sometimes they're formal and sometimes they're really informal. In South Africa Enos Mambuza [a psychologist and teacher who served as chief minister of the kaNgwane homeland] was kind of a godfather to us He didn't really do official stuff, but we'd have lunch with him and he'd give us different contacts. And we would be able to say well, is this really what we should be doing, and can you tell us is this playing into old apartheid when we're not meaning to be doing that?[5]

Wright's comments show how building alliances with supporters, such as Enos Mambuza, allowed Sesame Workshop to gain the trust of potential partners and build legitimacy for Sesame Workshop and the program.

Building Alliances with Governments

As described in the previous chapter, the process of building alliances and networks with government officials begins when Sesame Workshop enters a country. Sesame Workshop and its partners ensure that in every country, the curriculum for each program reflects the national educational curriculum. Sesame Workshop would not be allowed to enter a country without government support. Alliances with government officials are essential; they can provide legitimacy, alignment with government curricula, access to educational institutions and official gatekeepers, and access to state-owned broadcast channels. How alliances are deployed varies at different stages in the process of coproduction.

Alliances That Allow the Broadcast of Sesame Programs

In the dissemination stage, government alliances can be crucial to broadcasting the new program. As in Bangladesh, governments control public television stations that often broadcast local *Sesame Street* programs. In Bangladesh, finding a key government ally, such as the Minister of Women and Children's Affairs, facilitated the agreements and contracts necessary for broadcast. Without government approval, programs will not air. The first

[5] Personal interview, New York: 12/16/08.

iteration of Palestine's *Shara'a Simsim* was a joint project with the Israeli *Rechov Sumsum* team that the Palestinian government refused to broadcast. As Daoud Kuttab, the Palestinian producer of *Shara'a Simsim*, explained: "Palestinian television refused to show it because there were Israelis involved, which I had predicted, and I wasn't surprised."[6] Alliances with government broadcasters and officials are therefore critical in many countries.

In Mexico, government officials initially opposed the creation and broadcast of a Náhuatl version of *Plaza Sésamo* directly into public schools in indigenous communities through the government's educational television satellite system, Edusat (El Sistema de Televisión Educativa). Edusat was created in 1994 by Mexico's Ministry of Public Education. Martha Montemayor, the Mexican public relations director for *Plaza Sésamo,* described the first meeting with government officials, during which they openly expressed their disapproval of the idea: "We met with the people from Edusat and from the National Council for Educational Development [CONAFE] who are very dedicated to education in indigenous communities and with indigenous organizations. We went with some people from Sesame Workshop. And their initial reaction was: gringos, go home."[7]

The bluntness of the government officials she described surprised me, given that in my experience living in Mexico, formality is highly valued, particularly in professional settings. I pressed her, asking if they were that explicit or if that was their implicit message. She replied without hesitation:

TK: So at first they actually said, "Gringos, go home," in front of …

MM: Us. All of us, all the people. For me, no, because I'm not a gringo. But I was with the group of Sesame Workshop.

TK: So they said it to the people in New York? And the people in New York understood them?

MM: Yeah, of course. Of course.

TK: They literally said that?

MM: Yeah. "Gringos, go home." We don't want your education in Mexico. We have an Educational Ministry. We have schools. We don't need you.[8]

Montemayor then explained what she said to those government officials to change their minds, overcoming their strong initial resistance to the idea:

And then we started explaining how we do it locally with the local experts, that I was living here, I was a contact for them. We really pushed the fact that we did

---

[6] Personal interview, Amman: 2/28/09.
[7] Personal interview, Mexico City: 9/5/08.
[8] Personal interview, Mexico City: 9/5/08.

everything with local experts. I think that was the thing that convinced them in the end. Yes, it's people from Sesame Workshop, from New York. But we work together with the local people. We get together with the local experts like you, like all these people that were at the table. That's what we want exactly. And then they started to understand. And they said "Well, let's do a pilot project, and we'll see what happens."[9]

The Mexican government was so impressed by the results of the pilot project that it expanded it to include a Mayan version of *Plaza Sésamo*. And despite my surprise at how unfiltered the initial exchange between New York staff and potential partners was, it actually reassured me that potential partners—in this case, government officials—express their skepticism and reservations openly and honestly.

For *Iftah Ya Simsim*, a program involving governments across the Middle East, the process was even more complicated, requiring negotiations at national and transnational levels. Sesame Workshop and its partners built a network of nine regional stations to broadcast the program across the Gulf States region. That network was made possible with the support of key government agencies, both national and regional. Sesame Workshop signed an agreement with the Arab Bureau of Education for the Gulf States (ABEGS)—whose board of directors consists of the six GCC Ministries of Education—to collaborate on the program's educational curriculum. A document produced by Sesame Workshop reveals how critical the relationship with ABEGS and the educational seminar it convened was to diffusing the program and outreach projects: "This gathering also results in a regional content distribution plan taking into account varying needs and national priorities among the member states. In electronic media (broadcast and digital) Iftah Ya Simsim will serve as the Arabic language 'umbrella brand' representative of all Gulf Arab States and distributed through a coordinated effort by participating broadcast and digital partners to assure widest possible reach of content to children and families. Community engagement will take place at the national and local levels through networks of government and NGO partners."

By creating an alliance with ABEGS, Sesame Workshop and other local partners not only gained access to broadcasters but also to Arab policymakers, funders, and schools across the GCC.

The success of the educational seminar in Saudi Arabia—which included eighty education and media experts from across the Gulf region—attracted

---

[9] Personal interview, Mexico City: 9/5/08.

funders. A senior New York staff member made this clear in an email he sent to the Director-General of ABEGS: "It was the Educational Seminar in Riyadh that ultimately convinced [two potential supporters] that the new Iftah was a genuine and authentic effort. They took up the cause and through their own dedication and tenacity convinced Mubadala management to put up $12 million to make our dream a reality." As the case of *Iftah Ya Simsim* shows, building a broad network of support allows Sesame Workshop and partners who lack influence in key arenas (such as regional governance institutions) to build relationships with influential members (such as ABEGS), who can give them direct access to it and/or increase their legitimacy or influence within it.

Egypt and Palestine: Alliances to Align Curricular Goals

To address the needs of local children, Sesame Workshop and its partners create a curriculum for each program that conforms to, reinforces, or complements the national educational curriculum of every country in which it works. This kind of broad alignment is essential and a prerequisite to beginning work in any country. In Egypt, for example, partners identified girls' education as a key problem, as described in a report on the program's impact: "Research on this topic suggested a pressing need for educational television programming specifically directed towards girls, with data showing that girls in Egypt were enrolled in primary school at lower rates than their male counterparts ... Furthermore, research showed that within the adult population of the country, only 33.6 percent of Egyptian women were literate as compared to 60.4 percent of Egyptian men."[10]

Girls' education was already a central focus of the government. Partners, therefore, worked with government officials to align *Alam Simsim's* curriculum on girls' education with a new government agenda focused on addressing educational inequalities for girls, as the report explains:

> Production for *Alam Simsim* began in 1998 with a seminar held in Cairo to discuss the educational plan for the project. The seminar was attended by representatives of the Egyptian Ministry of Education, child psychologists, physicians and early education specialists. ... In developing the educational goals of the program the team aimed to support Egypt's national education agenda for its youngest citizens. At the time of curricular development, Egyptian officials were launching a series

---

[10] "'Maybe an Astronaut' The Measurable Impact of *Alam Simsim*", p. 10.

of national initiatives to support girls' education. Spearheaded by Mrs. Suzanne Mubarak, the First Lady of Egypt, and with support from the United Nations Girls' Education Initiative, there was a renewed effort to develop a national agenda to expand school access for girls in rural areas and address other educational inequalities that impact girls. ... To address this issue and bolster national initiatives, *Alam Simsim* integrated a special focus on girls' education.[11]

This process of alignment was critical to the success of *Alam Simsim's* curricular goals.

Dr. Cairo Arafat revealed, however, that the process of alignment can work in both directions. She explained that her outsider status with the Palestinian government allowed her to access and even influence its agenda: "During the second season we developed a very strong partnership with the Ministry of Education, put together an advisory board. And since that day, we've worked with them hand-in-hand. On an educational content level, it made the difference. It allows you to actually not only see where they're going in terms of curriculum for early childhood education and their priorities, but it also allows you to influence what their agenda should be."[12] As Dr. Arafat suggests, engagement is critical.

As in Egypt and Palestine, the support and participation of government officials allow Sesame Workshop and its local partners to develop curricular goals that may face resistance among particular groups or in certain areas. As former President/CEO Gary Knell explained: "I get this question all the time: do you run into big problems when you deal with gender and all these issues? The fact is—maybe I'm deluding myself—but we kind of haven't. And part of it is because we're given the cover of ministries of education in other places that have been promoting different educational agendas."[13] After attending the December 2012 meeting in New York for *Iftah Ya Simsim*, a potential partner echoed Knell's comment that government officials should provide "cover" for projects that seek to change societal values: "At the end of the day, if the officials and the educators and the government ministers that put together this educational objective, if they do want to create change, then they're going to have to obviously deal with some people who will be upset with watching this content. But at the same time, the majority of them will embrace it, and it would make a change."[14] The potential partner acknowledged that the

---

[11] "'Maybe an Astronaut' The Measurable Impact of *Alam Simsim*", p. 10.
[12] Personal interview, New York: 12/17/13.
[13] Personal interview, Cambridge: 11/14/07.
[14] Skype interview: 1/23/13.

program could face resistance but embraced the idea that it could also create meaningful changes across participating countries.

Jordan and India: Alliances to Disseminate Outreach Projects

Alliances with governments are also critical to the dissemination of outreach projects. In Jordan, access to government agencies and local NGOs requires the endorsement of the Kingdom's monarchy. Naila Farouky explained how only Khaled Haddad, the Jordanian producer with connections to the monarchy, could garner its support for *Hikayat Simsim*:

> So they called Queen Rania. And nothing ever happened for a long time. She really didn't come on board until Khaled Haddad brought her on board. They couldn't do it themselves. Sesame Workshop staff met with her. She developed an interest, but she wouldn't commit to anything. She wouldn't commit to being a patron on the project, she wouldn't commit to making an appearance, she wouldn't commit to anything. I think it just didn't click on her radar because it was like, well it's a bunch of Americans. But once they got a local producer on board here, then it became more interesting for her to be a part of it.[15]

The monarchy's support, through Queen Rania Al-Abdullah, enabled Sesame Workshop and its local partners to develop an ambitious outreach project with the Ministries of Education and Social Development, and to obtain local funding from Jordan's Hashemite Fund for Human Development. The outreach benefited the Ministry of Education—which opened Jordan's first public kindergartens in 1999—by complementing a nascent kindergarten curriculum and supplementing classroom materials. Together, they created outreach kits (including books, games, classroom materials, etc.) that were distributed to each child and teacher in every Jordanian public kindergarten (90,000 kits in 608 schools). Children's kits included a backpack, activity book, storybook, and parent's guide. Teachers' kits included a *Hikayat Simsim* DVD, teacher's guide, storybook, an educational classroom poster, word puzzles, board game, and blocks. Parent/teacher educational workshops were also held nationwide in Jordanian schools. The curriculum went beyond

[15] Personal interview, New York: 2/27/09.

just cognitive skills, literacy, and numeracy to cover broader topics like self-esteem, respect for others, and cultural tolerance.[16]

Hikayat Simsim became a widespread cultural icon and a national success.[17] Queen Rania Al-Abdullah commented on the program's contributions in a speech at the Mosaic Foundation's 9th Annual Benefit Dinner in Washington, DC: "Sesame programming in the Arab world [reflects] our region's culture and concerns: in the words of one Jordanian, 'it teaches children the alphabet of life by delivering messages of hope ... respect and understanding' ... These messages work, because the values behind them make sense in any language."[18]

In India, Sesame Workshop collaborates with the government on outreach projects in government-sponsored child/mother-care centers called Anganwadis. Ritesh Koshik, Chief Financial Officer for Sesame Workshop India, explained that working with the government is necessary to gain access and achieve scale: "You can't afford not to partner with the government because they are the ones who will ultimately be the change agents. We definitely get reach and scale. Unless you partner with the government, you can't enter any of the Anganwadis or the Integrated Child Development Scheme centers. You won't have permission to. That is where the kids of India go as their primary school, the first preschool that they are going to. But unless there is government buy-in, you are not talking about reach and impact."[19]

One of the key resources partners provide is access to government networks that would be difficult, if not impossible, for New York staff to penetrate on their own. Local partners are invaluable in building alliances with key government officials. Koshik described the process of identifying potential government allies:

> Actually, it only comes with the experience. When you are in this domain, you get to learn who are the people. In all spaces, there are bright people sitting there as well, who have the reputation of being the change agent for the society. So you would search out for those people. The reputation is something that precedes you, and you would come to know which government official is like what. You have this forum in which you are going and you know that the secretary of government of Gujarat is upstanding, he is a London School of Economics graduate and he will know these things and the other things, and you would like to meet him.[20]

---

[16] https://www.thefreelibrary.com/Hikayat+Simsim+Kicks+Off+Season+Three+on+Jordan+Television!!-a0227766791

[17] https://www.thefreelibrary.com/Hikayat+Simsim+Kicks+Off+Season+Three+on+Jordan+Television!!-a0227766791

[18] https://www.queenrania.jo/en/media/articles/mosaic-foundation-ninth-annual-benefit-dinner

[19] Personal interview, Delhi: 4/29/13.

[20] Personal interview, Delhi: 4/29/13.

Koshik also described how he persuades government gatekeepers to collaborate with Sesame Workshop—by highlighting that projects are customized and that their collaboration will give them access to a global network of Sesame Workshop partners and resources: "The other important part is that the government knows that *Galli Galli Sim Sim* is an Indian show, running in India on television. It's about education. So that is the first buy-in. The other buy-in is that we have access to international resources, so there is a bigger body, more countries, countries for training purposes. It's not that we only do it, and the world buys in from us. We also buy-in from other countries, understand from other countries what works and what doesn't work. So we have access to a larger resource pool, which they see."[21] As these data reveal, while Sesame Workshop and its partners value the networks that governments provide to disseminate programs and outreach projects, governments value the international networks that Sesame Workshop offers.

Although working with governments can provide tremendous opportunities, including legitimacy, resources, and the ability to scale, it can also present challenges. Government bureaucracies and rules can be difficult to navigate. And sometimes their reach may be limited, as New York staffer Daniel Labin and partners discussed during an outreach meeting in Israel, as recorded in field notes:[22]

ISRAELI PARTNER #1: The main problem that we had last season was with the distribution of the outreach because, in order to be in every kindergarten, you need to go through the local principalities. It was a huge problem that I would like to avoid this time. And that's why we thought maybe to do something more for families.

LABIN: For these different projects that are somehow associated with the Ministry of Education, how necessary is their involvement anyway? We've been—at least for the last two seasons—working with them enough so that they would endorse it, but not too much that they'd get involved.

ISRAELI PARTNER #1: If we want something to be distributed to kindergartens, we have to do the approval. The approval wasn't the problematic part, I think.

LABIN: No, that turned out okay, but it's distribution and the follow-through.

ISRAELI PARTNER #2: And at the end of the day, you want it to actually get to the family. I mean, the idea is that it get to the family, not that it stop with the kid in the [kindergarten].

LABIN: But how do you reach the families in a wide enough way without going door-to-door to every family?

ISRAELI PARTNER #2: You choose an area that, for a whole variety of reasons, will help you do this. And you start in one area.

21 Personal interview, Delhi: 4/29/13.
22 Field notes, Tel Aviv: 1/13/09.

New York staff lack direct experience in dealing with government stakeholders and lack knowledge about how to distribute outreach materials directly to families in Israel. Through this exchange, they develop a collective understanding about the limitations and possibilities of the dissemination strategy moving forward.

Palestine, Israel, Brazil: When Alliances Are Not Robust

The importance of building alliances with governments is best illustrated by the constraints faced when such alliances are absent or not sufficiently robust. In Bangladesh, if government officials had not agreed to broadcast *Sisimpur* on BTV, the program would likely not have aired at all, and months of work and significant amounts of money would have been wasted. In many countries, government approval not only provides the program with an audience but also gives its creators legitimacy. Daoud Kuttab, producer of *Shara'a Simsim*, explained how the lack of government support during the program's first year undermined the legitimacy of the project and its reach: "We produced a small video, we produced booklets and things like that. We couldn't get into the public school system. In the past we didn't have the legitimacy that we have now."[23]

Similarly, New York staff and Israeli partners faced problems when they failed to build collaborative ties with the Israeli Ministry of Education. In 2010, they created an Arabic-language DVD to address *Rechov Sumsum's* inability to meet the educational needs of Arab-Israeli children, many of whom do not speak Hebrew and do not have access to cable television, on which the program airs. The DVD's target audience was not Palestinians living in the West Bank or Gaza, nor Arabs outside of Israel. The content of the DVD was created by Arab-Israeli educators and scholars and was written and directed by Scandar Copti, who was nominated for an Academy Award for his film *Ajami*.

In order to distribute the DVD to each child and teacher in every Arab-Israeli public kindergarten and organize training sessions for 2,000 teachers, Sesame Workshop needed approval and assistance from the Arab department of the Israeli Ministry of Education. The Ministry was concerned with the use of spoken or colloquial versus literary Arabic. Sesame Workshop and Arab-Israeli partners included both forms of Arabic, but their choices

---

[23] Personal interview, Amman: 2/28/09.

were not completely in line with the Ministry, which required them to make changes. For one segment that could not be edited, the Israeli team and the Ministry came to an agreement that in written material accompanying the DVD, there would be a note explaining the language choice. Shira Ackerman, Content Director for *Rechov Sumsum*, described how the problems arose after they secured approval but failed to consult the Ministry during the early stages of the project:

> So they created a whole DVD without really including the Ministry in any of the planning stages. And then we get to the day where we can show them the rough cut, and the head supervisor in the Arab department comes. We finish, and she says I can't possibly approve this because it has this and this and this, and why didn't you talk to us before? But that's a kind of moment where you have to stop and think, would it not maybe have been better to bring them, on this particular project, to the table and at least hear some things than to afterwards have to make fixes that cost money that are over budget to finally get them to agree and to distribute it? And they finally agreed. But it took a really long time.[24]

These comments reveal not only the importance of government buy-in, but also how partners usually bear the largest burden of managing relationships with government officials.

In Brazil, Sesame Workshop's failure to develop and launch a local outreach project—discussed in detail in Chapter 4—severely constrained partners' ability to build alliances with government and civil society officials. Without an outreach project, partners had nothing concrete around which to build alliances. This example underscores the relationship between processes at each stage of coproduction; Sesame Workshop's failure to adapt outreach materials during initial stages limited its ability to build alliances during later stages, which would have helped facilitate dissemination.

Egypt, South Africa, Palestine: Alliances Help Build Local Capacity

Sesame Workshop also builds alliances with governments in order to transfer knowledge more effectively. Indeed, partners more frequently cited the value of receiving intellectual and technological resources rather than financial

---

[24] Personal interview, Jerusalem: 7/29/10.

ones, including training in production techniques, puppetry, script writing, and evaluative research. Sesame Workshop prioritizes using resources to build local capacity and sustainability, particularly in low-income countries. According to Dr. Cole: "Some of these development projects like our project in Egypt and South Africa and other places—Bangladesh—when we initially conceived of them we were conceiving of them as capacity building projects, so projects that would help bolster people locally to produce really good quality children's media. I think we're really committed to that."[25]

In a variety of countries, Sesame Workshop and its partners incorporate government educational and workforce goals into a strategic plan. For example, Dr. Cole described how Sesame Workshop worked with the South African government to create a certification program that institutionalized resources for outreach partners: "In South Africa, we used to actually run outreach programs ourselves, so we would train trainers to use *Sesame* materials in formal and informal school settings. And in fact in South Africa if you were part of *Sesame* outreach, you could become trained and actually get a government certification. So it's an official certification with the involvement of *Sesame*. And we'd often work with ministries of education and really try to have the information be something that is supporting government educational efforts."[26]

Sesame Workshop also frequently attempts to build capacity for disadvantaged populations. In the wake of apartheid, Sesame Workshop trained a largely Black South African production team, and in Tanzania, they chose a team of Black Tanzanians even though a funder preferred a more experienced company run by white Zimbabweans.

Capacity building was also a primary goal for New York staff and Palestinian partners, as a New York producer explained: "We created an infrastructure for the Palestinian team. They now knew how to produce television, they could do other programs. There were people who had a talent pool. That was also important."[27] Daoud Kuttab, the Palestinian producer, confirmed the value of this local production infrastructure:

> We didn't have our own studio. By 1995, 1996, Al Quds University had asked me to set up a media school and I said I'll only set it up if we can get a television station because I believe in training. And so they got me this piece of cardboard saying here

[25] Personal interview, New York: 1/17/08.
[26] Personal interview, New York: 1/17/08.
[27] Personal interview, New York: 1/17/08.

you have the tv station license, just do it for no money. We used *Sesame Street* to help us. The fact that I had to get equipment for the program meant equipment for the station. So everything that we did stayed on for our tv station so it was a great piggy back.[28]

Dr. Marcella Lembert described the impact of Sesame Workshop training in Latin America: "When we started in Mexico, there were no animators around. We started to prepare people in Mexico to do animation. Nowadays many people from other programs—the majority of programs on television that have to do with children and adolescents—have people making them who had *Plaza Sésamo* as their training ground. *Plaza Sésamo* marked a turning point for children's television around the world and especially for Mexico and Latin America."[29]

Indeed, many former partners I interviewed continued their careers at Disney, Nickelodeon, and other children's media companies. Some younger partners I interviewed from all over the world mentioned the influence of their mentors, who had worked on *Sesame Street* programs, and their own experiences working on local programs that used *Sesame Street* as a model.

Building Alliances with Civil Society Organizations

In addition to alliances with government officials, alliances with civil society organizations—including private companies, nonprofits, NGOs, and global governance institutions such as the UN—are also critical to the creation and dissemination of *Sesame Street* projects.

India: Alliances with Non-traditional Broadcasters

In India, many children do not have access to television. As discussed earlier, partners therefore launched the *Galli Galli Sim Sim* Radiophone project to bring *Sesame* content via community radio to 200,000 children in rural areas in the northern and central parts of the country.[30] Diffusing it required building alliances not with traditional broadcasters, but with local leaders and

---

[28] Personal interview, Amman: 2/28/09.
[29] Personal interview, Mexico City: 9/2/08.
[30] "The Radiophone Project: Technology and Storytelling, Together Changing Rural Children's Lives", Sesame Workshop India.

NGOs that run community radio stations. To facilitate their buy-in, partners introduced a unique format: each episode begins with pre-produced content from *Galli Galli Sim Sim* on a theme (such as vaccinations), moves to a community segment produced by the local radio stations themselves, and ends with a call-in interactive segment during which local audiences participate in the program with input and stories. By including the call-in segment that deals with relevant local issues related to each episode's theme, community radio stations built support for the program, enabling it to spread: "Community radio stations brought together local leaders, key opinion leaders, regular listeners of the ... program and other members of the community to discuss what had been identified through the program. The 10 community radio stations held 60 events. These events were designed to raise awareness around issues of local importance and relevance, such as various schemes announced by the Government of India to increase children's attendance in schools, information under the Right to Education Act, the need to improve sanitation and environmental conditions in the community, improving access to education for girls and others."[31] Working with community radio stations is an innovative response by partners to have an impact in low-resource areas. Engaging nontraditional broadcasters allows them to address critical needs that may not be addressed in other ways.

Jordan: Alliances with NGOs to Spread Outreach Projects

In Jordan, Nassma Halaseh, then outreach director of *Hikayat Simsim*, recognized critical educational needs among refugee children that were not being met. She explained how she built new alliances with NGOs to address these needs, which expanded the outreach project to new organizations and audiences:

> And we've been trying to find some NGOs linked with UNICEF and Save the Children because they do work with kids at this age. The other day we had somebody from the Relief International of United Nations High Commissioner for Refugees—for the Iraqi refugees—call me. Children come to their waiting rooms with their parents who have their passport work and papers done. And she said, "We have kids—like 100 kids a day, and really, we don't know what to do with them. Please help us." So we've sent her season two segments. And we've sent them some materials and

---

[31] "The Radiophone Project: Technology and Storytelling, Together Changing Rural Children's Lives", Sesame Workshop India.

she set up a viewing area for children. We told her what else do you need and what things would be improved by using our materials?[32]

The alliances she cultivated helped Sesame Workshop eventually scale up and diffuse an educational curriculum for children across the Middle East. In December 2017, the MacArthur Foundation announced that together, Sesame Workshop and IRC, through their humanitarian initiative to educate children affected by conflict and crisis, won its first and highly competitive and selective *100&Change* global competition "for a $100 million grant to fund a single proposal that promises real and measurable progress in solving a critical problem of our time."[33]

In addition, Sesame Workshop's Jordanian outreach director and her team conducted 180 four-hour workshops to train 1,400 teachers and 1,500 parents on how to use the materials in schools and at home, and worked with the Ministry of Social Development, which runs small NGOs, to train staff who work with orphaned and vulnerable children. Dr. Cole explained the importance of working with NGOs to customize outreach materials: "Where we work best is when our partners are actually involved in the development of the materials, so that they have some say into what's being produced, so that it fits into whatever it is that their existing programs are. The goal is to be able to provide something that actually is going to help local NGOs because it gives them a resource, but also that is something that they'll genuinely use and not just sit there on a shelf."[34] As Dr. Cole suggests, building alliances with local NGOs ensures not only the breadth but also the efficacy and relevance of outreach projects.

South Africa: Alliances with Civil Society to Pressure Governments

Partners are also able to build consensus among civil society organizations on controversial issues, particularly when there is resistance from government officials. During the 2013 writer's workshop for *Iftah Ya Simsim*, I asked the head writer for *Takalani Sesame* (who was training the Gulf States writers) if the South African team faced any resistance from South African President Thabo Mbeki's administration on the HIV/AIDS curriculum and its messenger, the female Muppet named Kami. As detailed in Chapter 4, President Mbeki did not accept established scientific research linking HIV and

---

[32] Personal interview, Amman: 3/5/09.
[33] https://www.macfound.org/programs/100change/
[34] Personal interview, New York: 1/17/08.

AIDS, nor medical protocols for its treatment. The head writer responded: "A lot of people will take credit for the HIV curriculum and Kami, but it was a group effort—*everyone* was on board. What was the tipping point for changing culture in South Africa on HIV was when notice went out to all NGOs about the *Takalani Sesame* curriculum and everyone was on board. There was total acceptance. And *Takalani* made a difference in changing things."[35]

The ability of partners to build relationships with civil society organizations is critical. Projects cannot succeed without partners' knowledge and skills. Robert Knežević, then senior vice president of Sesame Street International, attributed the success of Egypt's *Alam Simsim* to the invaluable resources of a key partner, Executive Producer Amr Koura: "Because of him we played it well in politics, we played it well in the private sector, we played it well with the ministries, we played it well with television, and all that stuff. It became immensely successful very, very quickly. It was the fastest that we have ever gone from launch of a project to practically universal awareness and viewership in the shortest time ever. Within eighteen months we were clocking 98 percent viewership and awareness of the program. The program instantly kind of became woven into the fabric of the Egyptian culture. The program became kind of iconic."[36]

Knežević explained more specifically what Amr Koura contributed to the project that no one in New York could: penetrating networks of potential civil society allies. New York staff could not effectively navigate the local political landscape to build strong alliances across a wide range of government and civil society organizations on their own, as Knežević emphasized: "Local partners can speak to someone else in a different organization or government agency or corporate sector or NGO or the civil society sector, and communicate to them: 'I have a vehicle that can address an issue that we're both interested in. And then we can explore ways together on figuring out how to use that vehicle to achieve a common goal.' That's where it all happens. That's where it all happens in terms of the relationships between people on the ground. It doesn't happen with us."[37]

This recognition of the value of partners' social capital, particularly in the form of local ties and networks, was ubiquitous among New York staff, who saw it as essential to their success.

---

[35] Field notes, New York: 12/17/13.
[36] Personal interview, New York: 1/17/08.
[37] Personal interview, New York: 1/17/08.

Aligning Interests and Building Alliances with Local Elites

In addition to alliances with government officials and civil society organizations, alliances with local elites are also critical to the dissemination of *Sesame Street* projects. Because of the deference and respect they are given in local communities, local elites can often help unlock doors to facilitate the dissemination of local *Sesame Street* programs and outreach projects.

India: Alliances with Local Elites

In India, partners constructed their community radio projects as tools for community organizing and advocacy—usually targeting local elites, particularly local politicians. Sarika Dubey, a member of the Indian team with expertise in child development and education, described how communities applied pressure on politicians to address health and gender inequalities in schools: "In addition to the programming, we also supported each community radio station in doing six community-level events. So they could call their local politician and say look, there are no soaps in the schools. You have the money so please give soaps. So we created a platform to do that. They've all organized events which are around these themes. It could be girls are not going to school. They have done these events. It's a local advocacy platform."[38]

Autonomy from local elites is also quite important. Dubey's experience exemplifies why her relative autonomy from them is critical to her ability to promote gender equality in India. When asked what she does if a teacher seeking a *Sesame Schoolhouse* franchise refuses to commit to an integrated classroom, she responded:

> We'll say sorry, then we can't work with you. So people who don't believe in what we're talking, we'll not give them a franchise, no matter what happens. That is why these areas have a little tough time getting their enrollments. Because parents may not really be up for it. We do understand that some grandmother would come up and say, don't let my boy sit with that girl—or maybe with that boy—because they belong to a different caste. But then, we can't [allow] these things because these are the things of the past, and we have to overcome this.[39]

By withholding a *Sesame Schoolhouse* franchise—which confers financial benefits and cultural status in India—Dubey can leverage those local elites who are not on board with gender-integrated classrooms. This highlights,

---

[38] Personal interview, Delhi: 4/29/13.
[39] Personal interview, Meerut, India: 5 /2/13.

again, how essential partners are to promoting gender equality norms through local *Sesame Street* programs.

As this chapter shows, alliances with governments, civil society organizations, and local elites are critical to coproducing and disseminating *Sesame Street* programs. Although alliances can develop at any time, those created during the initial stages can reap rewards at later stages. And it is partners who have the knowledge, skills, and resources to build them. Alliances build legitimacy for Sesame projects and provide necessary support for partners on the ground in their countries. Alliances with government ministries are particularly important because they provide cover to New York staff and partners when they need to make difficult and potentially controversial decisions. As we see in the next chapter, these decisions can also cause conflict between New York staff and partners.

7

Managing and Resolving Conflicts

> During the meeting, the Palestinian director expressed some nega-
> tivity when the team came up with ideas for using the Muppets, and
> skepticism that it could be done. He argued that there were limita-
> tions. A New York staffer told him to ask Noel MacNeal, a puppeteer
> who had come from New York, how to do things, since he was here
> to do it. The staffer and director went back and forth a bit, and peo-
> ple became a little uncomfortable. Finally, Noel pulled out the Muppet
> and showed people how to make it do the thing the writer wanted it to
> do. Soon after the incident, another New York staff member brought
> up the issue of bringing Noel or another puppeteer back later when
> they were in production. The Palestinian head writer was thrilled,
> saying "Yes, yes we need it." And the director also enthusiastically
> agreed.[1]

When I first conceived of this research project, I assumed that the process
of creating local versions of *Sesame Street* would require Sesame Workshop
and its partners to engage in constant and intense negotiations around issues
of control and autonomy. I imagined that partners might reveal to me—an
outsider and non-Sesame Workshop employee—stories of how they had to
push back against New York staff to claim and retain their autonomy, and
that at least for some, this caused some level of frustration and resentment.
My assumption was based on the power differentials between New York staff
and partners. *Sesame* is not a two-way street in terms of power; the model and
the initial resources to coproduce it come from the US, and Sesame Workshop
holds the intellectual property rights and controls the budget.

In addition, New York staff review content before partners can disseminate
it. This content review and oversight generally occurs extensively during the
first season a new program is produced, but is reduced, and even ceases, as
partners gain experience. It can include reviewing scripts, filmed segments,
outreach materials, etc. My assumption was that partners might resent this

---

[1] Field notes, Amman: 2/24/09.

Sesame Street Around the World. Tamara Kay, Oxford University Press. © Oxford University Press (2025).
DOI: 10.1093/9780190844325.003.0007

oversight and want less, not more, involvement from New York staffers like Noel MacNeal.

Although problems of control and autonomy did emerge, the story was more complex and nuanced than I had anticipated. During my first round of interviews in New York, when I asked about the nature of conflicts with partners and how they are resolved, New York staff revealed that the most contentious conflicts emerge with partners in high, not low-income countries. As Dr. Lewis Bernstein explained, "I think what happens is that it splits up to developing and developed countries. Developing countries want our input and the more they get the better. Developed countries are like, get off of our case we know how to do television."[2]

As I began interviews with partners around the world in low-income countries, a similar pattern emerged. I asked each partner two "Goldilocks" questions about control and autonomy: "Ideally would you want to have more autonomy, less, or are you happy with the level of autonomy?," and; "Overall would you like more, less, or the same amount of contact and input from New York?" The vast majority of partners reported that they were happy with the level of autonomy and wanted *more* contact and input from New York. Among a sample of 21 partners, only one said they wanted less autonomy, 12 reported they were happy with the level of autonomy, and 4 said they wanted more autonomy. The rest offered mixed responses, such as "just right but need more training and support."

When prodded to elaborate, partners explained that they wanted their program to be of very high quality, like the US version, and more input and support from New York staff were needed to achieve that. A Colombian partner explained her preference to have more contact with New York staff:

PARTNER: Yes, I would have liked to have more direct communication. It's like I told you— in the conferences we were working to be a little closer—so we can learn because they're experts. So it's their experience. I think it would be very enriching to be a little closer.

TK: So are you saying that you'd like to have more contact with Sesame and not less?

PARTNER: More contact. For me, I'd like more contact with Sesame Workshop. Definitely. Yes.[3]

This type of exchange with partners was quite typical across all regions and countries I studied.

---

[2] Personal interview, New York: 1/17/08.
[3] Personal interview, Bogotá: 6/25/09.

Partners' overall willingness to coproduce with New York staff, and their general satisfaction with the amount of autonomy they had, does not mean conflict is absent. During interviews, partners expressed their grievances and openly discussed complaints. And during my observations, I was privy to and witnessed a variety of interpersonal disagreements. But conflicts were managed such that they did not undermine projects between New York staff and partners. I was interested in how and why this occurred.

This chapter focuses on the nature of conflicts between partners and New York staff, and how conflict between them is managed and repaired. I had assumed that the most serious conflicts would arise over "big" issues: battles over budgets, educational goals and curricula, and creative control. The issues both New York staff and partners identified most frequently as causing conflict were related to creative control, but centered on two issues that actually surprised me: disagreements over what is funny, and modeling safety. Tension over the other issues existed, of course, but were not cited as regularly and consistently.

Understanding conflicts between New York staff and partners is critically important because, as scholars and activists rightly suggest, translation and adaptation processes can reflect the imposition and dominance of Western values, practices, and products. A focus on the power dynamics between organizational partners is critical, although we usually lack observational data in real time that exposes how it operates. In this chapter, I examine the nature of power asymmetries and how Sesame Workshop and partners manage them. My data also reveal the often hidden sources of partners' leverage, influence, and autonomy.

Managing Conflict

When I began field work, New York staff and partners were initially reticent to discuss conflicts. During my first few interviews, some expressed concern when I asked questions about how conflicts were managed. I gently prodded them, and they told me they were concerned that discussing conflicts felt like "gossip." I subsequently decided to preface the question by explaining that all relationships, including marriages, have conflicts. But it is how conflict is managed that reveals the nature and strength of any relationship. And because I was interested in how conflicts are managed in organizations, and particularly cross-culturally, their experience was instructive. This preface to the question instantly put people at ease, and, thereafter, they readily shared their experiences of conflict with me.

Psychologists suggest that productive conflict should create clarification; conflict clarifies our goals, values, expectations, boundaries, and limits. Ideally, conflict within teams should be managed rather than eliminated— because productive conflict can allow relationships to grow and lead to better outputs (Hackman 2011). In previous chapters, I articulate how coproduction engages practices of flexibility, trust, and mutual learning. Coproduction involves building relationships that allow partners to mitigate power asymmetries, misunderstandings, and conflict. Partners' knowledge provides them some leverage with Sesame Workshop because local *Sesame Street* programs cannot be created without them. What is distinctive about Sesame Workshop as an organization, however, is a willingness among many staff to acknowledge, reflect upon, and correct mistakes. Partners also engage in these practices regularly.

Variations on the Theme of Humor: What's Funny?

After my seven years in the field studying how Sesame Workshop and its partners coproduce *Sesame Street* programs around the world, one thing became very clear: creating *Sesame Street* is hard—really hard. And this is probably one of the primary reasons, in addition to its expense, that no other organizations produce anything like it. It is challenging in a way that is both concrete and abstract. Concretely, writing and producing a program that uses an educational curriculum to teach basic literacy, numeracy, and prosocial values—and entertain at the same time—is extremely difficult. As discussed earlier, it requires not only experts in production, but also in education to work together on the same team. Abstractly, writing funny and engaging segments for children that are also humorous to adults is a very heavy lift.

As in Mexico, I observed and participated in writers' workshops where new writers, over the course of multiple days, received training in how to conceive, conceptualize, and write *Sesame Street* scripts. The process was often extremely difficult and frustrating for new writers, particularly those who had not written for children and not written with an educational goal in mind. During these workshops, participants wrote draft scripts, and both New York staff and experienced partners gave feedback and advice. I often participated in these sessions, and I found writing *Sesame* scripts to be one of the hardest creative and intellectual exercises I had ever attempted. By far the most common issue that arose during these sessions was discussions of humor. As Naila

Farouky explained to partners at the beginning of a writers' workshop in Nigeria:

> We have to do a lot of thinking about what we have input on and what we, Sesame Workshop, don't have the right to comment on. Example of humor. We may not think it's funny, and the local team says, "We think it's hilarious." And the truth is, the way it should be is: you [Sesame Workshop] don't think it's funny is your problem. How can we give comments on something completely subjective?[4]

Because humor can be a proxy for understanding language and culture, lack of shared meanings in relationship to humor between New York staff and partners presents a challenge to coproduction.

Negotiations in relationship to humor were common during my observations of workshops and training sessions. After a New York producer showed a team of new Israeli writers a clip of the US program *Shalom Sesame* filmed in the 1980s, an Israeli partner remarked, "And maybe it's this different sensibility too. Maybe in the States that is funny, you know, and here, it's ... not so much. Another quipped, "Nothing was that funny in the '80s."[5]

Perhaps the most interesting example of variation in humor emerged during an interview with Bia Rosenberg, the former Brazilian producer of *Vila Sésamo*. I asked her: "Did you feel that the people in New York that you worked with understood Brazilian culture?" She immediately responded, "No." She then showed me an episode of *Cocoricó*, an acclaimed Brazilian children's program on which she had worked. The program uses puppets and is centered on a boy named Júlio, who moves to the Brazilian countryside to live on a farm with his grandparents. It promotes environmental stewardship and other prosocial messages.

Rosenberg described showing an episode of *Cocoricó* called "A História do Cocô"[6] to New York staff because it was so funny. In the episode, Júlio talks to a lump of animal excrement that sings of being mistreated and stepped on, and called names. It explains to Júlio that it is useful and should be respected because it can be used as fertilizer and is good for the earth. As they talk, pieces of the lump fall off, and it tells Júlio not to touch it and to always wash his hands. Rosenberg described the reaction of New York staff to the episode:

---

[4] Field notes, Abuja: 10/30/09.
[5] Field notes, Tel Aviv: 1/13/09.
[6] Episode is at: https://cultura.uol.com.br/videos/62402_videoclipe-a-historia-do-coco.html

And it's very funny. And it has won a prize in Germany. And when we showed that in New York, they were absolutely disgusted with it. Oh, they were like "How can you?" And they would show to other people, like, "See? I have copy of this poop from Brazil." Their reaction was—they were absolutely disgusted. "Oh that's awful. That's very bad." So we felt that they would never really get the Brazilian feeling and the irony of it.[7]

Despite their reaction, Rosenberg praised New York staff for how they worked with her team:

But during the work, during producing *Vila Sésamo*, it was very easy to deal with them. And it was a pleasure. You know, they would send us some ideas. And most of the time we would accept them. They were very good. But if we didn't accept them we would come back to them and then say, "We don't agree with you because of this, this and that." And they would say, "Okay."[8]

Another Brazilian partner foregrounded the issue of humor: "Also, our little jokes are different. What they think is really funny might not be that funny to us. So we need to scale it differently. Some things that we thought were really funny in the script, they looked at and they didn't think it was so good. This was one of the things we butted heads over. For us, this is funny—and for them it wasn't. This was one of the things that we sometimes clashed over." I then asked her: "And did they let you do it the way you felt it was funny in Brazil?" She responded: "Yeah, we defended it—this is good ...."[9]

Another Brazilian partner discussed how he managed competing conceptions of humor with New York staff by commissioning two advertising campaigns for *Vila Sésamo*:

Our advertising agencies here created two campaigns: one in New York style, another one in Brazilian style. We needed to show the campaign to the people in New York. They were completely different, because the Brazilian campaign used humor, used jokes. For instance, "Let our little monster enjoy yours." And the other one, in the New York style, was, "Watch *Vila Sésamo*, Cultura Television, 9 a.m., 3 p.m." Then I was in New York and I had to show the two campaigns. And I said, "Look, here I have two campaigns. One is a campaign with Brazilian style." And when I showed the campaign, they applauded the campaign that we chose to use here.[10]

---

[7] Personal interview, São Paulo: 6/19/09.
[8] Personal interview, São Paulo: 6/19/09.
[9] Personal interview, São Paulo: 6/16/09.
[10] Personal interview, São Paulo: 6/16/09.

In this case, New York staff accepted and appreciated what Brazilians found funny.

During my field work, I frequently observed partners requesting guidance as they learned to write humor for children. At a workshop for new Jordanian writers, a partner asked: "Can we have some guidelines on the do's and don'ts when you write funny stuff? I mean, things that we can do and be okay. Things that we cannot do it because it will ruin the segment, especially when you're writing something comic or funny."[11] Farouky responded by offering various options: "Characters can do what we call slapstick. It's physical comedy. So, accidentally carrying something too heavy and falling over and stuff going in the air. Then the character comes up and he's perfectly fine. That's all right. But the characters can never get hurt. You can't fall down and you hear an, "Ow!"[12] In general, partners were very responsive and excited about different ideas offered by New York staff, even though their humor was not always completely aligned.

Daoud Kuttab, the Palestinian producer of *Shara'a Simsim*, explained that his biggest concern was ensuring there was humor and fun in the program:

> Our big worry is to have creative writers who can come up with funny, interesting stories. The content is always there and will always be there and I'm not worried about it. My concern always is that there is good, funny, professionally well written, dramatically driven scripts. My problem is actually to get my writers and my head writer not to think so much of content. They're too content conscious. They're not as creative. So I want the opposite. Again, if you ask me what makes *Sesame* unique it's ability—and again publicly declared position—of matching drama and fun with education and content. That mix is a source of tension but it's also probably what makes the *Sesame* model so unique.[13]

The Palestinian team often struggled with writing a funny program for children because they questioned whether humor was appropriate, given the constant violence and oppression they endured. Research showed that almost a third of Palestinian children suffered from severe post-traumatic stress disorder (Afana et al. 2004). When the program filmed on location in the old city of Jerusalem, Saed Adoni, the show's line producer, heard comments such as "We are in a sad situation! Why are you bringing puppets here?" (Shapiro 2009). This general feeling of solemnity deeply affected the Palestinian team, as Adoni noted: "It's very hard here to ask writers to write something silly,

---

[11] Field notes, Amman: 2/27/09.
[12] Field notes, Amman: 2/27/09.
[13] Personal interview, Amman: 2/28/09.

because they are very worried about realism. If you watch American 'Sesame,' it's more lively and funny. The puppets aren't angry, and they sometimes do weird things, while we are more focused on realism, like Italian cinema in the 1950s" (Shapiro 2009).

The team in Palestine, like the teams in South Africa, Kosovo, and Northern Ireland, found themselves constantly at the whim of their political surroundings. And yet, every few months, the *Shara'a Simsim* team would bring life-sized walk-around[14] Muppets to greet seas of delighted children in Palestinian school auditoriums (Shapiro 2009).

Seatbelts, Life Jackets, and Knives: Modeling Safety

A quite unexpected source of disagreement among New York staff and partners centered on issues of children's safety. Research suggests that young children mimic what they see and hear, and Sesame Workshop therefore prioritizes modeling kindness, compassion, and other prosocial values. But New York staff also insist on modeling safety for children who view *Sesame Street* programs, and the cultural benchmark for safety is American. On the domestic program, for example, children are not shown playing with balloons, which can be a choking hazard. They are not shown using sharp objects, riding bicycles without helmets, or cooking without adult supervision.

And yet, many safety issues are culturally relative. Dr. Barbara Rogoff, a psychologist who studies cultural variation in what and how children learn, noted that in some cultures, children are taught how to use sharp objects when they have the strength and dexterity to hold them safely (2003). Dr. Cole, who frequently cites Rogoff's work, explained how she and other New York staff try to weigh issues of safety in relationship to local context:

> Safety I find even harder than violence because violence I think you can get a pretty good agreement pretty easily. But safety ends up being very culturally specific. We have kids wear helmets when they're riding bicycles in the US. In other parts of the world, kids don't wear helmets and it's a little weird to have them wear a helmet. So, on the one hand do you say, oh no, they have to wear a helmet because safety is safety and we shouldn't be sort of degrading our standards for kids in a different part of the world because all kids should be safe? Or is it just so ridiculous that

---

[14] A walkaround is a full body costume of a character inhabited by a person who walks around and interacts with people at events. An Elmo walkaround is therefore not the actual size of the Elmo character, which is a small rod Muppet.

it's just so out of context it doesn't make sense? And so we have a lot of these debates.[15]

Dr. Cole's comment reflects the difficulty for New York staff of balancing children's safety in relationship to cultural diversity. As I observed interactions around the world, New York staff often established hard lines on safety, but also attempted to be flexible.

During the workshop for new Jordanian writers, for example, two New York staffers emphasized non-negotiables in relationship to safety[16]:

NEW YORK STAFF #1: I just need to add, in regard to safety issue also. You cannot show the puppet jumping out of the roof or lighting a fire, you know?

NEW YORK STAFF #2: Well, yes. Another thing—it's like what you wouldn't want the child to do—carrying flaming torches down the street or things like that, no.

The following discussion between New York staff and Jordanian partners about modeling a child using a knife on the program illuminates the differences in cultural attitudes about safety:[17]

FAROUKY: You're not going to show them running around with scissors or chopping up vegetables, even if that's something they do at home. Because a seven year-old shouldn't necessarily be running around with a knife.

PARTNER: What would the—especially with the young child in cutting with the knife—if there is adult supervision, is it okay?

FAROUKY: For a kid?

PARTNER: Yeah.

FAROUKY: I would never show a kid with a knife. I would just really leave it up to the parent. But scissors, for example, a lot of preschools have child safe scissors.

PARTNER: Yeah.

FAROUKY: I don't see anything wrong with that. But in general, you have to make the decision, ultimately. And really, showing the kid cutting the cucumber versus the mother, it's not integral to the story. It doesn't matter who cuts it. That's not the story, unless your story was about chopping vegetables, in which case, that's not a film for a three year-old.

In this interaction, Farouky leaves the decision to partners, but provides different ways for them to weigh their options. Of course, children actually

---

[15] Personal interview, New York: 1/17/08.
[16] Field notes, Amman: 3/1/09.
[17] Field notes, Amman: 3/1/09.

do cut food in other cultures at the age of three. Teaching young children to cut is even integral to the Montessori method around the world—including in the US—as a way for them to develop and practice fine motor skills and foster independence and confidence.

In addition to safety in relationship to knives, on two separate occasions, I heard stories about how life jackets caused disagreements between New York staff and partners. Dr. Cole recalled a segment centered on a child who lived on a houseboat:

> Life preservers. I remember there was one time where there was a kid who lives on a boat who was featured—his home was on a boat. People were in an uproar because he doesn't have a life preserver on. And partners were like, it's his home. He doesn't wear a life preserver—that's ridiculous.[18]

During a workshop for directors in Jordan, Naila Farouky described a live action segment the Egyptian team shot centered on the son of a fisherman who goes with his father on a fishing trip, as recorded in field notes:[19]

> This segment gets sent to the US for content review. And the first thing the content people said was where are the life jackets? And everyone on the Egyptian team, the reaction was exactly the same—what life jackets? It's so removed from the reality of the situation. And so that's where you have this conflict of trying to figure out what is a safety issue that you should be modeling.

As she told the story, Jordanian partners laughed wryly, but Farouky carefully explained how the disagreement was resolved:[20]

> So in the end, what we ultimately concluded was okay—granted, if they were in the US, if they were in Europe, they probably would have had a life jacket because that's something that kids can understand. But for the Egypt side of it, the father was on the boat and that's okay. We would not have shown this kid fishing by himself because that could pose a safety issue. But his father was with him. You have to let it go. And so that's the kind of thing you need to be aware of, even within your own environment.

Farouky's advice to "let it go" in certain situations reflected the attitude of many New York staffers as they very carefully considered how to balance the challenges posed by different cultural environments.

But partners did describe situations in which New York staff exercised their veto power. Mariana Reichardt, Project Director for *Vila Sésamo*, described

---

[18] Personal interview, New York: 1/17/08.
[19] Field notes, Amman: 3/1/09.
[20] Field notes, Amman: 3/1/09.

what happened when TV Cultura chose photos of Garibaldo, a full body Muppet that looks like Big Bird, to use for the launch of *Vila Sésamo*:

> In one of the pictures Garibaldo was in roller-skates. And they were like, "Oh he's not wearing a helmet." And people said, we don't do that here, we would look like an American. Brazilian kids don't do that. But they didn't allow the pictures to be released. And we were like, okay we won't use it, we know it's safety and everything, but it's not the reality. It doesn't give the real picture of the Brazilian kids so they would not identify with Bel or Garibaldo because of that. So it happened, but it was not like major issue.[21]

In this case, because partners did not feel the decision undermined their project or their relationship with New York staff, they also let it go.

Like life jackets, seatbelts also present another challenge for New York staff and partners in relationship to safety. Dr. Cole described initial resistance from Egyptian partners to model seatbelt use:

> When kids are in cars or people are in vehicles, we do try to have them just sort of intrinsically put a seatbelt on. In Egypt, I remember being sort of adamant about that, like let's try to build that as something we model in Egypt because very few people do wear safety belts. And they were kind of like, ah, no one wears a safety belt, this is just ridiculous. But to their credit they did start doing it. You know, they would show somebody clasping together the belt.[22]

She explained how the local context eventually changed:

> And it was very funny because about three years into the project they passed a law in Egypt—a safety belt law in Egypt. And it became this joke that you have to have a sense of humor about. And they were like, oh well, I guess it was good that we were doing this. But understandably there was resistance to that because they're like, it's not part of the culture. And I think there it really has to be a discussion.[23]

Dr. Cole emphasized how working through difficult decisions depends on communication and exchanging critical knowledge about local contexts—both the local context of New York staff, and of partners:

> And it's all about helping each other understand the nuances and deciding together. And sometimes we're more successful at reaching a consensus and sometimes there's a point where it's kind of like, okay, I guess we're going to have to

---

[21] Personal interview, São Paulo: 8/6/08.
[22] Personal interview, New York: 1/17/08.
[23] Personal interview, New York: 1/17/08.

do it that way, because we can't come to an agreement that's sort of a compromise. But, if these things are discussed all the way through, there tends to usually be a way to solve it.[24]

Although conflicts about humor and safety do not make headlines around the world, those that engage politics can, and it is to these issues we now turn.

The Politics of Politics

New York staff and partners generally do not view the decisions they make every day as political. They do recognize, however, that working in a media space on children's education has inherently political implications. Sesame Workshop goes to great lengths to downplay politics, not only in the US, but also in local *Sesame Street* programs around the world. Politics, however, is ever present in the *Sesame* ether, particularly in programs focused on conflict zones and mutual respect and understanding. It is unavoidable, and New York staff and partners simply manage it.

As we saw in the case of the joint Israeli-Palestinian program, the choice of funders can be political. In Nigeria, for example, partners were willing to allow the Shell Corporation to fund their work, despite the harm the company had caused to the environment and to Nigerians, including workers. According to a senior New York staffer, a Nigerian partner told her: "If Shell was willing to give the money they should take it. If they want to get materials into the Delta region then they were going to have to work with Shell whether they took money from them or not because they basically have access to it."[25] Initially, Sesame Workshop explored the possibility of accepting funding from Shell. Ultimately, however, some New York staffers expressed concerns about taking money from Shell, as one explained: "I think the idea here is we're not going to help Shell clean up the reputation they've got, you know."[26]

Similarly, South African partners accepted funding from Sanlam Ltd., the country's second largest life insurance and financial services group, despite its former association with the South African National Party and its policy of apartheid. A New York staffer admitted that Sanlam "Partly funds *Sesame* to shore its image and doesn't hide it, but also does local community outreach and helps poor areas." When I asked a senior staffer about whether Sanlam's past in apartheid was a problem for partners, he said no.

---

[24] Personal interview, New York: 1/17/08.
[25] Field notes, Amman: 2/22/09.
[26] Personal interview, New York: 12/13/13.

Funding from USAID was seen by some partners as a form of soft power that is inherently political. New York staff were well aware of USAID's priorities, as a senior staffer explained about the agency's work in Nigeria: "USAID is focusing on northern states in Nigeria. I think we can guess why [she laughs]. We can guess that they're trying to have a positive impact on places where there is terrorism, there is low education levels, there is risk of children being recruited for local harm."[27]

Given USAID's history and mission, and the fact that many partners were distrustful of it, I asked New York staff and partners questions about tensions that may have developed in relationship to the agency. In 2006, USAID officials attempted to garner positive publicity for one of their projects by inviting US Secretary of State Condoleezza Rice to appear at an Islamic school in Jakarta to announce a USAID grant of 8.5 million dollars to fund an Indonesian version of *Sesame Street* for four years. The next morning, a major Indonesian newspaper printed a photo featuring a *Sesame Street* character[28] at the event. A New York staffer described what happened, and how senior staffers were apoplectic after seeing it:

> USAID had asked could we get an Elmo walkaround in time. It wasn't that we weren't open to it, but we couldn't get one done in time logistically. So they wound up getting a counterfeit one, a knock-off, without our knowledge. And they put an American flag in his hand, And it was a picture of Condoleezza Rice and in the background was Elmo holding up the American flag. We saw it and we were horrified. But one, it was a horrible looking walkaround, a horrible knock-off and second of all, we would never put an American flag in a walkaround's hand. We're not political, we do not do that. And so that one slipped away from us.[29]

I asked if Sesame Workshop had responded, and she said a senior staffer sent USAID a very polite letter saying "We were really surprised. It's not something we would normally do."[30] That her first concern, however, was that people saw an ugly walkaround, speaks volumes about Sesame Workshop's focus on quality.

New York staff also frequently expressed their concerns about maintaining control vis-a-vis funders. Dr. Lewis Bernstein explained how Sesame Workshop prioritizes autonomy from all funders, but focused on the unique issues with USAID:

---

[27] Personal interview, New York: 12/13/13.
[28] https://2001-2009.state.gov/r/pa/ei/pix/2006/63128.htm
[29] Personal interview, New York: 1/18/08.
[30] Personal interview, New York: 1/18/08.

USAID is looking for impact and what I think is the hard thing is to make sure that we don't become an agent of the US government. And the way we respond—we say we're our own entity. We create our own goals. If there's a mutuality of goals—so if you're interested in malaria in Tanzania, and they were—and you want to fund that, fine. So, so far we have overlapping interests. But we always have to watch out. We are willing to try to transcend politics in the way we deal with this. We tell partners we're Americans—sometimes we're naïve Americans, sometimes we're not so naïve. But we try to really be sensitive.[31]

Given that USAID's priority was supporting the mission of the US Department of State, it seemed inevitable that conflicts would emerge. And they did.

In 2012, *Shara'a Simsim* was temporarily suspended after USAID faced a massive funding cut. The United States Congress froze money to the region after Palestinians appealed to the UN for statehood and, as a result, *Shara'a Simsim* script writing ceased for months (Telegraph 2012). There was international outrage in response to this decision. Daniel Labin, then an executive for Israeli children's television channel HOP! that coproduced *Rechov Sumsum*, and who had previously worked as a producer for Sesame Workshop, protested, arguing: "Young children, whether Israeli or Palestinian, who are in need of educational tools to foster diversity appreciation and to prepare for life in a pluralistic society, should not be penalised or held accountable to the politics and political leadership, over which they have no control."[32]

Sesame Workshop's autonomy from USAID was tested in Bangladesh before production had even begun. In 2003, the democracy and governance office of the USAID mission in Bangladesh approached Sesame Workshop with a possible grant of six million dollars to create a new local *Sesame Street* program in Bangladesh. After an extensive and intensive search and vetting process, New York producer Naila Farouky chose a production company called Asiatic Marketing Communication Ltd., led by Sara and Aly Zaker, a couple who were very well known and respected artists and political activists in Bangladesh. Nayantara Communications is Asiatic's audio-visual production agency, responsible for coproducing *Sisimpur* with New York staff.

After Asiatic was chosen, problems quickly ensued with USAID, as Farouky foreshadowed: "I think in all the ten years that I have worked here, I never,

---

[31] Personal interview, New York: 1/17/08.
[32] https://www.theguardian.com/world/2012/jan/07/palestinian-sesame-street-us-congress

ever, ever had experienced a more difficult battle than the battle of setting up this team and sticking by this team."[33] Farouky explained that right before the educational content seminar, she was told that a managing director of Asiatic was also in the government—in the opposition party. According to Farouky, when the person in charge of the project at the USAID mission in Bangladesh was informed of this, they told the New York project manager: "That is a non-starter for this project. Your producer must come back and she must fire this company and she must find somebody new."[34] Farouky was alarmed when: "They asked us to cease and desist all activities on this project until I would do this." And she refused. She became visibly upset as she remembered and described her reaction:

> This man, A, lives in a democratic country. B, he has participated in the demo-cratic process in this country. How is the office of democracy and governance of the United States Agency for International Development punishing a democrat? It doesn't make sense. It's a scandal, quite frankly. So I refused. And we stopped for six months. USAID sent this letter, "Cease and desist all activities, the producer comes back and gets rid of this company." I said, no...[I] am not coming back and I am not changing this company. This is the company that we're going with and if you don't like it then you're very welcome to fire me and find yourself a producer who will, but this is not ethical. And honestly, God bless them, my bosses stood behind me one hundred percent.[35]

Farouky explained that having grown up in Egypt, she had a very different perspective of USAID than many of her US colleagues:

> I was constantly saying I understand what your perception of USAID is because you're American citizens, you've grown up in this country, you don't have this other perspective. But I have lived on the side of being a recipient of AID money, so it's a very personal thing to me and that's maybe why my stance is so much more adamant. I will not bow down to this, I'm not going to say it's okay. This is wrong. If he were a convicted murderer we might have a different conversation, but this guy's just a government employee, what the hell? What's your problem?[36]

Farouky revealed that the final decision about whether to retain the produc-tion company she chose was ultimately made at the highest level of Sesame Workshop, by President/CEO Gary Knell. She described how one night after

[33] Personal interview, New York: 1/16/08.
[34] Personal interview, New York: 1/16/08.
[35] Personal interview, New York: 1/16/08.
[36] Personal interview, New York: 1/16/08.

a work event, he asked her how things were going in Bangladesh, and she told him what had happened. This is how she described what happened next:

> We were in the street walking from the United Nations across to the subway station and I remember he stopped in the middle of the street and literally said, "I am telling you right now, I will not be strong-armed. If this is the situation, we walk away. We walk away from six million."[37]

Ultimately, Asiatic was retained, and *Sisimpur* became one of the most successful local *Sesame Street* programs New York staff and partners coproduced. They eventually opened Sesame Workshop's second local office in Dhaka, called Sesame Workshop Bangladesh.

The Politics of Place

In conflict zones, even the names of places can cause disagreements. According to multiple New York staffers, the word Palestine caused issues internally and with partners across the Middle East. Naila Farouky, who again is a native Arabic speaker who grew up in Egypt, is a US citizen, and whose family is Palestinian and Jordanian, described her many efforts to convince her New York colleagues that Palestine was the appropriate word to use. She was particularly adamant that Palestine be used with Middle Eastern partners and audiences.

Farouky revealed what transpired in 2006 when President/CEO Gary Knell gave a speech at the US-Arab Economic Forum in Detroit. He asked his speech writer to ask Farouky how he should refer to the place that creates the Palestinian project. She explained how she responded and what happened next:

> You have two options: Palestine or Occupied Territories. I know that there are many different opinions, but if you want to look at one, as neutral as can be, let's look at the United Nations. So that night before he gets up to give his speech, we have a talk, and he said what do you think I should say? And I said, I really think you should say Palestine. I don't think you should go to Occupied Territories. I think you want to be a little bit careful. And he says, okay, I'll think about it. The next day he gets up, gives a speech—Occupied Territories—and two New York staffers got up and walked out of the room. Just left.[38]

---

[37] Personal interview, New York: 1/16/08.
[38] Personal interview, New York: 2/27/09.

It is important to note that among Jewish staff in New York, there were very different views on Israel and the ongoing conflict. Gary Knell, for example, expressed deep concerns about the Israeli occupation and the situation Palestinians faced.

The politics of place in relationship to Palestine also surfaced in 2006. The Mosaic Foundation, a nonprofit founded by spouses of Arab ambassadors to the US, and dedicated to improving women and children's lives and fostering understanding between the US and the Arab world, chose to provide funds for Sesame Workshop's projects in the Middle East. A gala event was planned, and Farouky was asked to produce a highlight reel of Sesame Workshop's work throughout the Middle East. A senior staffer told her she could not use the word Palestine in her voiceover. She responded:

> You run this company, it's your call. I am telling you I think that it is extremely offensive. I think that going into a gala event where eighty percent of the people are Arabs and the queen of one of the countries that we're working with is in attendance as the guest of honor and you will not even say the name of her country? And then for the record, as an employee, I am offended.[39]

Farouky produced the reel, but she explained how she did the voiceover:

> I made the portion on the Palestinians the longest of all the pieces, and I said Palestinian as many times as I possibly could: our Palestinian Muppets, and our Palestinian coproduction with our Palestinian producer, and our Palestinian goals. And the producer, Daoud Kuttab, was the one person who got it and he went up to Gary and said I know what she did and I'm very grateful that she did that.[40]

In these two examples, the disagreement was among New York staff, not with partners. But Farouky's decisions to prioritize Palestinian partners and funders likely avoided conflicts between partners in the Middle East and New York staff.

When it came time to publicize *Sesame Tree*, the local program in Northern Ireland, the politics of place also emerged. Beatrice Chow, who was then Assistant Vice President of Strategic Communications, explained the care she used to ensure no mistakes were made: "If we have a press agency on the ground we'll share it with them to see the nuances of the localization. So we drafted something for Northern Ireland, and I wrote Belfast, Northern

---

[39] Personal interview, New York: 2/27/09.
[40] Personal interview, New York: 2/27/09.

Ireland. And I thought well, Belfast isn't really Northern Ireland, it's UK. I mean ultimately, it's the UK. But would I put Belfast, UK, or Belfast, Northern Ireland? And for me here sitting here in New York, I don't know which one I'm putting."[41] She explained that she asked the local team for advice, and they told her:

> Well, technically you're correct that you would say Belfast, UK. But because the folks here are particularly sensitive to it, and they would appreciate it if they were recognized for this work, you would say Northern Ireland. So something as small as that, we would check it just to make sure me sitting in an office in New York might not understand the nuances of working in that particular country.[42]

Chow's experience affirmed how important partners' expertise is to New York staff and suggests that asking them to share it helps build trust with partners and mitigate conflicts.

Autonomy and Control

As noted frequently in this book, there are significant power differentials between New York staff and partners. Sesame Workshop holds the intellectual property rights and often controls the budget, or parts of it. Partners consistently expressed frustration and discontent with the fact that even though they create content, they do not own their intellectual property. During a meeting in New York between potential and current partners, the former asked the latter about contracts, as recorded in field notes: "The current partner tells them they own their IP until they sign their contracts. So warns them to be careful about what they put forward as *Sesame*. Because if they include it in *Sesame* work they won't own it anymore. Says everything they produce *Sesame* owns. The current partner concludes: "But it's worth it. In the end, it will help you get other work and is great on your C.V."[43] A Colombian partner also echoed frustrations about intellectual property rights: "Because one of the things that we acknowledge is that the copyright rights are *Plaza Sésamo* even though the intellectual productions for doing them were ours. So I don't think that should be repeated."[44]

---

[41] Personal interview, New York: 1/18/08.
[42] Personal interview, New York: 1/18/08.
[43] Field notes, New York: 12/17/13.
[44] Field notes, Bogotá: 6/25/09.

Daoud Kuttab, producer of *Shara'a Simsim*, openly expressed frustration that until recently, he had never been provided the entire budget for the project:

> This season is the first season that I, as the executive producer of the Palestinian show, ever saw the full budget. They never shared it with us. They only send me my part of the budget. And you know why I saw this budget? Because I was involved with USAID. I literally sold the program to USAID and I also had Robert's [Knežević] help that they couldn't keep the budget away from me. I don't think there's a contractual obligation on their part to send me the full budget, but I think there's a moral obligation, even if there's no contractual obligation.[45]

Although Kuttab unequivocally supported coproduction, he articulated problems with equity between New York staff and partners:

> I truly believe in the value of coproductions on the quality of the programming, on the cross-cultural interchange, on the technology exchange part. Now, would I divide the budget the way it is divided now? No. I don't think that division is equitable. I don't think the share of Sesame in the overall budget is equitable. I mean, a junior administrator in New York is paid more than our best director here.[46]

Kuttab pointed out that there are "a lot of layers that for me they don't make sense," and a lot of money spent on "people in offices reading cc-ed emails"[47] rather than on production. Kuttab was not alone in articulating how Sesame Workshop's organizational structure and bureaucratic procedures created confusion and frustration for partners. It was often not clear to partners who in New York they should report to, which sometimes led to misunderstandings and chaos, as Kuttab explained:

> The first thing they taught us in management in college is that each person should have only one boss. If you have multiple managers it's a formula for disaster. So in New York we have a project manager, and two producers, and two finance people, and two public relations people. And it becomes overwhelming. And everybody's chiming in.[48]

[45] Personal interview, Amman: 2/28/09.
[46] Personal interview, Amman: 2/28/09.
[47] Personal interview, Amman: 2/28/09.
[48] Personal interview, Amman: 2/28/09.

A Colombian partner noted: "But inside *Sesame*, we have the idea that their divisions also have communication problems, and that there is a lot of bureaucracy. And that bureaucracy costs time and money. That was more or less what I think about it."[49]

Partners consistently articulated the need for more communication and clarity from New York staff. A Colombian partner offered suggestions for how to achieve this: "How to improve? By creating more channels of communication. That's the way I'd do it. And have a direct channel. But we don't have all the information. So if I don't have all the information, I don't know if the channel works because we don't all talk with each other."[50]

During my seven years in the field conducting research for this project, it became clear from interviews and observations that there were two camps of New York staffers who had very different views about the amount of control and autonomy partners should have. One group was concerned with brand management and worried that allowing partners too much autonomy could potentially lead to decisions that would undermine brand integrity. Their concrete concerns included: quality control (would characters "look" like Sesame characters), adherence to the mission (would educational goals and curricula be followed), and audience trust (would the brand be used in advertising and other endeavors that undermined parents' and caregivers' trust). Given the mistake made not by partners, but by USAID in Indonesia when Elmo was given a US flag to wave next to Condoleezza Rice, concerns about controlling the integrity of the brand are not insignificant.

Another group of New York staffers believed partners should be given more control and autonomy because it would support sustainability and scaling up, foster innovation, and deepen commitment to the brand. Robert Knežević, then Senior Vice President of *Sesame Street* International, was in this group, and he explained his position:

> Egypt is literally on its own. They're running the business, become an independent entity. I'm proud of that. They have their own funding. I've transferred all responsibility to these guys and they have secured funding through 2012. When you give people the right tools and autonomy they will do the self-policing. The Muppets become the brand integrity. Nothing special about us in New York. They are us. They are not them. They are us. This sets up completely different relations.[51]

[49] Personal interview, Bogotá: 6/25/09.
[50] Personal interview, Bogotá: 6/26/09.
[51] Personal interview, New York: 11/3/08.

Kneževic's comment also suggests that allowing for more autonomy helps build trust with partners.

President/CEO Gary Knell was also a firm supporter of allowing partners more autonomy. I asked him how Sesame Workshop builds autonomy, and whether "there is a point where you just sort of say, "We've been working with you for however many years and we sort of don't need to check the scripts"? He responded with a laugh:

> I'm laughing because we have these debates inside the company right now. And I'm of the school of, we don't need to read the scripts anymore. [TK: And why is that?] Because they've been doing it for thirty years—they know more than our people know. Some of these people in Germany have been living with Bert and Ernie longer than some of these producers on our side have been alive. So for us to be able to tell them what to do, it's insulting on some level. And I think we have to stand for respect also. And respect for our colleagues. And they have to own it primarily, and we need to be a coach, is how I would look at it.[52]

Knell's position reflects a tacit understanding that ultimately, it is likely that more equitable relationships between New York staff and partners lead to more successful project outcomes.

New York staff and partners shared many ideas about how to better balance autonomy and control. Naila Farouky advocated for providing more support during the early stages of a new program or for a new team. She concurred with other partners, quoted earlier in this book, that creativity is universal, but creativity in relationship to writing educational and funny television for children is specific and requires building particular skills:

> I've never come across a country that just doesn't have a creative population. It just doesn't exist. It doesn't matter if that creativity doesn't manifest itself in the way that we think of art. Every country has poets, puppeteers, has people that can move them. So they may not have the same skill, it may not be up to the same standard, but at the end of the day there is always a creative population that exists.[53]

She characterized her position as "always pushing for a change in the process whereby the New York team follows along at all stages more until the international team is able to get it." As she explained, "It took us twenty years to do it and it's hard. And why do we expect that an inexperienced team will be able

---

[52] Personal interview, Cambridge: 11/14/07.
[53] Personal interview, New York: 1/16/08.

to do it if we just spend a week with them and then say goodbye and good luck?" She argued that "it would save money anyway to do more trips during the early stages in the process because as it is now, they end up spending more time and money to help fix things in the end."[54]

But achieving that delicate balance between providing enough support while not impinging on partners' autonomy is difficult, and can be frustrating to both New York staff and partners. One New York staffer complained that a partner wants less oversight, but emails seventeen times a day for input: "If she wants me to just write it for her then she can't be upset about control, she should just have me review the finished product."[55] A Colombian partner (not the partner referenced above) had a very different perspective when describing the process of creating a teacher's guide. I asked her: "So in terms of creating this, the fact that you had to send things to New York constantly was okay, was too much, too little? She replied: "Too many steps. Too many revisions. It went to Geneva—the World Health headquarters—and back to New York, and back to Geneva, and back to Colombia. So in order to change some words, it could take a month or more."[56]

During more than one interview with partners, they suggested that sometimes they simply do not reveal to New York staff when they make changes to the program before it airs. As a partner explained: "Although we did change some things. We did cut some parts that we thought were very boring. But I think we never told them. I'm not very sure."[57] When I pressed for more detail, the partner walked the comment back. My interpretation is that on minor changes—not on those that would violate core principles—this may be common.

Building Trust

It became quite obvious early on that mentoring partners to coproduce a local *Sesame Street* program requires that New York staff express empathy and directness, and respect the expertise, skills, and talents of their partners. When asked how she measures success, producer Basia Nikonorow centered her response on relationships: "In our work it is the relationship that we create with the partner. That you feel that you can trust that partner and that

[54] Field notes, Amman: 2/24/09.
[55] Field notes, Abuja: 10/30/09.
[56] Personal interview, Bogotá: 6/26/09.
[57] Personal interview, São Paulo: 6/19/09.

they can trust you. That you can be honest with each other and that you're both aiming for the same goal."[58]

Building trust, however, is not easy and requires developing certain skills and engaging key practices. I observed Dr. Cole model mentorship during the writers' workshop in Abuja, Nigeria. As discussed in Chapter 4, a riveting discussion unfolded as partners expressed their desire to deal with corruption as a core theme in their curriculum. During the conversation, they shared knowledge about stereotypes they wanted to undermine, and New York staff shared knowledge about how to potentially accomplish that goal in their curriculum. Dr. Cole guided them as they articulated three potential themes.

When the session ended, Dr. Cole was speaking to the Nigerian producer and another partner, when a New York staffer interrupted the conversation and told Dr. Cole, "That was great, how you came up with those themes." Dr. Cole responded by refusing to take credit as the creative force, and instead highlighted her role as facilitator and mentor. As I wrote in my field notes: "Dr. Cole totally downplays it and says it was a group effort and emerged from the team and discussion. I was impressed by how she handled this. They were their themes but she helped direct them and focus it. She bases it on listening to what they are trying to express and go for."[59] Her decision to reject personal recognition and emphasize collaboration sent a strong signal to the Nigerian producer and partner that their contributions were primary, and that she recognized and respected their knowledge and expertise.

President/CEO Gary Knell provided an interesting example when I asked him how to build trust between New York staff and partners:

We have to walk the walk. Sometimes we have to convince our own people that you've got to step away from this. I'll give you a perfect example. We're in Japan. There's a segment on the show where the Japanese's Elmo is in a running race. It's a show on exercise or something. And he trips and falls down. And the adults standing around him are yelling at him "Get up! Finish the race, what's the matter with you!" And our educator is like, "You can't do that. He's four years old, this is terrible! His self esteem will be crushed." But in Japan the point they were trying to press was perseverance and drive—a totally different mentality. So what do we do? Do we put on a US hat on this or do we act like the Romans? And this came up to me for a decision. And it was like, we're going to do what they want to do. This is their show. There was a big debate about this.[60]

[58] Personal interview, New York: 1/18/08.
[59] Field notes, Abuja: 10/29/09.
[60] Personal interview, Cambridge: 11/14/07.

Knell acknowledged how difficult these decisions actually are:

> So anyway, he got over it. Elmo's okay. So that's a good example. And I think we have to walk the walk, and talk the talk. And it's hard, really hard. Especially when you're trying to control a brand. Not in the commercial sense as much as in the equity sense—that you can't have people messing around with the basic—what is Elmo's personality, what does *Sesame Street* stand for?[61]

Their willingness to grapple with these difficult choices shows that New York staff recognize their goal is not just to deliver an exceptional product—it is also to forge strong trust-based relationships with their partners, which ultimately increases the likelihood of creating successful local programs.

Sesame Workshop's Organizational Culture

This chapter illuminates the kinds of issues that more frequently emerge as conflictual and how New York staff and partners try to manage and resolve conflict. It is therefore an examination of Sesame Workshop's organizational culture. Sesame Workshop is not a perfect organization—none is—and New York staff certainly make all kinds of mistakes as they navigate coproduction with partners. To reiterate, what is distinctive about Sesame Workshop, however, is a willingness to acknowledge, reflect upon, and course correct when mistakes occur. Some of this must be built into the organizational culture through various policies and procedures. As Mariana Reichardt, the Brazilian Project Director for *Vila Sésamo*, explained:

> The good thing of Sesame Workshop is that we stop to think about it. So we know what are the problems. We are open to discuss them and even though we don't have a solution right away—maybe we never have a solution—at least we are aware of our weaknesses. I wouldn't even say weaknesses, but our critical points and you're open to discuss them. So who would do that? It's not easy. The easiest way would be, I'll give you the money and you do whatever you want, or do it my way. It's easier. It's easy for everyone. But no, we have this. At least everyone is allowing themselves to think about it and maybe change or not change their minds, but there is this respect in the difference in how to do that.[62]

---

[61] Personal interview, Cambridge: 11/14/07.
[62] Personal interview, São Paulo: 8/6/08.

Even though coproducing is difficult, as Reichardt suggests, almost all partners affirmed its value in creating a much better program.

But coproduction also largely depends on the skills and characteristics of individual staff members. Effective hiring, training, and evaluating are therefore critical to the process. As an organization, Sesame Workshop attempts to recruit staff who can engage effectively in transnational interaction. Staff who cannot do so are often removed from projects. At the end of one of my interviews in a South American country, I asked a partner to recommend his favorite restaurant for dinner. He expressed surprise that I was looking forward to local cuisine. He then told me about a New York staffer who refused to eat the local cuisine in his country, and who brought their own food from the US. He explained how insulting he found that behavior, and said the person did not last long on the project.

Like a marriage, the organizational relationships among New York staff and partners should not be evaluated based on the presence of conflicts, but rather on how those conflicts are managed and resolved. Sesame Workshop's organizational culture allows partners to navigate misunderstandings and conflicts that arise in those relationships and mitigate power asymmetries, even though it does not eliminate them. But partners' invaluable and crucial knowledge and expertise also provide them with leverage in their organizational relationships with New York staff and allow them to recalibrate the scales and to push back in order to set priorities and determine best strategies for their projects.

8

Conclusions

It was 2009, and we were in an elementary school in Ramallah, Palestine. Children exuded pure joy as they watched Haneen (a bright orange and pink girl monster) and Kareem (a green and blue rooster with a multi-colored tail)—the two main characters in *Shara'a Simsim*—wiggle and dance around their school's auditorium. Some of the younger children smiled broadly as they sat transfixed in their teachers' laps, and the older ones stood on their chairs to catch every detail as it unfolded around them. The children and their teachers' happiness was infectious. Watching them, I was filled with amazement that a Palestinian version of a children's program I had watched as a child had been created in a place so far from, and so different from, the place of its origin. This book is focused on how that outcome occurs and the processes that facilitate it.

I came to this project not focused on the issues that had drawn researchers to *Sesame Street* for decades since its inception in 1969—primary education, child development, and children's television and media. The dissertations, academic journal articles, and books on these topics could fill the electronic equivalent of entire library sections. I was interested instead in how Sesame Workshop functioned as an organization, specifically in relationship to its partners as they jointly created local *Sesame Street* programs together. The process by which Sesame Workshop and its partners all over the world engage in transnational collaboration to create a concrete hybrid cultural product intrigued me. And it was a topic that, to my knowledge, researchers had not examined empirically or theoretically.

Organizational Partnerships

But my interest went beyond Sesame Workshop's collaborative television and radio programs with partners, and extended to its community outreach projects with partners that intentionally prioritized and addressed many of the UN's Sustainable Development Goals, including quality education, health and well-being, gender equality, and environmental stewardship.

Sesame Street Around the World. Tamara Kay, Oxford University Press. © Oxford University Press (2025).
DOI: 10.1093/9780190844325.003.0008

This interest in Sesame Workshop's engagement in development work with partners in low- and middle-income countries emerged in large part from my frustration with the inadequacy of research on transnational organizational partnerships across various scholarly fields.

Although scholars who study global and transnational cultural production provide compelling insights into how cultural products change and spread, they focus very little attention on the role of collaborations among partner organizations in these processes. They ask what originators or adopters—separated by time and place—do to transform cultural products. They generally do not ask questions about how partners work together on the ground. World society researchers center their attention on macro-level questions, while translation and local adaptation scholars generally prioritize questions about processes at the meso-level. These very different vantage points prevent them from seeing how partners work together on the ground, and why examining their collaboration in real time is critical to understanding global and transnational cultural production.

While organizational scholars have examined collaboration within and among firms, they have focused primarily on corporate transnational collaborations—in the business literature as studies of international strategies, corporate governance in multinational firms, and organizational adaptation in emerging economies. Their research is largely retrospective, with analyses centered on the formation of subsidiaries and local franchises, and the adaptation of products for global markets by individual firms and for-profit organizations (Guillén 2000; Sklair 2001; Tihanyi et al. 2005; Lanchimba et al. 2025).

Analyses of the structure, performance, and effectiveness of transnational teams generally center on how individual firms construct them in order to develop and manufacture products for a profit (Snow et al. 1996; Earley and Mosakowski 2000; Verhoeven et al. 2017; Bjorvatn and Wald 2024). My analysis of Sesame Workshop's transnational teams is consistent with this scholarship; it shows that building trust and managing conflict are critical to creating effective transnational teams. Neither this research nor cultural globalization studies centers on how organizational partners create hybrid cultural products together in real time. Here, I expand on these bodies of work by showing how transnational teams that create hybrid cultural products together build trust and manage conflict through interactions. I can do so because I was in the room with them to observe those interactions as they occurred.

This book enters the debate on culture and globalization from an organizational perspective, devoting significant analysis to the relationship between organizations involved in constructing a hybrid cultural product. It therefore bridges cultural sociology and organization studies. Since Bielby and Harrington's (2008) *Global TV: Exporting Television and Culture in the World Market*, not many sociologists have brought these two subfields together. My focus on them is also rare among books on diffusion and local adaptation; it therefore makes a meaningful contribution to scholarship across these fields. An empirical examination of nonprofit organizations and NGOs offers a new and rich terrain for understanding how organizations collaborate when profits are not at stake.

Research on nonprofits and NGOs engaged in development work frequently focuses on whether they succeed or fail, but ignores how organizational relationships affect development outcomes. And across social science disciplines, explanations of development project failure too frequently identify their source as "cultural" differences (Landes 1998; Harrison and Huntington 2000), manifested by different values, religious traditions, and ethics, which result in underdevelopment and weak states. But the underlying message is that people and their environments in low- and middle-income countries are responsible for those failures. As many scholars have noted, this ignores history and historical processes, particularly the effects of colonialism, genocide, extraction and the theft of resources, exploitation, slavery and forced labor, coercion through multilateral free trade and investment agreements and institutions such as the International Monetary Fund and World Bank, cultural imposition and the destruction of cultural and religious practices.

To be sure, scholars have interrogated these practices and institutions and come to different conclusions (see Acemoglu, Johnson, and Robinson 2001; Swidler and Watkins 2009; Acemoglu and Robinson 2012). But given that most development projects occur between organizations in high and low-income countries, what aspects of those relationships affect project failures on the ground at the micro level? With few exceptions, we know relatively little about how NGOs in high-income countries interact and work with local partners in low- and middle-income countries. For example, what amount of control and autonomy do partners have? Can they determine needs and goals, set and change timelines, choose strategies and approaches, select funders, and make other critical choices? Because most research does not analyze the building of collaborative ties between organizations in high- and low-income countries, it misses the cultural environment in which transnational partnerships are constructed, and the dynamics that lead to the disarticulation between development strategies and local cultural environments in real time on the ground.

What many scholars have documented extensively are the failures of development projects between organizations in high and low-income countries. James Ferguson's seminal book *The Anti-Politics Machine: "Development," Depoliticization, and Bureaucratic State Power in Lesotho* (1994) set a gold standard for how to conceptualize and analyze development projects. He shows how development organizations' strategies and discourses depoliticized entrenched inequalities in Lesotho, many of which were rooted in lack of access to land, jobs, and other resources. Bureaucrats had little understanding of local cultural meanings and practices, which created perverse logics that damaged communities that had no control over decisions and ultimately increased the bureaucratic apparatus of the state. The failure of these projects did little to inspire change in discourse or strategy.

Scholars have also documented the billions of dollars of global aid money that is poured into public health awareness campaigns, many of which are intended to prevent HIV transmission. These campaigns often lack substantive efforts to include local communities in strategic goals or decision-making processes. And they are often "thin" attempts at local adaptation—devoid of substantive efforts to customize local health campaigns. This can result in unsuccessful and unexpected outcomes. For example, a billboard with local actors in "authentic" clothing behind a "use a condom" message is a thinly adapted attempt to influence behavior that rarely connects with people on the ground and therefore fails to produce meaningful change. In the case of McDonnell's (2016) superb analysis of the materiality of AIDS campaign objects, the introduction of female condoms in Ghana did not lead to widespread uptake in their use because gender inequality made it difficult for women to negotiate using them with partners. As a result, some women ingeniously repurposed and refashioned female condoms—specifically their hard plastic ring—into bracelets to wear and to sell.

Examining organizational partnerships would therefore help explain why, in contrast to world society arguments about the world converging around similar institutions, policies, and norms, they do not always flow seamlessly from high-income countries at the core to low-income ones at the periphery. Indeed, the Sesame Workshop case shows that even when we would expect frictionless convergence—given that Sesame Workshop does not go to a country hostile to its cultural product—conflicts still emerge and require negotiation to resolve. By placing knowledge exchange at the center of its analysis, this book offers promising avenues for new research on the success and failure, and the likelihood of the adoption of cultural products.

Culture in Transnational Interaction

Complex knowledge exchange is required at the point of production and at the point of consumption in order for partners to understand *Sesame Street,* and for New York staff to understand the context in which a new iteration of the program will be rooted. The exchange of complex cultural knowledge is embedded in the interactions between New York staff and partners as they work as a transnational team. It is important to emphasize that this involves very different processes from those engaged in by multinational corporations that do not coproduce. Disney, for example, employs cultural consultants and advisors for its films, including *Coco* and *Encanto.* These films were therefore not coproduced as a transnational team with Mexican and Colombian partners who lived and worked in those countries.

The *Sesame Street* case provides an opportunity to combine approaches from inhabited institutionalism—centered on social interactions among people in organizations—and cultural sociology—focused on "culture in interaction" (Eliasoph and Lichterman 2003), in order to theorize *culture in transnational interaction* at the organizational level. Both approaches examine people and organizations at the local or national level where people have shared cultures, collective meanings, and "group styles." But does this apply to people and organizations at the transnational level? I suggest that while interactions are still important at this level, the lack of a common culture means that collective identities and shared meanings must be forged. But how does this happen? Here, I address that question by offering a framework for understanding culture in transnational interaction that shows how organizational partners who do not share collective representations create them together through coproduction by constructing value to align their interests and exchanging complex cultural knowledge to both customize and build alliances.

The framework, therefore, foregrounds the *interactional* character of transnational ties that facilitate the coproduction of hybrid cultural products and the practices that allow partners to manage power asymmetries, misunderstandings, and conflict. Building a framework using interview and ethnographic data—much gathered from observations of real-time interactions between New York staff and partners—is essential because those meanings must be constructed in person in time and space. This framework offers an initial step toward developing more robust theories of how organizational actors connect as they collaborate transnationally, how they engage in mutual learning, and perhaps most importantly, how they build trust.

Although the process of coproducing *Sesame Street* involves the exchange of complex cultural knowledge, it moves beyond mere cultural exchange. Ultimately, Sesame Workshop and its partners must create something together. At its core, then, the framework I develop is an initial attempt to lay the foundation for understanding transnational interaction in relationship to cultural coproduction. This process privileges the creation of new knowledge that emerges from transnational interaction, and that is used to coproduce a hybrid cultural product that is transformed into more than the sum of its parts.

Indeed, this book is not about the global diffusion of a hybrid cultural product. Rather, it is about the coproduction of a cultural object that leads to multiple, different, and unique hybrid cultural products. Each local program resembles *Sesame Street* as an exceptionally abstract US cultural product; however, each program looks very different and cannot be substituted for another. The Irish and Indian programs, for example, are not interchangeable, although they are both recognizable as versions of *Sesame Street*.

The nature of interactions, or the coproduction culture, also varies between Sesame Workshop and partners across the seventeen countries I studied. For example, in India and Brazil, outreach projects were limited by institutional and legal constraints; only Indian and Brazilian organizations are permitted to engage in certain kinds of outreach work. In India, Sesame Workshop and its partners therefore had to create an Indian subsidiary and a trust to engage in outreach work. This provided Indian partners with increased leverage and autonomy, as was revealed by the data discussed in chapter three on how they negotiated their own revenue stream.

My framework, therefore, lays a foundation for scholars to theorize different kinds of coproduction cultures among transnational teams. The coproduction of *Sesame Street*, for example, results in multiple hybrid cultural products adapted for local audiences/markets, and power asymmetries are more salient because partners from the low-income countries must work around Sesame Workshop at the center. In contrast, film coproduction among European countries results in one hybrid product created for a global audience, and the power asymmetries are often less salient because there is no center.

Empirically and theoretically, a framework centered on transnational interaction in relationship to cultural coproduction is also useful because it lays a preliminary foundation for expanding our understanding of hybridization processes. Retrospective analyses of local adaptations and their progenitors can only provide hypotheses for how and why a particular cultural product mimics or strays from its original. Moreover, current research cannot trace how hybridity emerges, is constructed, resisted, or contested, thereby eclipsing the interactions and negotiations that result in a hybrid's final form. Néstor García Canclini laments how "studies about hybridization are usually limited to *describing* cross-cultural mixing," and calls for "studying processes of hybridization by locating these in structural relations of causality" (2005:xxix).

The Sesame Workshop case shows *how* partners negotiate to combine global influences with local specificity, resulting in multiple hybrids that promote both universality and particularity at the same time. Partners explained that they want to engage with Sesame Workshop because of its global reach and the universal values and quality they believe it represents. They simultaneously want to use their programs to highlight the beauty and distinctiveness of their own countries and cultures. Although Sesame Workshop and its partners each benefit from that universality and particularity, how they are expressed in individual local programs is not predetermined and varies by country.

In addition, placing transnational organizational interactions at the center of the analysis of cultural coproduction offers promising avenues for new research on the success and failure of local adaptation processes. While scholars have hypothesized that conditions and conflicts on the ground shape and mediate "the process of social construction that occurs with each and every adoption" (Simmons et al. 2008:354), micro-level processes can actually expose the nature of those conditions and the manner in which conflicts are intensified or resolved through organizational interactions.

This book, therefore, offers an initial response to the calls by researchers (many of whom study diffusion using quantitative data) for analyses of the micro-level interactions involved in diffusion (see Kogut and Macpherson 2008:106). Scholars generally agree that case studies and research that utilize observational data would contribute a great deal to our understanding of diffusion and localization processes. As Strang and Soule explain: "We typically know that potential adopters are brought into contact with the diffusing practice but do not know quite what they see, particularly whether they observe results. This inability to specify what is observed produces some theoretical fuzziness about the microprocesses involved in diffusion" (1998:269). Clarity requires understanding what they see, which requires observing it with them in real time.

Cultural Complexity and Friction

The *Sesame Street* case also raises interesting questions about the need to differentiate the *complexity* of different cultural products. For example, Sesame Workshop also produces cultural products that are not complex and not hybrids; *Sesame Street* plush toys, games, books, and other products sold around the world are minimally adapted and not coproduced by transnational teams. Clearly, the organization creating them has not changed, but the nature of the product and the market have. Alona Abt, the CEO of Channel HOP! that produces and airs *Rechov Sumsum*, explained why Israel imports plush toys of Elmo (who sometimes appears on the program) rather than create plush toys of *Rechov Sumsum* characters:

> We tried having a licensor for the Israeli characters but at the end of the day, he said it would be too expensive for them to create the characters in China, ship them in for the amount of units we could be selling. So I think in many small territories, it's easier to bring in Elmo or Cookie Monster or whatever is on the show because it's a big investment. And if it's a small country, you can't always make a return on an investment.[1]

As Abt reveals, selling US toys in Israel that require minimal adaptation makes economic sense because a market for these toys already exists; they are already considered locally valuable. The channel can tap into pre-existing commodity chains, without building new alliances. And toys do not need to be customized. They do not push new normative ideas or require coordinated interpersonal efforts.

Of course, the relative simplicity of *Sesame Street* toys is not a feature inherent to the toys themselves. Although in Israel, selling the toys did not create significant challenges, in India, an attempt to sell plush toys was problematic, as Sashwati Banerjee, the founder and managing director of Sesame Workshop India, explained:

> So we started looking at merchandising when Turner Entertainment had the merchandising rights. They did like two, three products. They were all wrong. From day one, I said, "Why do you want to launch a plush?" This is a country where 14 percent of children die from acute respiratory infections. It's highly polluted. Plush attracts dust. You shouldn't be doing plush in India really. They said, "Oh, no, it's our biggest selling toy." Nobody buys these things in India. I mean, it's a different

---

[1] Personal interview, Tel Aviv: 8/4/10.

culture. Kids sleep with their parents or their grandparents. They don't sleep in a different room with a toy. It's just not done. Toys are something you play with in the dust. Then they launched some Hokey Pokey Elmo or something. It was a complete disaster in India.[2]

The introduction of plush toys in India rubbed up against both norms related to family functioning in relationship to sleep, and to environmental health standards.

This variation suggests that complexity does not inhere in the cultural product itself. Rather, it inheres in the *relationship* between the product and the environment. The more a cultural product challenges aspects of the local environment, the more friction is generated in the encounter. When a cultural product confronts pre-existing cultural and moral frameworks, it can create normative friction, and when it challenges pre-existing social arrangements, it can generate relational friction. The relationship between a cultural product and the local environment, in turn, shapes the way originators, distributors, local partners, target users, and local audiences localize products in different contexts.

Sesame Street programs generate both normative and relational friction, making it necessary for New York staff and partners not only to construct value and build alliances but also to customize the cultural product together. There are other cultural products that generate varying degrees of normative and relational friction. The Suzuki method for music education, for example, is the same around the world but generates normative friction; music teachers must convince parents and child students of the value of learning music during the initial stages, by ear. And advanced medical equipment generates relational friction, requiring interactions to teach physicians, nurses, and technicians how to use and maintain it. *Sesame Street* is not the only cultural product to generate both normative and relational friction at the same time. Magazines such as *Vogue*, for example, are routinely customized to fit local contexts through repeated interactions—*Vogue Italy, Vogue China, and British Vogue,* among others.

Power Across Borders

Because a driving question that motivated the research for this, and my two previous books, is how organizations can build more equitable ties with transnational partners, the primary focus here is on relationship building.

---

[2] Personal interview, New York: 12/3/12.

Power is a critical component of all relationships, but particularly those among partners with very unequal resources. It is crucial to emphasize again that *Sesame* is not a two-way street in terms of power. As previous chapters highlighted, the model originated in the US, the initial resources to coproduce it came from the US, and Sesame Workshop retains control of the intellectual property rights, even to material produced by partners.

Partners openly expressed their feelings about the power dynamics with Sesame Workshop; they criticized the unequal distribution of financial resources, a lack of transparency of budgets, the oversight of their work, and their lack of control over intellectual property. These are not small concerns. Other legitimate concerns, though not raised by partners, are also worth mentioning. For example, can Sesame Workshop escape the soft power of the US government if it accepts money for projects from agencies such as USAID? Is it problematic to define success as the invisibility of Sesame Workshop's origin and not critically engage how designing the kitchen, as Gary Knell described it, might have an impact on what is cooked in that kitchen? And, of course, it is reasonable to ask whether six million dollars is better spent on building schools, training and paying teachers, and providing books and learning materials in Palestine and South Africa than on creating an educational television program—for which a large portion of the budget goes to New York staff. These are all questions that deserve critical engagement.

The fact that I do not engage them adequately here does not mean I think they are unimportant, or that I even disagree with them. Rather, it reflects a focus on a different question: given that Sesame Workshop coproduces with partners, how effectively do they do it? The ubiquity of organizational attempts to move cultural products from North to South—often in ways that produce no results or worse, harmful ones—means it is critical to understand how these processes work on the ground between organizational partners. Is there a way to create more equitable partnerships between organizations in high and low-income countries? If so, how would it be achieved, and what would they look like?

As James Ferguson makes very clear, "development" usually depoliticizes, imposes, disempowers, and creates more problems than it solves (1994). But development is not just a project or a discourse; it is also a practice—or a set of practices. And interrogating those practices is critical to rejecting them or improving them. In essential ways, *Sesame Street* is unlike Ferguson's case of an agricultural project that is imposed in Lesotho by a Canadian development organization. Sesame Workshop does not have the power to impose a local program in Palestine, for example, because it does not have the access, knowledge, cultural understanding, skills, and networks to create a local program on its own. It must engage in coproduction with partners in order for the cultural product to resonate locally. This affords partners a significant (though not total) amount of power. Like development, coproduction is also a set of practices. And some of those core practices involve managing and resolving conflict. Conflict is inevitable in any relationship; the strength of which can be measured by how effectively conflict is managed. Productive conflict, organizational psychology research suggests, produces stronger relationships and better outcomes among teams (Hackman 2011).

In this book, I provide many examples to show how coproduction engages practices of flexibility, trust, and mutual learning. These practices allow partners to manage power asymmetries, misunderstandings, and conflict. Without changing Sesame Workshop's structures, however, no practice can eliminate power differentials. And yet, partners' knowledge—which is indispensable to creating a local program—provides some leverage to mitigate power imbalances with Sesame Workshop.

My interviews and observations show how New York staff regularly engage in introspection that allows them to acknowledge mistakes and attempt to correct them. Whether it was senior New York staff admitting that they made mistakes in Brazil or used stereotypes of Egyptian culture, they consistently engaged in self-reflection on their behavior and choices. This analysis of Sesame Workshop and its partners is an initial attempt to first examine those practices in the context of one organization, with the recognition that research on additional organizations is necessary to more fully understand them.

Implications for Other Organizations

What, then, can other organizations engaged in transnational relationships or working as transnational teams learn from Sesame Workshop? One of the key lessons from Sesame Workshop's engagement in coproduction is that it takes a lot of time, effort, and financial resources. It is not a process for organizations that wish to produce a product quickly. Despite the sensitive nature of children's education and prosocial values, in over five decades, Sesame Workshop has never been forced to end production of a local program or leave a country as a result of political strife or contention. Local programs generally end when resources do. As discussed earlier, some Palestinians did not accept the program coproduced with Israelis. *Shara'a Simsim*, which replaced it, however, was widely accepted and earned the support of Palestinian educators and government officials. *Sim Sim Hamara*, a Pakistani program that debuted in 2012, ended after the first season while the funder, USAID, investigated corruption allegations against its producer, the Rafi Peer Theater Workshop, which denied them. The program, like *Sisimpur* in Bangladesh, was unique because it featured puppets created by Rafi Peer, rather than only Muppets created by the Jim Henson Company. Of course, the end of *Sim Sim Hamara* did not result from political or creative differences.[3]

Sesame Workshop's coproduction model is rooted in building the right team over time and entrusting that team to identify and evaluate possible pitfalls and points of contention. It involves trusting their knowledge, encouraging their input and feedback, and valuing their creativity, skills, and opinions. The model does not attempt to thwart all conflicts, but rather creates productive ways of managing and resolving them. Sesame Workshop's coproduction model is built on a foundation of mutual learning. And that also helps balance the scales between New York staff and partners. In Lesotho, Canadian development workers and agricultural experts attempted to "teach" and convince people to change their practices, and the underlying values in which those practices were rooted, by improving the management of their livestock and growing cash crops. They failed miserably and actually caused harm. A relationship constructed where one partner has all the knowledge—or more accurately, the only knowledge considered important and valuable—and the other does not, cannot be equitable. And the outcomes of a partnership rooted in inequality are arguably less likely to succeed across a variety of dimensions, including satisfaction among partners and the local population.

The practices that Sesame Workshop incorporates into its coproduction process ensure that local programs are less likely to fail and less likely to generate dissatisfaction among their partners. They are also all practices that organizational scholars recognize as making teamwork and collaboration more successful. Research shows that well managed conflicts within teams can result in more creative outcomes, that teams that stay together longer do better than teams that do not, and that the "most powerful thing a leader can do to foster effective collaboration is to create conditions that help members competently manage *themselves*" (Hackman 2011:3). After disassembling and reconstituting *Sesame Street*, partners can effectively manage themselves.

And in fact, they can also manage others. When the team in Afghanistan, coproducing a new local program *Baghch-e-Simsim*, needed community outreach training, the Indian team trained them in Delhi. And when the Bangladeshi team could not get visas to travel to New York for their

[3] https://world.time.com/2012/06/11/why-is-the-u-s-no-longer-funding-pakistans-sesame-street/

educational content seminar—an extensive and crucial training for the entire team—the *Takalani Sesame* team successfully planned, hosted, and conducted the workshop in South Africa with two weeks' notice. As Robert Knežević recognized, partners were not a separate, "other" entity: "They are us." After my many discussions with partners in very different parts of the world, I would argue that a majority also recognized that: "They (New York staff) are us."

Mutual Learning

The process of coproduction involves a two-way exchange of complex knowledge between New York staff and partners. One of the last questions in my interview schedule encouraged partners to reflect on knowledge that originated with them and flowed to New York staff: "You've told me a lot about what you and your team learned from New York staff. What do you think or hope they have learned from you?" Their responses illuminated how their contributions went far beyond sharing knowledge about their own culture; they also contributed technical, business, artistic, and educational innovations. For example, when Mexican partners asked how to manipulate Muppet Lola's feet so they would appear to be pushing the pedals as she rode a tricycle, New York staff said they had not done that. They filmed Elmo riding a tricycle from the waist up—no feet—they said. The Mexican team solved the technical issues so that Lola's feet could be filmed pushing pedals. This innovation was then shared with the New York team and partners all over the world. And Elmo was no longer filmed riding a bicycle from the waist up.

The Indian team developed a range of innovations, from *Sesame Schoolhouse*, educational digital applications, and educational outreach products. Their ingenious "Story Pond" is an extremely well-received outreach product used in pre-schools to teach children basic vocabulary, sentence construction, and storytelling, before they can read (Cole and Lee 2016). A five-by-five-foot vinyl floor mat reminiscent of the game "Twister" is covered in colorful illustrations of stones, each bearing an image—various people, animals, flowers, fruit, toys, a house, and more. To teach storytelling, children are instructed to move from stone to stone and tell a story based on the image as they go (Figure 8.1).

Research on Story Pond's effects showed that children exposed to it in low-resourced Indian pre-schools increased their narrative skills compared to children who were not exposed (Cole and Lee 2016:199).

Figure 8.1 Story Pond (Sesame Workshop India)

New York staff were so impressed with Story Pond that they featured it during workshops and trainings with partners around the world. And soon, those partners wanted to create their own versions of Story Pond. Local adaptations of Story Pond have been created by partners in China, Israel, Nigeria, Indonesia, Bangladesh, Afghanistan, and Ireland—and each team has made it their own. In Nigeria, for example, where the television program is called *Sesame Square*, a tree rather than a pond is depicted, and children move from leaf to leaf while recounting their stories (Figure 8.2). Sesame Workshop's model of coproduction allows for knowledge and innovation to flow from New York staff to partners, and from partners to New York staff and to other partners around the world.

Figure 8.2 Sesame Square (Nigeria) version of Story Pond

Partners' willingness to make *Sesame Street* their own, and Sesame Workshop's recognition of partners' invaluable contributions to it, highlights how the process of coproduction can also produce a shared commitment to and investment not only in that product, but also the relationship that created it. It is through transnational interactions that New York staff and partners construct collective meanings and representations. And it is through coproduction that two interacting teams are transformed into one transnational team.

While many factors spark local resistance to cultural globalization, many also constrain it. By attempting to shift the analysis here to transnational interaction in relationship to cultural coproduction, I attempt to identify and explore where agency is located in these processes. The experience of Sesame Workshop and its partners suggests that in an era in which cultural products can be so quickly dispatched across the globe, creating locally acceptable hybrid forms may depend upon the construction of more equitable transnational ties between transnational organizational partners. The Sesame Workshop case illuminates how coproduction is at least one way to construct them.

9

Epilogue

The Sesame Model, Sustainability and Scale

It is always difficult for me to complete fieldwork for a project, largely because it never feels complete. In an organization like Sesame Workshop, things change every day; new projects and initiatives begin or end, staff and partners come and go, and the organization's priorities can shift with new challenges and new opportunities. I am always concerned that when I leave the field, I will miss these changes, some of which may be important or even critical to my analysis.

After leaving my fieldwork for this project, Sesame Workshop changed in large and small ways: departments were reorganized, new staff and leadership were hired or moved on to other jobs, priorities shifted, new grants were secured, and new projects were initiated. The world also changed, resulting in social, economic, and political shifts that affected Sesame Workshop, which is embedded in multiple institutional environments at national and transnational levels.

Given these changes, I thought an epilogue was necessary to bring the Sesame Workshop story up to date. Writing an epilogue required that I conduct approximately 20 additional interviews with New York staff and partners between 2021 and 2024. This provided me with the exciting opportunity to have a foot in the field again, albeit briefly. But even after I finished those interviews, the fieldwork did not feel complete. I begrudgingly accept that it never will.

Economic Challenges and Reorganization

When the financial crisis struck in 2008, Sesame Workshop was hit hard. I was in Israel with New York staff when executives announced there would be significant layoffs in the days to come and that the nonprofit would be restructured. It was agonizing for New York staff as they continued to do their jobs in Israel without knowing what would happen to those jobs on their return to

Sesame Street Around the World. Tamara Kay, Oxford University Press. © Oxford University Press (2025).
DOI: 10.1093/9780190844325.003.0009

the US. Ultimately, the international department was reorganized, and some projects were reallocated to different departments.

When former CEO of Nickelodeon, Jeffrey Dunn, was chosen to lead Sesame Workshop in 2014, the nonprofit had experienced eight years of its operating expenses exceeding its operating revenues. Dunn divided Sesame Workshop into two divisions: 1) Media and Education and 2) Social Impact and Philanthropy (SIP). This solidified the restructuring that Gary Knell had started, and that H. Melvin Ming had continued during his tenure as CEO/President from 2011 until he retired in 2014.

Dunn divided the CEO/President role into two positions (CEO and President). He assumed the role of CEO, and Sherrie Westin and Steve Youngwood were both named Presidents of their divisions: Westin became President of Global Impact and Philanthropy, and Youngwood became President of Media and Education and COO.[1] One of the most impactful ways Dunn dealt with Sesame Workshop's dire financial situation was to broker a deal with HBO (now HBO Max) in 2015. The agreement was for new seasons of *Sesame Street* to launch first on HBO and then, nine months later, on PBS. Under Dunn's leadership, the HBO deal and two successful $100 million grants—one from the MacArthur Foundation and one from the Lego Foundation—allowed Sesame Workshop to cease operating at a loss.

Changing Technologies and Consumption Patterns

In addition to financial challenges, Sesame Workshop—like all companies producing television programs for children, such as Nickelodeon and Disney, also has to contend with new technologies that change how audiences view and consume content. Starting in the mid-2000s, children's media exploded with the introduction of new digital formats, including online, as cell phone applications, and on other digital devices. Carolina Casas, then Regional Director of Education and Research for Latin America explained: "The demand of our audience—which now has moved away from television more to digital devices—has required us to rethink the format of our content, how it's packaged, and how it's promoted to reach our audience, which is now consuming media in very different patterns as they used to when we developed Plaza Sésamo back in the 1970s."[2] Children are no longer glued exclusively to television sets, but also to computers, tablets, cell phones, and gaming devices.

---

[1] In February 2024 Youngwood announced he was leaving Sesame Workshop.
[2] Zoom interview: 9/8/21.

Even in low- and middle-income countries, where Sesame Workshop began to focus more targeted attention during this same time period, people were consuming a significant amount of content on cell phones because they were affordable and accessible. Children in households with fewer resources, and/or in rural areas, were less likely to have access to any television at all. Carolina Casas described the limitations Sesame Workshop faced by only focusing on television:

> I think trying to address the educational needs of children in the region through a television program is just very challenging in the sense of needs and opportunities. The television platform is always valuable as part of our kind of contribution and one of the things that people associate with our organization. But it also has a lot of limitations in terms of delivering impact. You know, you are kind of dependent on your distribution partners. You're dependent on media consumption trends, accessibility. So for example, a lot of the populations that we prioritize are not necessarily in a position to kind of have access to our media regularly if we're just depending on television.[3]

Casas explained that technological trends forced Sesame Workshop to reconsider its focus on television and expand its reach into digital formats, while still maintaining a television presence: "So I think we shifted from our priority from television production to other delivery mechanisms that allow us to reach children more directly, more specifically, I guess in a more targeted way, thinking about their needs. But also just bringing kind of that added value of television."[4] Sesame Workshop staff recognized that the organization could not survive if it failed to create content and innovate for new and evolving technologies.

Globalization and Competition

In 2009, I invited CEO/President Gary Knell to give the keynote talk at a week-long event in Puerto Rico as part of Harvard's Puerto Rico Winter Institute, which I organized and directed that year. One of the first things he noted for the audience was how much the landscape of children's programming in the US had changed in the previous twenty years. In 1990, he said, there were two preschool programs on television: *Sesame Street* and *Mr. Rogers' Neighborhood*. In his PowerPoint presentation, he then showed the audience the

---

[3] Zoom interview: 9/8/21.
[4] Zoom interview: 9/8/21.

table below (see Table 9.1), and explained that by 2009, forty-seven preschool programs were being aired for children. Staying relevant, he explained, was a constant challenge.

During my seven years conducting research on Sesame Workshop, New York staff consistently expressed concern about *Sesame Street's* ability to compete in an increasingly competitive global media environment for children's programming. I was privy to their conversations about whether Sesame Workshop should change *Sesame Street's* format, place less emphasis on the Muppets, eliminate human characters, and even move to a fully animated version of the program. But the internal resistance to making what many staff considered to be drastic changes—that could potentially damage brand recognition and confidence—was intense.

Sesame Workshop's Research and Evaluation team decided to conduct a study to figure out what made certain popular children's programs engaging for children. Dr. Jennifer Kotler Clarke, Vice President of Research &

Table 9.1   47 Preschool Shows Today vs. 2 in 1990

1990	2009		
• Sesame Street	• Arthur	• Wow Wow	• The Land
• Mr. Rogers	• Barney	Wubzzy	Before Time
	• Callilou	• Yo Gabba	• 64 Zoo Lane
	• Clifford	Gabba	• Franklin
	• Curious	• Bunnytown	• Lazytown
	George	• Charlie and	• Little Bear
	• Dragon Tales	Lola	• Little Bill
	• It's a Big Big	• Doodlebops	• Jack's Big
	World	• Handy Manny	Music Show
	• Sesame Street	• Higglytown	• Maggie and
	• Super Why	Heroes	the Ferocious
	• Teletubbies	• JoJo's Circus	Beast
	• Word World	• Koala Brothers	• Maisy
	• Blues Clues	• Little Einsteins	• Miss Spider's
	• Dora the	• Mickey Mouse	Sunny Patch
	Explorer	Clubhouse	Friends
	• Wonder Pets	• My Friends	• Oobi
	• Go, Diego, Go	Tiger and	• Oswald
	• Max and Ruby	Pooh	• Pinky Dinky
	• Ni Hao,	• Stanley	Doo
	Kailan	• The Wiggles	• Upside
	• Backyardigans	• Mr. Men Show	Down Show

Evaluation, shared the findings that children enjoyed programs with a clear beginning, middle, and end, and a story helped them internalize educational objectives. The research also suggested that short, unrelated content did not help children internalize educational objectives unless it centered on familiar characters in a recurring format that was predictable for them. These findings were momentous for Sesame Workshop, creating a reexamination of *Sesame Street's* magazine format and the research from the 1970s that had supported it. Ultimately, these findings led the organization to do what many New York staff thought was unimaginable: begin changing *Sesame Street's* format.

The Impact of Domestic Changes on International Programs

Partners, of course, had been experimenting with different formats for years before New York staff changed *Sesame Street's* format in the US. In the mid-2000s, Germany's *Sesamstrasse* program moved from short interconnected Muppet (or street story) segments spread throughout an episode to longer segments that combined beginning-middle-end segments into one. The Indian team found success expanding the length of the street story segment of *Galli Galli Sim Sim* and experimenting with longer and comprehensive storylines, after finding the magazine format to be less effective in their local context. In Ireland, partners chose an innovative format for *Sesame Tree* that centered around guiding questions that were introduced at the beginning of each program and addressed through different segments throughout it. Partners, then, were the first innovators of *Sesame Street's* format, and they succeeded in creative ways and in different environments around the world.

Changes to *Sesame Street's* format, however, had a significant effect not only on local programs but also on Sesame Workshop's international work more generally. The first impact was on how global content was produced. Sesame Workshop had always produced global content that was generated by *Sesame Street* and local programs' use of the magazine format. Short segments, particularly Muppet and animation that could be easily dubbed, were incorporated into the Sesame library and were available for New York staff and partners around the world to use in their programs. Once the magazine format was abandoned, there was significantly less content being produced in New York that could be repurposed by partners for their programs. Daniel Labin, Sesame Workshop's former Vice President of International Social Impact, explained the problem this created:

And the net impact for international was that there was a lot less content that really could be extracted and used in the way that we were using it a lot. So it wasn't that the need for global content was a new need—there always has been a need for global content—but the supply chain for that global content was no longer pumping out the content that we needed. So we needed really to think about a new way of creating content that could be shared and that could really help supply the additional segments that weren't being created locally.[5]

As Labin suggested, a lack of content would present an enormous problem for *Sesame Street's* sustainability.

But again, it was partners who were already pushing the envelope and experimenting with creating global content, meaning content that could be used in different places all over the world. In India in 2018, for example, Sashwati Banerjee and her team at Sesame Workshop India produced a series of short segments called *I Heart Elmo*, with the intention of using them globally. Each Muppet segment focuses specifically around resilience in the face of difficult and adverse experiences for children by presenting a life challenge that Elmo and his parents face and overcome. Examples include dealing with conflict among friends, learning to share, and expressing anger in healthy ways.

As Labin pointed out, this first foray into creating global content was successful—the series went global—appearing in over 40 countries in at least 18 languages. He also explained how it was an important first step in developing a more standardized way of creating global content across Sesame Workshop:

So, in essence, it became a global block because we've now used it globally. But there were not advisors around the world who weighed in on it and it wasn't tested up front. That was sort of an interesting stop along the way of the journey of what that model of production would look like—about how do we create content for global audiences that's actually made and tested with global audiences in mind.[6]

But Labin also acknowledged that the repurposing of the Sesame library for almost five decades was neither an intentional nor a strategic way to create global content:

The Sesame Workshop coproduction model was predicated on the fact that about half the content was generated by the US and by the US *Sesame Street*. And that was the library material that, in essence, formed the "co" aspect of the coproduction

---

[5] Zoom interview: 10/18/21.
[6] Zoom interview: 10/18/21.

because that's what Sesame was contributing to augment and supplement the local content. And one could ask why was that model created? It was probably created because of scarce resources, which continues to be a driving motivating reason for this model 50 years or so later.[7]

That this model worked so well for so long, and that characters created for the US were seen as universal and "ended up working internationally was just like a wonderful, happy accident," Labin explained.

Experimenting with the Sesame Model

Given the global competition in children's media, changing technologies, and Sesame Workshop's financial challenges, how to intentionally and strategically evolve its international work became a priority under Dunn's leadership. Dr. Jennifer Kotler Clarke and her team's research on children's engagement with popular programs provided a road map for that process of refocusing. Because the research suggested a core set of characters well known to audiences was key, senior New York staff decided to experiment with eliminating some characters from global productions. For some projects, the focus and strategy of localizing content, which had been the hallmark of the coproduction model, would shift to a focus and strategy of globalizing content, as Labin explained:

> So what does creating content for global audiences really mean from a production standpoint? It means gravitating more toward animation but not entirely because animation has a more global look and feel. And then it really means not producing content with humans or with hyper-localized settings. Like the Lola Adventures takes place in a hot air balloon or in a garden. I mean nothing's generic because even a garden has place specificity and the garden looks different in different places, but there is an attempt made to not overly localize, from the background to the props.[8]

Shari Rosenfeld, promoted in 2016 to Senior Vice President of International Social Impact, explained that a "block format" was chosen for its versatility:

> Everyone sort of settled on let's do global content and let's bring together experts and kind of figure out what can travel. I think it evolved from various discussions and around creating what we call a block format so that the local content is all like

[7] Zoom interview: 10/18/21.
[8] Zoom interview: 10/18/21.

five minutes so that you can plug and play—you can choose from your different curricular goals and put together a show that addresses the specific goals that someone would be most interested in. And building out a library that would allow local producers to work with, and to choose together with local education experts, what are the needs that they want to address.[9]

The idea underlying this evolution was that truly global content could be used in any location, from Bangalore to Botswana, because it would be read by audiences as neutral, and therefore as universal. This new strategy would solve the core problems that had plagued local *Sesame Street* programs—they were incredibly expensive to consistently fund and staff year after year, which resulted in significant gaps in production. Rosenfeld summed up the financial challenge: "It's hard to justify that expense in the eyes of funders. So the value for money isn't there in the same way as when you are creating more evergreen content that can serve multiple audiences."[10]

This did not mean, however, that Sesame Workshop would abandon local *Sesame Street* programs, but rather, selectively choose to produce them when funding was available and when particular goals required that format. So when Sesame Workshop and the International Rescue Committee won the MacArthur Foundation *100&Change* $100 million prize in December 2017, they used it to create *Ahlan Simsim*, a Cadillac version of the regional production across the Middle East focused on the needs of children, many displaced by conflict and experiencing humanitarian crises in the Syrian response region.[11] A $100 million grant from the Lego Foundation in 2018 also supported *Ahlan Simsim*, and later supported the creation of a program to address the needs of Rohingya children living in refugee camps in Bangladesh. Rosenfeld explained how the strategy for creating local content was developed for this program:

In Bangladesh with the Rohingya population, they don't have access to mass media and they have limited access to mobile phones. So in deciding to do this content—which we're going to deliver through direct services in order to make the investment worthwhile—we're creating some localized content. And we've created two Rohingya Muppets named Noor and Azeez—they're a pair of twins—and locally produced live action puppet-based segments that will be the wrap around for the animated content. But the animated blocks will then serve other crisis-affected settings as well as other development settings. So we'll be able to use it in

---

[9] Zoom interview: 6/4/21.
[10] Zoom interview: 6/4/21.
[11] https://sesameworkshop.org/our-work/what-we-do/ahlan-simsim/

Afghanistan, we'll be able to use some of it in the Middle East. We'll be able to use it in the Bangladesh program. So we're going to find a lot of utility. It's not going to replace all of the local content. But instead of the US library content that we used to use and dub, it will replace that.[12]

The approach to this project reflects a recognition of local needs and constraints, and prioritizes experimentation by creating multi-purpose content that can be used with different audiences.

Relationships with Partners

As Sesame Workshop began to create more global content, a debate about the decolonization of aid also emerged among development organizations, practitioners, recipients, and scholars. The debate centers on a critique of how ongoing structures and ideologies of colonialism and racism affect the entire aid enterprise and reinforce inequalities between the Global North and the Global South. A 2021 report titled "Time to Decolonize Aid: Insights and lessons from a global consultation," published by Adesco, Alliance for Peacebuilding, Peace Direct, Women of Color Advancing Peace, Security and Conflict Transformation (WCAPS), calls on donors, international NGOs (INGOs), and policymakers to reconsider how they conceptualize and deliver aid. The report devoted specific recommendations to INGOs, including "Re-evaluate partnerships with local organisations":

> INGOs should end the practice of seeking short-term 'implementing partners' and instead establish long-term strategic partnerships that are not determined by project cycles. Peace Direct's nine partnership principles of effective partnerships might be a good place for INGOs to start. These are 1) Acknowledge and challenge power imbalances; 2) Confront racism and prejudice; 3) Support and invest in local leadership; 4) Strive for mutual accountability and learning; 5) Establish long term partnerships; 6) Provide unrestricted funding; 7) Be adaptable, and promote adaptability and resilience with your partners; 8) Consider nonfinancial resources as part of any partnership; and 9) Ensure that partnership transitions are a collaborative endeavor.[13]

---

[12] Zoom interview: 6/4/21.

[13] "Time to Decolonize Aid: Insights and Lessons from a Global Consultation Executive Summary." Adesco, Alliance for Peacebuilding, Peace Direct, Women of Color Advancing Peace, Security and Conflict Transformation, 2021, p. 10. Available at: https://resourcecentre.savethechildren.net/pdf/time-to-decolonise-aid-executive-summary.pdf/

In this context, Sesame Workshop's leadership began to reassess how the organization could strengthen and promote more autonomy for its partners, as Carolina Casas explained:

> [In relationship to] this whole decolonization of aid process I think we're trying to take our kind of historical practices a step further and making sure that decisions not only are being made in the communities for which we're creating content, but also that we're moving away from a project- by-project approach to more long-term programs. So we're not just creating a production that has two or three seasons in it and then moving on to the next territory, but really keep bringing out how we leverage those productions to create a broader presence that allows us to kind of leverage all the resources that the organization can bring and use it to be like a force of good in those spaces.[14]

To create a broader presence through long-term programs would mean prioritizing locally driven decision-making.

This new experiment with global content and long-term programs, however, did not imply that Sesame Workshop would eschew the coproduction model that focused on building strong and more equitable relationships with partners. Rather, they would use that model to innovate alternative ways to deploy it within the organization and throughout their work. For example, they created a team of educational experts chosen from around the world to evaluate and provide feedback on content that is produced with the intention that it will be distributed across multiple regions and cultural contexts. So, for example, partners would be involved in developing and shaping global content as part of a global advisory team, as Labin explained:

> So these blocks that are part of *Play to Learn* were created with a global advisory. I think that is sort of like our best foot forward in really having created a new way of developing global content that isn't just a repurpose—like oh let's try to use this in another country—but knowing up front that it's intended for lots of other countries.[15]

Shari Rosenfeld responded to my question of whether the evolution to a more global strategy has changed how Sesame Workshop interacts with partners:

> No, not really. I mean, we're vetting our content with education experts from multiple countries to ensure cultural relevance. So we have a team of educators that are

---

[14] Zoom interview: 9/8/21.
[15] Zoom interview: 10/18/21.

reviewing, for example, the *Play to Learn* content, which is really being designed as global content. So there are about, I think, maybe six or seven educational experts that represent a cross-section of geographic areas that are reviewing all of the scripts, as well as the rough cuts of what we do to make sure that we're not stepping into anything that sort of is either culturally insensitive or culturally irrelevant.[16]

This model, however, constructs different kinds of relationships with partners. One of the primary ways Sesame Workshop is experimenting with partner relationships is by integrating them more formally into the organization. Carolina Casas explained why they prioritized hiring educational experts as part of the staff, rather than as consultants:

We have a stronger Latin America education team which is the team I manage. And we have our own in-house expertise that includes educators from Mexico, Brazil and Colombia right now. So that's kind of an internal capacity that didn't exist before. Before we were always looking for all that external expertise and bringing it together to develop a curriculum whereas now we have more internal capacity to take the lead and then have a more kind of symmetrical consultation process where we can approach other experts but we also have some capacity in-house.[17]

Casas explained how integrating local partners into the organization increases their influence within Sesame Workshop:

I would say that it's even become more of a sustained process than it was before because before you would have these convenings maybe once or twice and then you would just go into production. Whereas now that we have a stronger footprint within the region it's an ongoing conversation with our partners—our ministries of education, our secretaries of education. We have stronger connections with local expertise that is kind of constantly being cycled into what we do. So it's less of a one-off check-in and more of an ongoing kind of discussion about where we should be headed and what we could be doing.[18]

Lesley Bourns, who was promoted to Senior Vice President of International Social Impact in August 2024, highlighted how experimentation allows Sesame Workshop to reach more children with fewer resources:

When we were recently asked to work in a new place such as Ukraine, we could say we have already made this investment in this global library. We want to look at it

[16] Zoom interview: 6/4/21.
[17] Zoom interview: 9/8/21.
[18] Zoom interview: 9/8/21.

with you and see how does it meet the needs you're facing at the moment. So we're not saying we need this big up front investment to do anything at all—we have kind of an accelerated starting point and and it's turned out to allow for much greater access for more children globally.[19]

But Bourns' comments also suggest the broader implications of these recent innovations: they allow Sesame Workshop to be more nimble and to build more relationships by having the ability to address partners' needs quickly.

Creating a Path Forward As Streets Diverge

Since I began this project, friends and colleagues often alert me—in a deluge of text messages and emails—to breaking stories about *Sesame Street*. They want to make sure I caught that story about Elmo's viral tweet, the new character who is unhoused, or the impact of *Ahlan Simsim*. They often pass along news I have not yet heard. But in December 2024, when news broke that HBO/Max (now owned by Warner Bros. Discovery) would not renew its contract to produce and stream new episodes of *Sesame Street*, I had already known for months from a former New York staffer who told me in confidence.

Social media immediately exploded with the news. Parents and fans expressed their disbelief and despair that one constant during the last 56 years was vulnerable to ending its long run, which was now the fourth-longest scripted program in US television history (the first three are soap operas). Alan Sepinwall, *Rolling Stone's* TV critic, captured this collective distress: "But the mere possibility that there may only be one season left of this national treasure, at a dark moment in the world when we need *Sesame Street* more than ever before, is awfully troubling."[20]

The Washington Post's Laura Meckler explained that HBO/Max did not see a future in children's programming: "Examining its internal data, the company concluded that HBO—home to some very adult content—was not a destination for young viewers looking for shows like "Sesame Street." She quoted an HBO/Max spokesperson: "We've had to prioritize our focus on stories for adults and families, and so new episodes from *Sesame Street*, at

---

[19] Zoom interview:11/5/24.
[20] https://www.rollingstone.com/tv-movies/tv-movie-features/sesame-street-contract-expire-save-where-to-watch-1235218815/

this time, are not as core to our strategy."[21] The company would, however, continue to make past episodes available until 2027.

Reporters noted, as I have here, that *Sesame Street* faces many challenges: the high cost of producing the program, increased competition resulting in fewer children and parents watching it, particularly among younger generations of viewers, and fewer children of *Sesame Street's* target age of 2–3 years old tuning in overall.[22] Then in early 2025, only a month into his term, the president and his administration dealt another blow by defunding and dismantling USAID, thereby ending humanitarian and aid projects around the world, including some of Sesame Workshop's international work. Local *Sesame Street* programs became the center of news stories as the president and Republican members of Congress cited them as examples of USAID waste and used them to justify why it should be shuttered. To many, *Sesame Street's* future looked bleak. Then on May 19, 2025, Sesame Workshop announced that it had struck a deal to produce and air new episodes of *Sesame Street* worldwide on Netflix. The deal also allows new episodes of *Sesame Street* to be released and available simultaneously on PBS and its digital platforms.

Missing from all the mainstream news during the tumultuous five months of uncertainty over *Sesame Street's* future, were the contributions of Sesame Workshop's local partners around the world. Their role and perspective was eclipsed, their contributions ignored. To my knowledge, only *Shara'a Simsim* producer and esteemed journalist Daoud Kuttab gave voice to local partners.[23] In an article he published in *The New Republic* titled: "I Worked on the "Arab *Sesame Street*." It Was *Not* a Waste of Money,"[24] he described the impact the program had on Palestinians, including Palestinian children, and the team that produced it.

The ommission of partners from the US *Sesame Street* narrative is particularly disheartening, and deeply ironic, given what partners have produced and contributed to it and Sesame Workshop since 1970: almost half a century of content, strong and sustainable networks of local allies, and new markets and audiences across the globe. In addition, partners successfully modeled for New York staff how new paths can be taken without compromising the organization or its brand; they have been at the forefront of experimenting

---

[21] https://www.washingtonpost.com/style/interactive/2024/sesame-street-wellbeing-hbo-struggles/

[22] https://www.washingtonpost.com/style/interactive/2024/sesame-street-wellbeing-hbo-struggles/

[23] From an academic's perspective, Dr. Naomi Moland wrote about her research on Nigeria's *Sesame Square* for an editorial published in the *Philadelphia Inquirer*. See https://www.inquirer.com/opinion/commentary/sesame-street-anniversary-international-funding-20191126.html

[24] https://newrepublic.com/article/192426/arab-sesame-street-not-waste-money

with new formats, prioritizing sustainability for their programs, innovating novel curricula to meet the needs of children in their environments, and utilizing new technologies and creating new content for them. As a result, its engagement in coproduction with local partners is a core part of what Sesame Workshop *is* as an organization and trusted brand, and will be essential to Sesame Workshop's ability to continue its mission and strategy far into the future.

APPENDIX I

Data and Methods

Fieldwork and Data Collection

I interviewed New York staff in key leadership positions from at least one core division of Sesame Workshop (e.g. international, marketing, international education, research and outreach, etc.) who had decision-making power, and who interacted regularly with partners. I also interviewed New York staff with leadership positions from each of the content, production, and research teams who were involved in coproduction. The sample of New York staff was therefore quite representative.

I compiled the sample of international partners from: 1) official rosters of Sesame Workshop partners for then-current programs, 2) names of key partners who had participated in previous seasons of programs provided by New York staff and archival documents, and 3) names of key partners who had participated in previous seasons of programs provided by partners. I had a very representative sample; it included partners from each of the content, production, and research teams, almost all of whom played crucial roles, had decision-making power, and interacted regularly with New York staff (such as producers, directors, head writers, educational content specialists, etc.).

While in the field, my role was a participant observer and interviewer. Sesame Workshop allowed me to interview any New York staff or partner (past or present) I wished without restriction. All respondents with whom I requested interviews granted them. I relied on in-depth, semi-structured interviews, for which I developed and used two standard interview questionnaires: one I utilized for New York staff and one for partners. This was necessary because some of the questions were quite specific to the experience of partners (e.g. how they wanted to represent their culture, issues with different languages, etc.). The questionnaires covered background information and career histories, work experiences with Sesame Workshop, and relationships with counterparts and partners.

Although I used two standard questionnaires, most interviews went well beyond them as I asked for clarification, sought concrete examples, pushed to understand interpretations and meanings, and gently prodded about underlying thoughts and feelings about events that were described to me. Some questions varied by the role and responsibilities of the respondent. For example, I asked respondents with administrative and decision-making authority questions about budgets and finances, but I did not ask these questions of puppeteers. The Institutional Review Board at Harvard University, at which I was employed when I began the research for this project, approved this study.

To gain the trust of partners in various countries, I decided to conduct interviews in each country in the days after I had observed a joint event between New York staff and partners. This allowed respondents to get to know me a little bit and feel comfortable with me as I was participating and observing each event. At the beginning of each event, New York staff always introduced me to partners as a professor and observer, and I was given a name tag with my observer status. When I introduced myself at events and at the beginning of interviews, I reminded partners that I was an independent researcher and did not work for Sesame Workshop. Because partners revealed conflicts and concerns with Sesame Workshop, I believe my role as observer allowed me to collect data from partners that they otherwise would not have revealed if I had been working for Sesame Workshop. I told partners I would be writing academic articles and a book based on my observations and interviews. This put them at ease, and most expressed excitement about the possibility of being included in the book.

Almost all respondents gave me permission to use their names in publications. I have decided to exercise extreme care and caution in protecting their anonymity, however, particularly that of partners. For that reason, I use names only when I am certain the data would not be harmful to reveal, and have decontextualized the data where appropriate to ensure respondents' confidentiality. Tables A.1 and A.2 provide lists of job titles—for New York staff and partners, respectively—to give readers a sense of the breadth and depth of the respondents I interviewed. Because revealing the country and year of the interview (and specific government and NGO names and job titles) would identify them, I refrained from including that information in the table.

There are many challenges to conducting multi-sited ethnography, particularly when sites are located in multiple countries or regions. The logistics of traveling to different countries, often with little notice, required assistance from someone who could liaise between me and various New York staffers. I was very fortunate that Sesame Workshop assigned Jodi Lefkowitz that responsibility. Jodi was a young and enthusiastic corporate communications manager who, among other things, helped write President and CEO Gary Knell's speeches. In addition to arranging almost all of my interviews in Sesame Workshop's office, she regularly checked in with New York staff to find out when trips were planned so that I could make arrangements to travel with them. She sent me hotel and flight information, schedules, and dates, which enabled me to always stay in the same hotel as New York staff.

Another complication of this multi-sited ethnography in multiple countries is that observations usually occurred in places that were unfamiliar to both New York staff and partners. To accommodate the large number of participants, most of the workshops, seminars, and planning meetings I observed took place in big hotels or event venues where many of the participants had never been. This meant that participants did not feel completely at home in their own spaces when I observed them. It also meant that they rarely occupied the same space at the same time. During each research trip—both to the New York office and abroad—various meetings and side discussions often occurred simultaneously. Since I could not observe multiple meetings at once, I chose those I felt were most crucial to the research. That meant I focused on the primary event itself—educational content seminar, writers workshop, directors workshop, etc. I generally did not observe meetings about budgets or finances, marketing, or licensing, which meant the only data I have on these issues is from interviews. When I observed in the New York office, I had to choose between various meetings to attend because many happened simultaneously. My role as observer rather than employee, therefore, shaped the data I could collect —I was not privy to everything that was happening and every communication in the New York office. Of course, this is the case for all ethnographers in large and complex organizations and in multi-sited field locations.

All meetings between New York staff and partners were conducted in English. Simultaneous translation was generally provided for participants who did not speak English. I noticed that smaller side discussions and meetings often occurred between partners and New York staff who spoke the same language, including in Israel, Mexico, Colombia, Palestine, and Jordan. A limitation of this multi-sited ethnography was that I could not understand what was being said in these discussions and meetings and therefore could not observe them, except for those in Spanish, which I speak.

Among the most important events I observed were meetings and training sessions held in New York for partners from around the world. These included a three-day event in December 2012 with potential partners for *Iftah Ya Simsim*, a program among the Gulf States. This case is particularly important because it allowed me to observe interactions among New

Table A.1 Job Titles of Sesame Workshop New York Staff

President & CEO
Vice President, International Project Management
Vice President, International Television Distribution
Vice President, Global Production
Vice President, Education and Research
Senior Vice President, International Social Impact
Assistant Vice President, Publicity
Executive Vice President, International
Vice President, International Social Impact
Vice-President, Corporate Sponsorship
Vice President, Worldwide Television
Executive Vice President of Education, Research and Outreach
Executive Vice President, Creative
Vice President & General Manager, Global Consumer Products
Vice President, Brand Strategy
Vice President, Production Operations, Global TV
Vice President, Global Education
Senior Vice-President, Impact Programs
Senior Vice President of International Social Impact
Regional Director of Education and Research for Latin America
Regional Director, International Strategies Group
Director, International Education, Research and Outreach
Director, International Projects
Director, International Coproductions
Country Director, International
Director of Research, Global Education
Assistant Director of Education and Research
Educational Content Specialist, International Education, Research and Outreach
Script Editor, Global Production
Producer (Executive Producer, Senior Producer)
Producer, International Global Production
Producer, International
Producer (multiple)
Director (multiple)
Head Writer (multiple)
Writer (multiple)

[i]Multiple means I interviewed various people with this job title, for example, a director in Palestine and Mexico

York staff and potential partners who had not yet committed to participating in the program. While observing in the field, I took detailed and exhaustive contemporaneous field notes that included my observations and thoughts. I was allowed to audio record some events.

Building trust with New York staff and partners was incredibly important. I found that doing so was made easier by the fact that we were all together every day from seven in the morning until approximately ten o'clock at night. This allowed us to talk about our lives and get to know each other. I stayed in the same hotel (and while in Israel, also a kibbutz) as New York staff, ate all my meals with New York staff and partners, shared transportation with and spent almost all

Table A.2 Job Titles of Sesame Workshop's International Partners

Managing Director (multiple)
Project Director (multiple)
Chief Financial Officer
Director of Outreach (multiple)
Project Coordinator
Director of Educational Content and Research (multiple)
Head Content Advisor
Education Specialist (multiple)
Executive Producer/General Manager
Research and Digital Initiatives Manager
Assistant Producer/Line Producer
Creative & Art Director
Program Manager
Content Manager
Research Manager
Producer (multiple)
Director (multiple)
Puppeteer (multiple)
Head Writer (multiple)
Writer (multiple)
Director of Music
Musician
Director of Public Relations (multiple)
Marketing Manager
Advisors/Consultants (multiple, including doctors, pediatricians, psychologists, teachers)
NGO representative (multiple)
Government representative (multiple)
General Manager, Nonprofit
CEO, Television Company
Head of Television, Television Company
Director of Children's Television, Television Company
Director of Innovation, Television Company
VP of Program Acquisition and International Strategy, Television Company
Director General, Television Company
Director of Fund Raising and Marketing, Television Company
Director of Projects, Television Company
Director, Consulting Firm
Education Coordinator, Consulting Firm
Health and Education Advisor, Consulting Firm

waking hours with New York staff and partners (e.g. attending a play in Mexico City, shopping in Amman, and visiting historic sites in Israel). New York staff treated me as part of the team in the sense that I was always included in activities and social events—even in partners' homes. And because I always offered to help, I could contribute to the team by providing additional assistance with copying, distributing, and carrying materials and equipment, and setting up before or cleaning up after events.

Table A.3 Sesame Workshop Events Attended

Event Name	Location	Date
Kosovo and Bangladesh Research Results meeting	New York	January 2008
Plaza Sésamo 35th Anniversary Celebration	Mexico City	August 26, 2008
Plaza Sésamo Curriculum Development meeting	Mexico City	August 27–28, 2008
Plaza Sésamo Writers' Workshop	Mexico City	August 29, 2008
Colombia Healthy Habits for Life Meeting	New York	September 9–10, 2008
Plaza Sésamo Partners' Meeting: Healthy Habits for Life Initiative, Colombia	New York	December 9–10, 2008
First conference call with Israeli team to plan content seminar	New York	December 16, 2008
Sesame Workshop All Staff Meeting	New York	December 16, 2008
Sesame Street English: Educational Content Seminar	New York	December 17, 2008
Israel Content Seminar and Writers Workshop Meetings	Tel Aviv, Israel	January 11–13, 2009
Israel Research and Outreach Ideas Meetings	Tel Aviv, Israel	January 11–13, 2009
Puerto Rico: Meeting on Dengue Fever Prevention Public Service Announcement	San Juan, Puerto Rico	February 12, 2009
Puerto Rico: Education Committee, Puerto Rican Television Meeting	San Juan, Puerto Rico	February 18, 2009
Palestine Writer's Workshop	Amman, Jordan	February 23–25, 2009
Jordan Writer's Workshop	Amman, Jordan	February 26–28, 2009
Palestine and Jordan Puppeteer Workshop	Amman, Jordan	February 28, 2009
Jordan Directors Workshop	Amman, Jordan	March 1, 2009
Colombia Healthy Habits for Life Launch Event	Bogotá, Colombia	June 24–25, 2009
Nigeria Educational Content Seminar and Writer's Workshop	Abuja, Nigeria	October 28–29, 2009
Iftah Ya Simsim: Welcome to Sesame Workshop	New York	December 12–14, 2012
Sesame Workshop India site visit to Sesame Schoolhouse	Meerut, India	May 2, 2013
Iftah Ya Simsim Writing Workshop	New York	December 10–17, 2013

This research centered on interviews with and observations of elites—both skilled New York staff and partners. Because they were offering me access to them and their work, and could deny it at any time, I felt that I held much less power than they did. But because I had absolutely no experience or expertise in any aspect of their work and stayed in my lane, I was not seen as a threat or as someone who could legitimately judge or evaluate their work. In fact, I regularly asked a lot of questions to understand the nature of that work, the larger context in which it was embedded, and the challenges and opportunities they faced. Respect is an integral part of building trust, and I made it clear through my interactions with New York staff and partners that I deeply respected them and their work.

Data Coding and Analysis

The ten-page coding dictionary has approximately 14 coding categories (e.g. New York Internal Organization and Structure) with various sub-categories under each (e.g. Educational and Professional Background), and individual codes under these sub-categories (e.g. Background education; Comparing other jobs to Sesame). The coding dictionary has a total of 316 individual codes. Various coding clusters, however, apply only to certain respondents. For example, certain codes relate to New York staff, and others to partners. I also developed a variety of codes to be able to aggregate data (e.g. on specific countries and programs).

Many coding categories have multiple codes. For example, the coding category for "diffusion" has ten individual and distinct codes: 1) negotiation: terms of adoption; 2) negotiation: alliance building mechanisms; 3) negotiation: resources; 4) negotiation: training; 5) negotiation: customization; 6) general negotiation and/or other; 7) diffusion of local content to other developing country; 8) desire for local content versus imported content; 9) New York learning from local partners; 10) diffusion from developing country to New York. Other codes capture additional aspects of localization and adaptation processes.

Sources

Abu-Lughod, Lila. 2005. *Dramas of Nationhood: The Politics of Television in Egypt*. Chicago: University of Chicago Press.

Acemoglu, Daron, and James A. Robinson. 2012. *Why Nations Fail: The Origins of Power, Prosperity and Poverty*. New York: Crown Books.

Acemoglu, Daron, Simon Johnson, and James A. Robinson. 2001. "The Colonial Origins of Comparative Development: An Empirical Investigation." *American Economic Review* 91(5): 1369–1401.

Acharya, Amitav. 2004. "How Ideas Spread: Whose Norms Matter? Norm Localization and Institutional Change in Asian Regionalism." *International Organization* 58(2): 239–275.

Afana, Abdel Hamid, Samir Qouta, and Eyad El Sarraj. 2004. "Mental Health Needs in Palestine." Humanitarian Exchange Magazine. 28(10): 28–30.

Ames, Morgan G. 2019. *The Charisma Machine: The Life, Death, and Legacy of One Laptop per Child*. Cambridge, MA: MIT Press.

Anderson, Daniel R., Aletha C. Huston, Kelly L. Linebarger, and John C. Wright. 2001. *Early Childhood Television Viewing and Adolescent Behavior: Monographs of the Society for Research in Child Development*. Wiley-Blackwell. 66: 1–147.

Ang, Ien. 1985. *Watching Dallas: Soap Opera and the Melodramatic Imagination*. New York: Routledge.

Appadurai, Arjun. 1996. *Modernity At Large: Cultural Dimensions of Globalization*. Minneapolis: University of Minnesota Press.

Barrington, DJ, R. C. Sindall, A. Chinyama, T. Morse, M. N. Sule, J. Beale, et al. 2025. "The Persistence of Failure in Water, Sanitation and Hygiene Programming: A Qualitative Study." *BMJ Global Health*. 10: e016354.

Becker, Howard S. 1982. *Art Worlds*. Berkeley: University of California Press.

Berman, Elise. 2019. *Talking Like Children: Language and the Production of Age in the Marshall Islands*. New York: Oxford University Press.

Bhabha, Homi K. 1994. *The Location of Culture*. New York: Routledge.

Bielby, Denise D. and C. Lee Harrington. 2008. *Global TV: Exporting Television and Culture in the World Market*. New York: New York University Press.

Binder, Amy. 2007. "For Love and Money: Organizations' Creative Responses to Multiple Environmental Logics." *Theory and Society* 36(6): 547–571.

Boellstorff, Tom. 2003. "Dubbing Culture: Indonesian Gay and Lesbian Subjectivities and Ethnography in an Already Globalized World." *American Ethnologist* 30(2): 225–242.

Bogatz, Gerry Ann, and Samuel Ball. 1971. *The Second Year of Sesame Street: A Continuing Evaluation. Volume 1*. Princeton, NY: Educational Testing Services.

Bjorvatn, Torbjørn and Andreas Wald. 2024. "Antecedents of Knowledge Transfer Effectiveness in International Teams." *European Journal of International Management* 23(4): 622–647.

Boli, John, and George Thomas. 1997. "World Culture in the World Polity: A Century of International Non-Governmental Organization." *American Sociological Review* 62(2): 171–190.

Bourdieu, Pierre. 2005. *The Social Structures of the Economy*. Polity Press.

Brienza, Casey and Matthias Revers. 2016. "The Field of American Media Sociology: Origins, Resurrection, and Consolidation." *Sociology Compass* 10(7): 539–552.

Bromley, Patricia, Evan Schofer and Wesley Longhofer. 2020. "Contentions Over World Culture: The Rise of Legal Restrictions on Foreign Funding to NGOs 1994–2015." *Social Forces* 99(1): 281–304.

Buchholz, L. 2016. "What is a Global Field? Theorizing Fields beyond the Nation-State." *The Sociological Review* 64(2): 31–60.

Burke, Peter. 2009. *Cultural Hybridity*. Cambridge, UK: Polity Press.

Campbell, Catherine. 2003. *Letting them Die: Why HIV/AIDS Prevention Programmes Fail*. Bloomington: Indiana University Press.

Canclini, Néstor García. 2005. *Hybrid Cultures: Strategies for Entering and Leaving Modernity*. Minneapolis: University of Minnesota Press.

Capoor, I and Gade, J. 2004. "Gender in equalities matters! A situational analysis of gender discrimination in India." Unpublished report for Sesame Workshop.

Cole, Jennifer, and Deborah Durham, editors. 2007. *Generations and Globalization: Youth, Age, and Family in the New World Economy*. Bloomington, IN: Indiana University Press.

Cole, Jennifer, and Deborah Durham, editors. 2008. *Figuring the Future: Globalization and the Temporalities of Children and Youth*. Santa Fe: School for Advanced Research Press.

Cole, Michael. 2005. "Culture in Development." In Marc H. Bornstein and Michael E. Lamb (Eds.) *Developmental Science: An Advanced Textbook* (45–101). Hillsdale, NJ: Lawrence Erlbaum.

Cole, Charlotte F. and Lewis Bernstein. 2016: "Ripple Effects: Using Sesame Street to Bridge Group Divides in the Middle East, Kosovo, Northern Ireland, and Elsewhere." In Charlotte F. and June H. Lee. 2016. *The Sesame Effect: The Global Impact of the Longest Street in the World*. New York: Routledge, 154–180.

Cole, C. F., Arafat, C., Tidhar, C., Tafesh, W. Z., Fox, N. A., Killen, M., Ardila-Rey, A., Leavitt, L. A., Lesser, G., Richman, B. A., & Yung, F. 2003. "The Educational Impact of Rechov Sumsum/Shara'a Simsim: A Sesame Street Television Series to Promote Respect and Understanding among Children living in Israel, the West Bank and Gaza." *International Journal of Behavioral Development* 27(5): 409–422.

Cole, Charlotte F. and June H. Lee. 2016. *The Sesame Effect: The Global Impact of the Longest Street in the World*. New York: Routledge.

Cooper, Elissa. https://www.jta.org/1999/02/12/lifestyle/behind-the-headlines-muppets-cross-the-street-to-join-israelis-palestinians

Cowen, Tyler. 2004. *Creative Destruction: How Globalization Is Changing the World's Cultures*. Princeton: Princeton University Press.

Crane, Diana, Nobuko Kawashima, and Ken'ichi Kawasaki. 2002. *Global Culture: Media, Arts, Policy, and Globalization*. New York: Routledge.

Davis, Kathy. 2002. "Feminist Body/Politics as World Traveler: Translating our Bodies, Ourselves." *European Journal of Women's Studies* 9(3): 223–247.

Dezalay, Y., and B. G. Garth. 2002. *The Internationalization of Palace Wars: Lawyers, Economists, and the Contest to Transform Latin American States*. University of Chicago Press.

Earley, P. C., and E. Mosakowski. 2000. "Creating Hybrid Team Cultures: An Empirical Test of Transnational Team Functioning." *The Academy of Management Journal* 43(1): 26–49. https://doi.org/10.2307/1556384

Eliasoph, Nina and Paul Lichterman. 2003. "Culture in Interaction." *American Journal of Sociology* 108(4): 735–794.

Evans, Peter B. 1995. *Embedded Autonomy: States and Industrial Transformation*. Princeton: Princeton University Press.

Fang, J. 2024. "The Culture of Censorship: State Intervention and Complicit Creativity in Global Film Production." *American Sociological Review* 89(3): 488–517. https://doi.org/10.1177/00031224241236750

Felps, Will, Terence R. Mitchell, Eliza Byington. 2006. "How, When, and Why Bad Apples Spoil the Barrel: Negative Group Members and Dysfunctional Groups." *Research in Organizational Behavior* 27: 175–222.

Ferguson, James. 1994. *The Anti-Politics Machine: Development, Depoliticization, and Bureaucratic Power in Lesotho*. Minneapolis: University of Minnesota Press.

Finnemore, Martha and Kathryn Sikkink. 1998. "International Norm Dynamics and Political Change." *International Organization* 52(4): 887–917.

Fligstein, Neil. 2001. "Social Skill and the Theory of Fields." *Sociological Theory* (19(2): 105–125.

Fluent Research. 2008. "Assessment of Educational Impact of *Rruga Sesam* and *Ulica Sezam* in Kosovo: Report of Findings." January.

Gettas, Gregory J. 1990. "The Globalization of "Sesame Street": A Producer's Perspective." *Educational Technology Research and Development* 38(4): 55–63.

Gladwell, Malcolm. 2000. *The Tipping Point: How Little Things Can Make a Big Difference*. Little, Brown and Company.

Glaser, Barney G., and Anselm L. Strauss. 2009. *The Discovery of Grounded Theory: Strategies for Qualitative Research*. New York: Aldine de Gruyter.

Go, J. 2008. "Global Fields and Imperial Forms: Field Theory and the British and American Empires." *Sociological Theory* 26(3): 201-229.

Gorn, Gerald J., Marvin E. Goldberg, and Rabindra N. Kanungo. 1976. "The Role of Educational Television in Changing the Intergroup Attitudes of Children." *Child Development* 47(1): 277–280.

Grindstaff, Laura. 2002. *The Money Shot: Trash, Class, and the Making of TV Talk Shows*. Chicago: University of Chicago Press.

Griswold, Wendy. 1987. "The Fabrication of Meaning: Literary Interpretation in the United States, Great Britain, and the West Indies." *American Journal of Sociology* 92(5): 1077–1117.

Guillén, Mauro F. 2000. "Business Groups in Emerging Economies: A Resource-Based View." *Academy of Management Journal* 43: 362–380.

Hackman, J. Richard. 2002. *Leading Teams: Setting the Stage for Great Performances*. Cambridge: Harvard Business Review Press.

Hackman, J. Richard. 2011. "Six Common Misperceptions about Teamwork." *Harvard Business Review*. Published on hbr.org. Reprint 2–4.

Haedicke, Michael A. 2012. "Keeping our Mission, Changing our System": Translation and Organizational Change in Natural Foods Co-Ops." *The Sociological Quarterly* 53(1): 44–67.

Hallett, Tim, and Amelia Hawbaker. 2021. "The Case for an Inhabited Institutionalism in Organizational Research: Interaction, Coupling, and Change Reconsidered." *Theory and Society* 50: 1–32.

Hallett, Tim and Marc Ventresca. 2006. "Inhabited Institutions: Social Interactions and Organizational Forms in Gouldner's Patterns of Industrial Bureaucracy." *Theory and Society* 35(2): 213–236.

Hamelink, Cees J. 1983. *Cultural Autonomy in Global Communications*. Longman Group United Kingdom.

Hannerz, Ulf. 1996. *Transnational Connections: Culture, People, Places*. London: Routledge.

Hannerz, U. 1987. "The World in Creolisation." *Africa* 57(4): 546–559.

Haraway, Donna. 1985. "Manifesto for Cyborgs: Science, Technology, and Socialist-Feminism in the 1980s." *Socialist Review* 15(2): 65–107.

Haraway, Donna Jeanne. 1976. *Crystals, Fabrics, and Fields: Metaphors That Shape Embryos*. New Haven: Yale University Press.

Harrison, Lawrence E. and Samuel P. Huntington. 2000. *Culture Matters: How Values Shape Human Progress*. New York: Basic Books.

"Human Rights in Palestine and other Occupied Arab Territories: Report of the United Nations Fact-Finding Mission on the Gaza Conflict." United Nations Human Rights Council. September 25, 2009.

Jameson, Fredric, and Masao Miyoshi. 1998. *The Cultures of Globalization*. Durham: Duke University Press.

Kameo, Nahoko. 2024. *Cosmopolitan Scientists: How a Global Policy of Commercialization Became Japanese*. Stanford: Stanford University Press.

Kaufman, Jason, and Orlando Patterson. 2005. "Cross-National Cultural Diffusion: The Global Spread of Cricket." *American Sociological Review* 70(1): 82–110.

Kay, Tamara. 2011. *NAFTA and the Politics of Labor Transnationalism*. New York: Cambridge University Press.

Kay, Tamara. 2012. "Educating Children on the Longest Street in the World." *Global Dialogue* 2(5):10–11.

Kay, Tamara and R.L. Evans. 2018. *Trade Battles: Activism and the Politicization of International Trade Policy*. New York: Oxford University Press.

Kay, Tamara. 2023. "Culture in Transnational Interaction: How Organizational Partners Coproduce *Sesame Street*." *Theory and Society* 52(4)711737.

Kay, Tamara and Isabel Jijon. 2025. "Theorizing "Cultural Friction": Or, How Norms, Technologies, Media, and Commodities Spread"(unpublished manuscript).

Kearney, Melissa S., and Phillip B. Levine. 2019. "Early Childhood Education by Television: Lessons from Sesame Street." *American Economic Journal: Applied Economics* 11(1): 318–50.

Kibria, Nazli, and Sonali Jain 2009. "Cultural Impacts of *Sisimpur, Sesame Street*, in Rural Bangladesh: Views of Family Members and Teachers." *Journal of Comparative Family Studies* 40(1): 57–75.

Kogut, B., and J. Muir Macpherson. 2008. "The Decision to Privatize: Economists and the Construction of Ideas and Policies." in *The Global Diffusion of Markets and Democracy*, edited by Simmons, Beth A., Frank, and Geoffrey Garrett, 104–140. New York: Cambridge University Press.

Kraidy, Marwan M. 2005. *Hybridity, or The Cultural Logic of Globalization*. Philadelphia: Temple University Press.

Kuipers, Giselinde. 2015. "How National Institutions Mediate the Global: Screen Translation, Institutional Interdependencies, and the Production of National Difference in Four European Countries." *American Sociological Review* 80(5): 985–1013.

Kymlicka, Will. 2007. *Multicultural Odysseys: Navigating the New International Politics of Diversity*. New York: Oxford University Press.

Landes, David S. 1998. *The Wealth and Poverty of Nations: Why Some are so Rich and Some So Poor*. New York: W. W. Norton & Company.

Lareau, Annette. 2003. *Unequal Childhoods: Class, Race, and Family Life*. Berkeley: University of California Press.

Larkin, E., Connolly, C., and Kehoe, S. 2009. "A Longitudinal Study of the Effects of Young Children's Natural Exposure to Sesame Tree on their Attitudes and Awareness (Report 2)." Belfast: Centre for Effective Education, Queen's University Belfast.

Latour, Bruno. 1993. *We Have Never Been Modern*, translated by Catherine Porter. Cambridge, MA: Harvard University Press.

Latour, Bruno. 2000. "When Things Strike Back: A Possible Contribution of 'Science Studies' to the Social Sciences." *British Journal of Sociology* 51(1): 107–123.

Lavie, Noa, and Simone Varriale. 2019. "Introduction to the Special Issue on Global Tastes: The Transnational Spread of Non-Anglo-American Culture." *Poetics* 75: 101388.

Lechner, Frank, and John Boli. 2005. *World Culture: Origins and Consequences*. Oxford: Blackwell Publishing.

Lederman, Sara. 2012. "Transmitting the Critical Community: Muppets, Migrant-Labor, and Indian Radio." unpublished B.A. thesis. Barnard College.

LeVine, Robert A., and Rebecca S. New, eds. 2008. *Anthropology and Child Development: A Cross-Cultural Reader*. Malden, MA: Blackwell Publishing.

Levitt, Peggy. 2020. "Becoming a 'Cultural Destination of Choice': Lessons on Vernacularization from Beirut and Buenos Aires." *International Journal of Cultural Policy* 26(6): 756–770.

Levitt, Peggy and Sally Merry. 2009. "Vernacularization on the Ground: Local Uses of Global Women's Rights in Peru, China, India and the United States." *Global Networks* 9(4): 441–461.

Liebes, Tamar and Elihu Katz. 1990. *The Export of Meaning: Cross-Cultural Readings of Dallas*. New York: Oxford University Press.

Lightfoot, Cynthia, Michael Cole, and Sheila Cole. 2018. *The Development of Children* (8th ed.). New York: Macmillan Learning.

Liu, Meng, Yanhong Hu, and Minli Liao. 2009. "Travelling Theory in China: Contextualization, Compromise and Combination." *Global Networks* 9(4): 529–553.

Lanchimba, C., J. Kaswengi, & E. J. Silva-Bitti. 2025. "Strategic Participation and Local Assets: Key Drivers of Franchise Performance in an Emerging Market." *Journal of Strategic Marketing* 33(5), 620–638.

Mares, M., and Woodard, E. 2005. "Positive Effects of Television on Children's Social Interactions: A Meta-analysis." *Media Psychology* 7: 301–322.

Mares, Marie-Louise and Zhongdong Pan. 2013. "Effects of *Sesame Street*: A Meta-Analysis of Children's Learning in 15 Countries." *Journal of Applied Developmental Psychology* 34(3): 140–151.

McDonnell, Terence E. 2016. *Best Laid Plans: Cultural Entropy and the Unraveling of AIDS Media Campaigns*. Chicago: The University of Chicago Press.

Meckler, Laura. "Inside 'Sesame Street' as it fights to survive." *The Washington Post*. December 22, 2024.

Merry, Sally E. 2006. *Human Rights and Gender Violence: Translating International Law into Local Justice*. Chicago: University of Chicago Press.

Menon, Alka V. 2019. "Cultural Gatekeeping in Cosmetic Surgery: Transnational Beauty Ideals in Multicultural Malaysia." *Poetics* 75: 101354.

Meyer, John W. 2010. "World Society, Institutional Theories, and the Actor." *Annual Review of Sociology* 36: 1–20.

Meyer, John W., John Boli, George M. Thomas, and Francisco O. Ramirez. 1997. "World Society and the Nation-State." *The American Journal of Sociology* 103(1): 144–181.

Miles, Matthew B., and A. Michael Huberman. 1994. *Qualitative Data Analysis: An Expanded Sourcebook*. Thousand Oaks: SAGE.

Miller, Marjorie. 1998. https://www.latimes.com/archives/la-xpm-1998-apr-01-ca-34706-story.html

Moland, Naomi. 2020. *Can Big Bird Fight Terrorism?: Children's Television and Globalized Multicultural Education*. Oxford: Oxford University Press.

Molnár, Virág. 2005. "Cultural Politics and Modernist Architecture: The Tulip Debate in Postwar Hungary." *American Sociological Review* 70(1): 111–135.

Morfit, N. Simon. 2011. ""AIDS is Money" How Donor Preferences Reconfigure Local Realities." *World Development* 39(1): 64–76.

Morrill, Calvin. 2008. "Culture and Organization Theory." *The Annals of the American Academy of Political and Social Science* 619: 15.

Mukerji, Chandra. 2016. *Modernity Reimagined: An Analytic Guide.* New York: Routledge.

Naples, Nancy A. and Manisha Desai, eds. 2002. *Women's Activism and Globalization: Linking Local Struggles and Transnational Politics.* New York: Routledge.

Ostrom, Elinor. 1996. "Crossing the Great Divide: Coproduction, Synergy, and Development." *World Development* 24(6): 1073–1087.

Pieterse, J. N. 1994. "Globalisation as Hybridisation." *International Sociology* 9(2): 161–184.

Peterson, R. A. 1976. "The Production of Culture: A Prolegomenon." *American Behavioral Scientist* 19(6): 669–684.

Platón, Y., and M. Lembert 1999. Encuentro de Género [Gender Seminar Report], unpublished Document. New York: Sesame Workshop.

Polanyi, Michael. 1958. *Personal Knowledge: Towards a Post-Critical Philosophy.* Chicago: University of Chicago Press.

Rimal, Rajiv N, Maria Elena Figueroa, and J. Douglas Storey. 2013. Character recognition as an alternate measure of television exposure among children: Findings from the Alam Simsim program in Egypt. *Journal of Health Communication* 18: 594–609.

Risse, Thomas, Stephen C. Ropp, and Kathryn Sikkink. 1999. *The Power of Human Rights: International Norms and Domestic Change.* New York: Cambridge University Press.

Ritzer, George. 1995. *The McDonaldization of Society: An Investigation Into the Changing Character of Contemporary Social Life.* Rev. ed. Thousand Oaks: Pine Forge Press.

Robertson, Roland. 1994. "Globalization or Glocalization?" *Journal of International Communication* 1(1): 33–52.

Rogers, E. M. 2003. *Diffusion of Innovations.* New York: Simon and Schuster.

Rogoff, Barbara. 2003. *The Cultural Nature of Human Development.* New York: Oxford University Press.

Rosenau, James N. 2003. *Distant Proximities: Dynamics Beyond Globalization.* Princeton: Princeton University Press.

Rouchdy, M. 1998. "Girls' Education in Egypt", paper commissioned by the Children's Television Workshop, New York.

Saguy, Abigail C. 2002. "International Crossways: Traffic in Sexual Harassment Policy." *The European Journal of Women's Studies* 9(3): 249–267.

Sedano, Livia Jiménez. 2019. ""From Angola to the World", From the World to Lisbon and Paris: How Structural Inequalities Shaped the Global *Kizomba* Dance Industry." *Poetics* 75: 101360.

Seidman, Gay W. 2012. "Regulation at Work: Globalization, Labor Rights, and Development." *Social Research* 79(4): 1023–1044.

Sepinwall, Alan. "Can you Tell me how to get someone to save 'Sesame Street'?" *Rolling Stone.* December 30, 2024.

Shapiro, Samantha. "Can the Muppets Make Friends on the West Bank?" *New York Times Magazine.* Oct. 4, 2009, 38.

Sides, John. January 19, 2024. "Right-wing Populist Parties have Risen. Populism Hasn't." *Good Authority.* https://goodauthority.org/news/right-wing-populism/

Simmons, Beth A., Frank Dobbin, and Geoffrey Garrett. 2008. *The Global Diffusion of Markets and Democracy.* New York: Cambridge University Press.

Sims, Christo. 2017. *Disruptive Fixation: School Reform and the Pitfalls of Techno-Idealism.* Princeton: Princeton University Press.

Sklair, Leslie. 2001. *The Transnational Capitalist Class.* Oxford: Blackwell.

Snow, Charles C., Scott A. Snell, Sue Canney Davison, Donald C. Hambrick. 1996. "Use Transnational Teams to Globalize Your Company." *Organizational Dynamics* 24(4): 50–67.

Storey, John. 2003. *Inventing Popular Culture: From Folklore to Globalization.* Oxford: Blackwell.

Strang, David, and Sarah A. Soule. 1998. "Diffusion in Organizations and Social Movements: From Hybrid Corn to Poison Pills." *Annual Review of Sociology* 24: 265–290.

Strangaard Jensen, Helle. 2023. *Sesame Street: A Transnational History*. Oxford: Oxford University Press.

Strasburger, Victor C., Amy B. Jordan, and Ed Donnerstein. 2010. "Health Effects of Media on Children and Adolescents." *Pediatrics* (125)75: 767.

Swidler, Ann and Susan Cotts Watkins. 2009. ""Teach a Man to Fish": The Sustainability Doctrine and Its Social Consequences." *World Development* 37(7): 1182–1196.

Swidler, Ann and Susan Cotts Watkins. 2017. *A Fraught Embrace: The Romance and Reality of AIDS Altruism in Africa*. Princeton: Princeton University Press.

Tarrow, Sidney. 2005. *The New Transnational Activism*. Cambridge: Cambridge University Press.

"Palestinian Sesame Street shuts after UN statehood bid punishments." *The Telegraph* January 9, 2012.

Thayer, Millie. 2000. "Traveling Feminisms: From Embodied Women to Gendered Citizenship." in *Global Ethnography: Forces, Connections and Imaginations in a Postmodern World*, edited by Michael Burawoy et al. Berkeley: University of California Press: 203–233

Tihanyi, Laszlo, David A. Griffith, and Craig J. Russell. 2005. "The Effect of Cultural Distance on Entry Mode Choice, International Diversification, and MNE Performance: A Meta-Analysis." *Journal of International Business Studies* 36: 270–283.

The World According to Sesame Street. Directed by Linda Goldstein Knowlton and Linda Hawkins Costigan, International Street Productions and Participant, 2006.

Tsing, Anna Lowenhaupt. 2005. *Friction: An Ethnography of Global Connection*. Princeton: Princeton University Press.

Van Maanen, John. 1992. "Displacing Disney: Some Notes on the Flow of Culture." *Qualitative Sociology* 15(1): 5–35.

Verhoeven, D., Cooper, T., Flynn, M. and Shuffler, M.L. 2017. "Transnational Team Effectiveness." In *The Wiley Blackwell Handbook of the Psychology of Team Working and Collaborative Processes*, edited by E. Salas, R. Rico and J. Passmore, John Wiley & Sons Ltd. (Hoboken, New Jersey), 73–101.

Warshel, Yael. 2009. "How Do You Convince Children that the 'Army,' 'Terrorists' and the 'Police' Can Live Together Peacefully? A Peace Communication Assessment Model." Dissertation, University of California, San Diego.

Warshel, Yael. 2021. *Experiencing the Israeli-Palestinian Conflict: Children, Peace Communication and Socialization*. Cambridge: Cambridge University Press.

Watson, James L. 1997. *Golden Arches East: McDonald's in East Asia*. Palo Alto: Stanford University Press.

Wright, J. et al. 2001. "The Relationship of Early Television Viewing to School Readiness and Vocabulary of Children from Low-Income Families: The Early Window Project." *Child Development* 72(5): 1347–1366.

Yúdice, George. 2004. *The Expediency of Culture: Uses of Culture in the Global Era*. Durham: Duke University Press Books.

Zelizer, Viviana A. 1994. *Pricing the Priceless Child: The Changing Social Value of Children*. Princeton: Princeton University Press.

Zielinska, Ida Eva, and Bette Chambers. 1995. "Using Group Viewing of Television to Teach Preschool Children Social Skills." *Journal of Educational Television* 21(2): 85–99.

Zwingel, Susanne. 2011. "How Do Norms Travel? Theorizing International Women's Rights in Transnational Perspective." *International Studies Quarterly* 56: 115–129.

Index